CHANGES OF STATE

CHANGES OF STATE

NATURE AND THE LIMITS OF THE CITY IN
EARLY MODERN NATURAL LAW

ANNABEL S. BRETT

PRINCETON UNIVERSITY PRESS
PRINCETON AND OXFORD

Published by Princeton University Press,
41 William Street, Princeton, New Jersey 08540

In the United Kingdom:
Princeton University Press,
6 Oxford Street, Woodstock, Oxfordshire OX20 1TW

Second printing, and first paperback printing, 2014
Cloth ISBN: 978-0-691-14193-0
Paper ISBN: 978-0-691-16241-6

Library of Congress Control Number: 2010940945

British Library Cataloging-in-Publication Data is available

This book has been composed in Bembo with Avenir display
Printed on acid-free paper ∞
press.princeton.edu
Printed in the United States of America
3 5 7 9 10 8 6 4 2

For Hilary

CONTENTS

A NOTE ON THE TEXT

Most of the texts in this book are quoted in translation, which is my own except where otherwise stated. Where I do quote from the Latin, I have normalised spelling, expanded contractions, and omitted accents in accordance with modern conventions, but have kept the original punctuation. For ease of reading I have transliterated the few words of Greek that occur. In terms of editions, I have used a modern critical edition where possible; where not, I have used the first edition or the earliest available to me. I have in almost all cases preferred the vernacular form of proper names; where I have felt that there is a perhaps confusing difference between the vernacular and the Latin form, I have given the latter in brackets. The major exception to this policy is Hugo Grotius, who is so well-known by the Latin form of his name that to use the vernacular would be obstructive. Classical works are cited from the Oxford Classical Text, Teubner or Loeb series, without further details of publication, and by the single name of their author (e.g., Cicero or Seneca). A bibliography of all other works cited appears at the end.

ACKNOWLEDGEMENTS

This book has its origin in the series of six Carlyle Lectures that I gave at the University of Oxford in the early months of 2008. I would like to express my warmest thanks to George Garnett, who offered me the invitation, and to the Warden and Fellows of All Souls College, who extended to me the hospitality of the college during the period of the lectures. I would also like to thank all those whose conversation made my days in Oxford such a pleasure and a profit, especially Colin Burrow, John Elliott, Joanna Innes, Ian Maclean, Noel Malcolm, John Robertson, Keith Thomas, Ronald Truman, and Brian Young. In Cambridge my research has been supported by the Faculty of History and by Gonville and Caius College. I would like to offer my thanks to both institutions, and also to the exemplary staff of the Rare Books Room of Cambridge University Library. I would also like to thank the Pierre Trudeau Foundation of Canada for supporting my visit to the University of Victoria in September 2008.

Many people have taken time and trouble to give me their comments and suggestions for improvement. As always, I owe a great debt of gratitude to Quentin Skinner for his unfailingly generous and thoughtful response. David Armitage and Ian Hunter read the text of the lectures for Princeton University Press, while Martin van Gelderen, Martti Koskenniemi, and James Tully commented on the whole book in draft form. I cannot thank them enough for the acuity of their insight and understanding. For the faults that remain I alone am responsible. I am deeply appreciative of the benefit I have received from conversations and exchanges with many others, including Duncan Bell, David Colclough, Michael Edwards, Andrew Fitzmaurice, Tim Harper, Steve Hindle, Kinch Hoekstra, Duncan Ivison, Julius Kirschner, Sachiko Kusukawa, Melissa Lane, Sarah Mortimer, Douglas Osler, Philip Pettit, Magnus Ryan, Peter Schroeder, Benjamin Straumann, and Jo Whaley. I would also like to mention my graduate students Anna Becker, Justin Jacobs, Sophie Nicholls, Sophie Smith, and Lauri Tähtinen. Chris Clark has been an inspiring interlocutor, and Shelley Lockwood read the typescript with her habitual clarity of mind; to both of these I owe special thanks. Finally, I could not have wished for a better editor than Ian Malcolm: perceptive, understanding, and enthusiastic from first to last. My warmest thanks go to him, and also to my copy editor, Marsha Kunin, for her careful attention to the text.

Above all, however, my work would never be done without the un-limited support and encouragement that I receive from all my friends and especially my family, which I can never sufficiently acknowledge. Their infinite care, affection, generosity and wit I treasure every day, and so my ultimate and most inadequate thanks go to my parents, to Alex, to Judy, to James and Stuart, and to my sister Hilary. This book is for her, with love.

CHANGES OF STATE

INTRODUCTION

ON THE THRESHOLD OF THE STATE

This is a book about what the sixteenth-century philosopher John Case called "the sphere of the city."[1] By it he meant, and I mean, the political space that human beings have constructed as a space in which to live a distinctively human life. "City" here is not "city" in the sense of an urban environment, *urbs* in the Latin. "City" is instead the Latin *civitas*, a civic not a stone structure. Again, this is not, at least in the first instance, *civitas* in its sense as a city like London, but in its sense as synonymous with the *respublica*, the commonwealth. It is what, at the end of our period, Thomas Hobbes would define as nothing other than the state: "that great Leviathan called a Common-Wealth, or State, (in latine *Civitas*)."[2] It is a metaphysical, not a physical place. And yet it is central to this idea of the city that it is not something immediately given in nature but something that has to be built out of it, just as the walls of the *urbs* have to be built on a patch of ground. Both are constructed by a peculiar kind of agency, human

[1] John Case, *Sphaera civitatis* (Oxford 1588). See fig. 1. The sphere of the city is here depicted by analogy with the celestial sphere, with Elizabeth I as the *mobile primum* or "prime mover," as the accompanying poem makes clear.
[2] Thomas Hobbes, *Leviathan* (1651), ed. R. Tuck (Cambridge: Cambridge University Press 1996), p. 9.

Figure 1 John Case, *Sphaera civitatis* (Oxford 1588) © The British Library
Board. 8006.b.8.

agency, which itself has to be theoretically constructed as something that is not *un*natural but is nevertheless distinguished from or discontinuous with all other kinds of natural agency. It is here that the focus of this study lies: not on "the sphere of the city" in itself, but in its aspect as something that is brought into being through processes of differentiation and exclusion on multiple levels.

In this sense, the central theme of this book is the conflicted relationship between nature and the city—the fraught intersection of the political and the natural world—in the natural law discourse of the later sixteenth and early seventeenth centuries, roughly the one hundred years between Francisco de Vitoria and Thomas Hobbes. In the course of this extraordinary century, marked by the outward expansion of European states across the globe and simultaneously by their internal implosion into civil war, the boundaries of political space were fundamentally contested not only at a practical but at a theoretical level, and the dominant (though by no means exclusive) idiom of that contestation was the universalising juridical language of natural law. What was forged in the process, culminating iconically in the Peace of Westphalia of 1648 and Hobbes's masterpiece *Leviathan* of 1651, is commonly taken to have been nothing other than the modern, territorial nation-state. Here we have, at least in theory, the sovereign state, clearly demarcated as a juridical entity both against other sovereign states and against other kinds of human association; and a fortiori against the world of non-human nature, dominion over which it protects, facilitates, and indeed claims for itself. Three or four hundred years later, however, these clear lines of demarcation that define the state seem decidedly more fragile. They are under pressure conceptually from new theories of international relations, of cosmopolitanism and global justice, and of the moral, juridical, and political status of non-human nature, all of which question the sharp break between "inside" and "outside" upon which the modern state in theory rests.[3] And that sharp break, that line of demarcation, is equally under pressure on the ground: from the waves of economic migrants who cross the frontiers of richer states, from the waves of the sea that threaten simply to wash away those of the poorer. It seems an apt moment, then, to look back at the formative moment of the modern state, training our focus precisely on the way that its

---

[3] For "inside" and "outside," see R. Walker, *Inside/outside: International relations as political theory* (Cambridge: Cambridge University Press 1993); for the challenge to boundaries in multiple senses, see for example S. Caney, *Justice beyond borders* (Oxford: Oxford University Press 2005), and M. Nussbaum, *Frontiers of justice: Disability, nationality, species membership* (Cambridge, Mass.: Belknap Press 2006). James Tully's *Public philosophy in a new key* (Cambridge: Cambridge University Press 2008), esp. vol. II, draws these several dimensions together in a conception of political philosophy that itself centres upon the crossing of boundaries—*franchissement*—as a practice of freedom.

Figure 2 Thomas Hobbes, *De cive* (Paris 1642). Reproduced by kind permission of the Syndics of Cambridge University Library.

boundaries were theoretically constructed. What we find is not a settled conception but a tense negotiation that is still fruitful for our political thinking today.

I take as the central problem with which natural law discourse in this period wrestles that the city or state must pull away from nature to form itself at the same time as being grounded in nature to motivate and to legitimate it. The Hobbesian colouring of the way I have framed this problematic should be acknowledged at the start. If we look at the famous frontispiece to the first edition of *De cive* of 1642, we can see that it depicts three zones or spheres of being: *Libertas* or freedom, which governs the notorious "condition of meer Nature," a state of war of all against all; *Imperium* or sovereign power, which governs the civic state of peace that flows from the institution of a sword of justice; and *Religio*, religion, which is a depiction of the Last Judgement, above and beyond the two human worlds shown beneath.[4] The border between the human and the divine—that middle dividing line—is not the subject of this book, deeply ambivalent and contested though it too was and is. Rather, we are concerned with the interface between the two lower pictures, the two figures that look out at us and challenge us for our choice. They are wholly distinct in every respect; the conditions they govern, seen in the background, are equally so. The city defines itself against nature in this sense. And yet at the heart of Hobbes's theory is the possibility of passage between the two, from nature to city and back again: the seeds of each are in each. A distinction that allows for passage, an either/or that is at the same time a mutual implication: this is the fine line that Hobbes's political theory treads; this is the uneasy frontier with which we are overall concerned.

Now it might be objected here that to use Hobbes to frame the entire question is to traduce all the other writers with whom we shall be concerned. For I have so far failed to define precisely what I mean by "nature," and herein lies the whole issue. Hobbes gets his definitional extremes, his either/or, by an animalisation—as his own words suggest, a brutalisation—of human nature outside the sovereign state, where "man is a wolf to man."[5] But our other authors do not recognise the problem in these terms, because they will never concede that humanity stops at the city gates. Human beings differ from animals not through common subjection to a sovereign, but intrinsically, of their essence: *human* nature

[4] Thomas Hobbes, *De cive* (1642), from the Latin text as edited by H. Warrender (Oxford: Clarendon 1983). See fig. 2.
[5] Hobbes, *De cive*, dedicatory epistle to William Cavendish, 3rd earl of Devonshire (ed. Warrender, p. [73]).

is never "*nature* nature." In consequence, there is a whole sphere of inter-human relationships outside the sphere of the city, governed by a common human nature and a common human justice that is more than simply where the sovereign's sword falls. Passage between cities is *not* the same as passage between the city and nature: it is illegitimate, and dangerous, to run the two together. By all means talk about the boundaries of the state, but recognise that the boundary between the sovereign state and the broader human community is not the same as the boundary between the state and nature. It is on precisely this distinction that the cosmopolitanism of Francisco de Vitoria and his colleagues—which will constitute our starting point—rests.

These objections are entirely to the point. We shall be talking about legitimate travellers going about their business between cities, about transgressive vagabonds who roam around in the manner of wild beasts, and about the wild beasts themselves. There is a difference that it would be wrong to elide. But I would defend my theme nonetheless. In the first place, to insist on the distinctiveness of human nature does not take away the problem of the interface between the city and nature—the political and the natural—but pushes it one level lower, from the city limit to the limit of the universal human community. That limit is equally constructed and equally contested, as the continuing early modern debate over the existence of natural slaves, and their juridical and political status, so clearly shows. The distinction between human nature and "nature nature" is not always so clear-cut. And the boundary of the human in any case implicates the city, for part of what is seen to be distinctively human is the motivation and the capacity to form into political commonwealths. For most of our non-Hobbesian-minded authors, human beings are not only naturally capable of, but naturally desirous of forming into such communities; those who are not are not only on the margins of the state but on the margins of humanity. Finally, Hobbes's determined stripping-away of the conventional pieties surrounding human nature speaks to a critical sensibility on the whole question of the human, its relationship to citizenship and to rights and its distinction from the animal. By using Hobbes's polarity as an axis for my own analysis, I do not mean to subordinate the whole of the early natural law tradition to his problematic. Nor do I want to endorse his solution. As we shall see, that solution carries its own difficulties, problems that are more promisingly dealt with in other kinds of contemporary natural law theory. Rather, I use his line of attack to open up some of the key assumptions and lines of argument that structure these theories and give them their characteristic shape.

With this in mind, this book examines the pressures on the relationship between nature and the city, between "inside" and "outside," from two angles. In a first move, it traces the genesis of the "sphere of the city" as a distinctive sphere of being contradistinguished against natural being, starting with human nature itself and moving from there to trace the complex juridical universe in which humans alone act and in which they build the political spaces that are commonwealths or states. It is thus about the metaphysical boundaries of the city, the ontological ground on which its structure of laws and rights is erected, and it is about the complex negotiation involved in maintaining those limits in the face of a human life that can be neither wholly naturalised nor wholly politicised. But the book goes on from there to explore "inside" and "outside" in another sense, the sense in which a traveller goes "out" of one city and "into" another. Local motion or locomotion of this kind, metaphysically under-privileged in almost all of our authors because it is not an exclusively human phenomenon, is nevertheless an essential component of political or civilised life as they envisage it. By pressing on the city as a place of travel and stay, the book explores a further dimension of the interface between the political and natural lives of subjects, exposing a critical early modern tension between the commonwealth as a situated space and as a body that of its essence defies situation. It is here that the two senses of *civitas*, a city like Paris and a commonwealth like France, collide. The first kind of city is firmly situated within the walls of the *urbs*. It welcomes or excludes strangers at its gates, and travel is primarily per-ceived as being between cities in this sense.[6] The second kind of city is in one way parasitic upon the first, its juridical structure represented by walls and turrets,[7] its rationale borrowed from the protection and defence offered by those physical barriers. *Civitas* as commonwealth is unthink-able without such cities, places in which people live a civilised life and that spill over from the walls to civilise their environs, as the vista in the background to *Imperium* on Hobbes's frontispiece so clearly shows.[8] And yet, as we shall see, the local fixity that marks this kind of city challenges the juridical self-definition of the commonwealth, which must transcend place if it is to constitute itself a self-sufficient or sovereign juridical struc-ture. In Carl Schmitt's terminology but against his conclusions, *Ordnung* and *Ortung* do not fall easily together in this period; the wall is both repre-sentative and insignificant, the commonwealth both placed and placeless.[9]

[6] See further below, ch. 7, p. 174, n. 23.
[7] For the representation of *civitas* in this way, see Q. Skinner, *Hobbes and republican liberty* (Cambridge: Cambridge University Press 2008), pp. 47–50.
[8] From a different perspective, Saskia Sassen stresses the importance of the political econ-omy of urban territoriality, with its associated political culture and judicial structures, to the emergence of the national territorial state: *Territory, authority, rights. From medieval to global assemblages* (Princeton: Princeton University Press 2006), pp. 53–73.
[9] C. Schmitt, *Der Nomos der Erde im Völkerrecht des Ius Publicum Europaeum*, 4th edition (Berlin: Duncker & Humblot 1997), esp. pp. 13–20, 36–48.

Thus, while the central chapters of this book are occupied with tracing the construction of the state as a juridical entity that fundamentally abstracts from place, I begin and end with models of political community that in their very different ways take place seriously. I start with a sixteenth-century version of juridical cosmopolitanism that, uniquely in my reading of the period, turns the cosmopolitan argument against the frontiers of Europe itself in the course of arguing for the rights of beggars. But I close with two authors who re-conceive the juridical model of the city on the basis of a relationship of "living together" or "living alongside," bringing the physical and essentially situated aspect of human life into the commonwealth at its foundation. Crucially, however, none of the theorists with whom we are concerned could ever accept that the sphere of the city might simply reduce to a matter of lives lived in different places, nor politics to the management of their mutual circulation or "Traffique" by government conceived as "that rod of Circes, that tameth both men, and beasts."[10] Michel Foucault has shown how the "reason of state" tradition that is exactly contemporaneous with this discourse creates, as the field for these new techniques of government, a new kind of "naturalness": what happens spontaneously when human beings live together, work together, produce things, exchange things. This is no longer "nature" in the sense of natural existence, a primitive condition, but a social kind of nature, the nature of the population that is the object of government. Significantly, the necessity to regulate and to police urban space, *la ville*, plays a central role in this new conception.[11] But our authors distinctively insist on the commonwealth as a shared juridical space that transcends the natural being of its subjects, "natural" here meaning the physical, the necessitated, what is shared with the animal that is the figure of the anti-political. What I hope to show is the ways in which nature in this sense is *involved* in political space even while it is on one level excluded.[12] It is this negotiation over the boundary between the two, rather than its disappearance into the population at large, that makes

[10] The terms are taken from William Jones's 1594 translation of Justus Lipsius's *Politica*, bk. II, chapter 1, in which Lipsius argues that civil society consists in two things, "Traffique," and "Government"; in the Latin, *commercium et imperium*. Justus Lipsius, *Sixe bookes of politickes or civil doctrine* (London 1594); ed. J. Waszink (Assen: Van Gorcum 2004), bk. 2, ch. 1, p. 295.

[11] Michel Foucault, *Sécurité, territoire, population. Cours au Collège de France, 1977–1978* (Paris: Seuil/Gallimard 2004), pp. 357–359; 14–21.

[12] In this respect I have found some of the lines of analysis in Giorgio Agamben's *Homo sacer. Il potere sovrano e la nuda vita*, 2nd ed. (Turin: Einaudi 2005), suggestive. But I specifically do not want to endorse his Schmittian, and reductive, language of "exception" for the relation between natural life and the city in the early modern period, or the absolute contrast he draws between Greek *zoē* and *bios*, which overrides the complexity of what our authors want to say, in Latin, about human life (*vita*). See below, ch. 6.

the natural law discourse of the late sixteenth and early seventeenth centuries a resource and a critical tool today.

I want to close this introduction with a few words concerning my procedure and my choice of authors. As will be evident from what I have already said, my aim has been to open up and explore what I see as the central theme of the particular political-philosophical discourse that we know as "natural law," in the formative century of its early modern career. I have approached this mass of literature from a critical perspective provided both by contemporary and by modern political theory, in an analysis that is thus intended to be both historical and philosophical. It is trained upon the characteristic argumentative motifs of this idiom or "way of talking" as a whole, rather than on particular authors as agents within their specific contexts—although, since a political language is constituted (even as it is modified) in the discursive moves of those who deploy it, contextual considerations necessarily come into play to explain the moves they make. This focus also accounts for why I have chosen to concentrate on academic or at least theoretical treatises to elucidate the contours of the language, rather than on the myriad strategic deployments of natural law arguments and principles in the practical political conflicts of the period.

Even at this more abstract level, however, there are different kinds of natural law thinking developed from different intellectual heritages within different textual genres and different institutional milieus, as well as some individuals and their works that do not fit easily into any particular school of thought. I have tried to do justice to the range, complexity, and fluidity of the discourse by moving between schools and authors, juxtaposing their different premises and strategies, showing where they come together and where they diverge, and what is at stake therein. For the sake of coherence, however, I have worked with a loose categorisation of authors into three broad affiliations. The first two are familiar in this context: the Catholic scholastic tradition of natural law writing, stemming ultimately from Thomas Aquinas's *Summa theologiae*, and what I have reluctantly and with several caveats acquiesced in calling "Protestant natural law," which includes the major figures of Hugo Grotius and Thomas Hobbes. Perhaps less obviously, I have added in the political treatises of Johannes Althusius and Henning Arnisaeus, together with a range of contemporary commentaries and near-commentaries on Aristotle's *Politics* that stand in the background to their work.

Of these three loose groupings, only the first is a tradition in any recognisable sense, comprising authors trained in the same way, in dialogue with the same source—Aquinas's handling of law and right in the *Prima secundae* and *Secunda secundae* of his *Summa*—and also with each other. Of the hundreds of writers who belong in this tradition, I have concentrated on a handful of the most influential and the most philosophically acute, taking the view that it is better for the reader to become reasonably well acquainted with a few brilliant contributors to the genre, whose works are moreover related to one another, than to be introduced sketchily to the bewildering and often rather derivative mass of the generality. "Protestant natural law," by contrast, though a fairly familiar label, is a much more fluid category. Its most famous representatives for the period with which we are concerned are Hugo Grotius and Thomas Hobbes, and yet just how "Protestant" either of them is is open to question, as it is for a wide range of legal scholarship on the part of Lutheran and Calvinist authors whose principal debts are to humanist jurisprudence. I discuss these difficulties of categorisation in chapter 3, even though I have ultimately chosen to stay with the label to mark a style of natural law reasoning that differs significantly from the Catholic tradition in certain respects. Finally, the contributors to the genre of *politica* (taken very broadly to include commentaries as well as free-standing treatises) that I consider might appear to be even more of a mixed bag; indeed, such works might not be thought to be part of the discourse of natural law at all. But I am interested in them for the characteristics that they share as more or less distant meditations upon the natural politics of Aristotle, and for their consistent deployment of natural law arguments in elucidating this conception. They form an important part of the early modern conversation on the relationship between nature and the city with which this study is overall concerned, and—as my appeal to Case's title itself suggests—the sphere of the city cannot be understood without them.

CHAPTER ONE

TRAVELLING THE BORDERLINE

We begin, then, in the middle of the sixteenth century, in Spain, with Francisco de Vitoria (ca. 1485–1546) and his Dominican colleagues at the university of Salamanca. They are famous for their reconstitution and redeployment of Thomas Aquinas's theory of natural law to address the new problems of the sixteenth century, problems that beset Spain along with the rest of Europe: the power of the crown both within its own commonwealth and in relation to other commonwealths, and these powers both within Europe and overseas. This was a century of conflict in which European states fought within themselves for control of the political order, between themselves for control of European territory, and beyond Europe for new realms and new subjects that had previously been unheard of. As internal and external war re-formed the political map, so it pressured the inherited languages of legal and political legitimacy.[1] Modifying and enlarging Aquinas's juridical vocabulary through the deployment of later medieval conceptions of rights as belonging to the individual, the Dominicans of the Spanish School of Salamanca provided one model of how natural law reasoning might be applied to address the

---

[1] For the relationship between war and political languages, see James Tully's introductory essay in *Meaning and context* (Cambridge: Cambridge University Press 1988), pp. 23–24.

competing claims of states, subjects, and non-subjects in a rapidly-changing world.[2]

For the School's most celebrated member, Francisco de Vitoria, natural law is the law of reason by which all human beings are naturally governed—the law of humanity as such—and, for him as for Aquinas, it ultimately determines the legitimacy of any subsequent human institutions and laws.[3] Closely connected with natural law is the *ius gentium*, traditionally but not very accurately translated as the "law of nations," since *gentes* is not always best understood as "nations" and *ius* can mean both "law" and "right."[4] Here, Vitoria's engagement with Aquinas's complicated pronouncements on the subject drew him in a new (if not entirely clear) direction. Aquinas had handled the question both in the *Prima* and the *Secunda secundae*, that is, in his discussion of law as well as in his discussion of *ius* or right. The definition in the *Secunda secundae* followed a discussion of the division between natural and positive right, in which Aquinas characterised the latter as something introduced by agreement, be it private or public.[5] In this schema, Aquinas took his prompt from the Roman jurist Gaius to place the *ius gentium*, as a function of natural reason, on the side of natural *ius*.[6] However, it is still not the *same* as natural *ius*, for this is (following Ulpian rather than Gaius) something common to all animals and not just to human beings.[7] By contrast, in the treatise on laws in the *Prima secundae* Aquinas appeared to see it rather as a species of positive law, although in so doing he still distinguished it from civil law

---

[2] I have discussed some of these issues in *Liberty, right and nature. Individual rights in later scholastic thought* (Cambridge: Cambridge University Press 1997), as has Brian Tierney in his *The idea of natural rights* (Atlanta, Ga.: Emory 1997). A comprehensive overview of the School with a rich bibliography can be found in Juan Belda Plans, *La escuela de Salamanca* (Madrid: Biblioteca de Autores Cristianos 2000). Biographical and bibliographical information on all the late scholastic authors mentioned in this study can be found on Jacob Schmutz's indispensable website *Scholasticon* (http://www.scholasticon.fr).

[3] It is important that although the law of nature is natural to us or "impressed" upon us by nature, this does not mean that it is innate in the sense of born with us. "Natural law is not so-called because it is in us from birth, for children do not have natural law nor the disposition [for it], but because from the inclination of nature we judge those things that are right": Francisco de Vitoria, *Comentario al tratado de la ley*, ed. V. Beltrán de Heredia (Madrid: CSIC 1952), q. 94, a. 1. See further below, ch. 2, pp. 57–58.

[4] For more on this distinction and the relations between the two terms, see below, chs. 3–4.

[5] Thomas Aquinas, *Summa theologiae* (henceforth *ST*), ed. altera Romana (Rome: Forzani 1894), 2a2ae, q. 57, a. 2.

[6] Ibid., a. 3. The text of Gaius (D.1.1.9) reads: "that which natural reason established among all men, this is kept equally by all and is called the *ius gentium*, as if the law [*ius*] that all nations [*gentes*] use."

[7] Ibid. For Ulpian's definition of the *ius naturale* as something common to all animals, see below, p. 23 and, in more detail, ch. 3, p. 99.

by the manner of its derivation from natural reason, that is, as conclusions from principles.[8]

In his commentary on the *Secunda secundae*, Vitoria followed Aquinas in seeing the *ius gentium* as a function of natural reason but departed from his position in this part of the *Summa* by understanding it as a kind of positive right. Furthermore, he provided a new source of its positivity in the consensus of all mankind.[9] However, in his lecture *De indis* ("On the American Indians"), Vitoria was less clear on the difference between natural law and the *ius gentium*. Here he said that the law of nations "either is, or is derived, from natural law,"[10] following the definition offered by Gaius as "what natural reason has constituted among all men." Nevertheless, Vitoria altered the original phrase *inter omnes homines* ("among all men") to *inter omnes gentes* ("among all nations"), prompting a tradition of interpretation that saw Vitoria as the originator of a modern understanding of the law of nations as a law between sovereign states.[11] But this is misleading. Vitoria saw the *ius gentium* as a law neither between individual men, nor between sovereign states, but between all human beings as forming one community: "The whole world, which is in a sense a commonwealth, has the power to enact laws which are just and convenient to all men; and these make up the law of nations."[12] The worldwide community is structured into different peoples without detracting from its essential juridical unity, and it is in this sense that Vitoria could characterise the *ius gentium* equally as the consensus of "all peoples and nations" or of "the whole world."[13] Without it, "the law of nature could hardly be preserved,"[14] and it governs all inter-human relations prior to and outside the laws of particular sovereign states.[15] It both legitimates

---

[8] Aquinas, *ST* 1a2ae, q. 95, a. 4.

[9] Francisco de Vitoria, *Comentarios a la Secunda secundae de Santo Tomás*, ed. V. Beltrán de Heredia (6 vols., Salamanca: Apartado 17 1934), vol. III, q. 57, a. 3, nn. 1–5.

[10] Francisco de Vitoria, *Relectio de Indis*, ed. and tr. in A.R.D. Pagden and J. Lawrance eds., *Francisco de Vitoria. Political writings* (Cambridge: Cambridge University Press 1992), 3.1, § 2, p. 278.

[11] For a clear and concise summary of this tradition of interpretation and the arguments for the contrary opinion, which I follow here, see H.-G. Justenhoven, *Francisco de Vitoria zu Krieg und Frieden* (Köln: Bachem 1991), pp. 64–71. See also the discussion of the original meaning of Gaius's text, together with Vitoria's interpretation, in P. Haggenmacher, *Grotius et la guerre juste* (Paris: Presses Universitaires de France 1983), pp. 313–25, 334–41.

[12] Francisco de Vitoria, *Relectio de potestate civili* ("On civil power"), 3. 4, § 21, tr. Pagden and Lawrance, p. 40.

[13] Vitoria, *Comentarios a la Secunda secundae*, vol. III, q. 57, a. 3, n. 4: *consensus omnium gentium et nationum*; ibid., n. 5: *consensus totius orbis*.

[14] Ibid., n. 4.

[15] Cf. Justenhoven, *Vitoria zu Krieg und Frieden*, p. 70: "Es ist eher angemessen, Vitorias Völkerrecht als vorstaatliches denn als zwischenstaatliches Recht zu bezeichnen."

division between properties and peoples and at the same time limits the claims they can make to exclude other members of the universal human society. On the surface, then, this mid-century Dominican meditation has an attractive dimension of what we now call "cosmopolitanism."

Vitoria used both natural law and the *ius gentium* to address the legitimacy of the Spanish conquest of the Indies. Thus, he argued, all justifications of conquest founded on the presupposition that the Indians are not properly human, not part of the universal society, and that therefore their commonwealths are not proper commonwealths, their property not properly owned, are illegitimate. There *are* no natural slaves, not at least in the Aristotelian quasi-bestial sense of natural chattels.[16] Vitoria suggested that if you thought the American Indians were natural slaves in this sense, you would have to think the same of Spanish peasants, many of whom "are little different from brute animals."[17] However, precisely their humanity, their membership in the universal society, equally demands that these Indian commonwealths allow "travellers"—and the irony here is very familiar—the right to use their harbours and rivers; the right to any "unoccupied"—more irony—deposits of precious metals; and the right to marry, to settle, and to be given citizenship in their towns and cities.[18] That is, to our modern ears, a quite astonishing degree of permeability of one state by the inhabitants of others. It is no surprise, then, that Vitoria's *ius communicandi* or "right of inter-communication" was seen at the time, and has been seen since, simply as a green light to imperialism and colonialism.[19] He would never, his contemporaries at Salamanca

---

Nonetheless, it is important that Vitoria's *ius gentium* is still not a wholly pre-*political* law, as shown by his reference to its source in the whole world as "in a sense a commonwealth."

[16] Francisco de Vitoria, *Relectio de Indis*, q. 1, aa. 4–6 and conclusion, tr. Pagden and Lawrance, pp. 231–92. As Brian Tierney has shown, Vitoria did not abolish the category of "natural slaves" in favour of "nature's children" for the American Indians, as Anthony Pagden argued in *The fall of natural man. The American Indian and the origins of comparative ethnology* (Cambridge: Cambridge University Press 1982). Instead, he reinterpreted the category (following Aquinas) as those free human beings who are naturally in need of the guidance of the wiser. See B. Tierney, "Aristotle and the American Indians—again. Two critical discussions," *Cristianesimo nella storia* 12 (1991), 295–322, and *The idea of natural rights*, ch. 11.

[17] Vitoria, *De Indis*, tr. Pagden and Lawrance, p. 252.

[18] Vitoria, *De Indis*, q. 3, a. 1, tr. Pagden and Lawrance pp. 278–84, and see the discussion in G. Cavallar, *The rights of strangers. Theories of international hospitality, the global community, and political justice since Vitoria* (Aldershot: Ashgate 2002), ch. 2; A.R.D. Pagden, "Dispossessing the barbarian," in A.R.D. Pagden ed., *The languages of political theory in early-modern Europe* (Cambridge: Cambridge University Press 1987), 79–98.

[19] As argued forcefully in A. Anghie, *Imperialism, sovereignty and the making of international law* (Cambridge: Cambridge University Press 2002), ch. 1. But the argument is too strong as it stands. Anghie ignores the *Relectio de Temperantia* (tr. Pagden and Lawrance "On dietary

objected, make that argument if it were the commonwealth of *Spain* that were in question.

I want to pursue the ramifications of this neo-Thomist theory of natural law and the *ius gentium*, with its conception of the permeability of borders, not from the more well-known writings of Vitoria but from those of his now lesser-known Salamancan colleague Domingo de Soto (1495–1560). Soto precisely did bring the argument into a European context, in the course of arguing the rights of another kind of suspect human being: beggars. He published *The deliberation in the cause of the poor* simultaneously in Latin and in Spanish early in 1545. Its immediate context was the poor law that was passed in Spain in 1540, but only published in 1544. The law was drawn up following representations to the emperor from several Spanish cities asking permission to institute measures to deal with the increasing problem of mendicancy and vagrancy. Charles V had already sanctioned poor law reform in Flanders, and the measures implemented by the Spanish cities as a consequence of the 1540 law have a generic similarity with the pattern that we find both at Ypres and in other European cities (both Protestant and Catholic).[20] As Soto summarised them, the contentious points of the law were six: (1) that the poor shall not be allowed to beg before they have been through an examination to determine whether they are genuine paupers; (2) that even if they are, they cannot beg except in their place of birth, and within certain limits (with exceptions for serious famine or plague); (3) that even in their place of birth, they shall not go out without official

---

laws, or self-restraint"), q. 1, a. 5, with its insistence that what Anghie calls "cultural difference," or practices contrary to natural law in Vitoria's terminology, do not in themselves justify conquest. What justifies intervention is strictly the violation of right involved in human sacrifice and cannibalism. Secondly, while there is certainly an element of dual construction of the Indian—both as (culturally) "other" and as (juridically) "same"—this does not lead so clearly to a juridico-cultural fusion to the detriment of the Indian. Anghie does not acknowledge (pp. 21–22) that Vitoria's understanding of the Indians as "timid" *does* affect the Spaniards' right to wage war on them based on their violation of the *ius communicandi*, which Vitoria does *not* construct as barbarian aggression: "the barbarians may be *understandably* fearful" (emphasis mine), and these "understandable fears made them innocent. So the Spaniards must take care for their own safety, but do so with as little harm to the barbarians as possible since this is merely a defensive war....This is a consideration which must be given great weight." (*De Indis*, q. 3, a. 1, 5th conclusion, tr. Pagden and Lawrance, p. 282.)

[20] For the Spanish case, see the general discussion by J. Arrizabalaga, "Poor relief in Counter-reformation Castile: An overview," in Ole Peter Grell, Andrew Cunningham, and Jon Arrizabalaga eds., *Health care and poor relief in Counter-reformation Europe* (London and New York: Routledge 1999), 151–76, and the earlier but more detailed studies by Maureen Flynn, *Sacred charity. Confraternities and social welfare in Spain, 1400–1700* (London: Macmillan 1989), and Linda Martz, *Poverty and welfare in Habsburg Spain* (Cambridge: Cambridge University Press 1983).

papers; (4) that they shall not be given these papers until they have been confessed by the Church; (5) that pilgrims to Santiago shall not diverge more than four leagues from the *camino real*; (6) that officials shall reform the hospitals so that the poor are fed and cared for there, rather than begging at the doors of houses.[21]

Soto's *Deliberation*, addressed to the young prince Philip—the future Philip II of Spain—is a passionate attack on all these measures, and it provoked an angry response from Juan de Robles (or de Medina), a Benedictine monk involved in the reform of poor relief at Zamora.[22] Opinions differ as to how to evaluate the debate between them. Some see Soto's defence of mendicancy as the survival of an essentially medieval Christian mindset, in which the poor shall be with us always and perform a moral function in pricking the consciences of the rich and inspiring them to charity. Certainly, this is one of Soto's themes. But a glance at a work written ten years earlier by a Franciscan friar in the same city of Salamanca shows how far Soto's tract is from simply perpetuating this inherited framework. Gabriel de Toro's defence of mendicancy is called *A treasure of divine and human mercy*, anchoring poverty in the life of Christ and defending the twin statuses and virtues of rich and poor. Soto is equally certain that charity is a duty and mercy a virtue, and he has some sharp things to say—in his responses to the third and fourth of his points of contention—about the hypocrisy of those who insist on examining the morals of the poor while turning a blind eye to their own. But the main theoretical focus of his argument—in his replies to the first, second, fifth, and sixth points of contention—is explicitly on the rights of the poor rather than the duties of the rich. Again, those rights are explicitly seen as operating in the context of territorial commonwealths structured internally into provinces and cities, and externally in relation to other territorial commonwealths. These features link his evaluation of mendicancy with the broader juridical analysis of the commonwealth, its constituent members, and the *ius gentium* that he developed in his later work, *On justice and right*, first published in 1553. In this connection it is Linda Martz's assessment that still seems the more acute:

> To those of us who know the end of the story—state taxation and the implementation of welfare—Domingo de Soto appears to be

[21] The Spanish text is edited in F. Santolaria Sierra ed., *El gran debate sobre los pobres en el siglo XVI. Domingo de Soto y Juan de Robles 1545* (Barcelona: Ariel 2003); these provisions at pp. 53–54.

[22] See the authors cited above, n. 20, as well as Santolaria's introductory study and, in most detail, J. N. Garrán Martínez, *La prohibición de la mendicidad. La controversia entre Domingo de Soto y Juan de Robles en Salamanca (1545)* (Salamanca: Ediciones Universidad Salamanca 2004).

arguing for an outdated system. However, the Dominican raised some issues that continue to be of interest for later generations ... if freedom of movement within the confines of national borders is now a generally accepted premise in most of the developed countries of the world, the immigration policies of those same countries are devoted to limiting outsiders, especially those who are poor and unskilled. Nor have the obligations of the rich developed countries to the poor undeveloped ones received any accepted or comprehensive definition. Thus the problems brought up by Domingo de Soto in the sixteenth century linger on, though juridical boundaries have been enlarged from cities and provinces to countries.[23]

Martz does not, however, pursue her analysis beyond the *Deliberation* into Soto's legal-theoretical writings, especially *On justice and right*, or into the broader context of the second scholastic meditation on the rights of states both internally and externally. Perhaps for this reason, she misses the extent to which the international perspective is in fact present in the work.

We can find many elements of the debate between Soto and Robles in a more embryonic form in the literature generated by the contested introduction of poor law reform at Ypres.[24] As this controversy involved the Dominican Order along with the other mendicant orders of the city, and was sent to the Sorbonne for adjudication, Soto may well have seen some of the actual documents involved; at the very least, we know from his text that he was well aware of the Ypres legislation.[25] The principal aim of the reform was to prevent begging in the streets of the city and at the doors of houses. But the implementation of such reforms within the city meant dealing with the large numbers of people coming into the city from outside, both natives and foreigners.[26] The new regulations were finally published in 1531 under the title *Forma subventionis pauperum*.[27] Here, the lives of beggars who heretofore have "roamed around" (*circumvagabantur*) are presented not only as un-Christian, "without any order to their life," but as only half-human: they are like "shorn sheep," or "the shadows of the dead," "more than orphans," "whose life and well-being lies in the help of others."[28] This miserable condition of mendicancy is

[23] Martz, *Poverty and welfare*, p. 28.

[24] A history of this process and a valuable collection of related documents is furnished in J. Nolf, *La réforme de la bienfaisance à Ypres au XVIe siècle* (Ghent: E. van Goethen & Co. 1915).

[25] Soto refers to Ypres in chapters 11 and 12 of the *Deliberation*.

[26] Nolf, *Réforme*, xvi, xxvii–xxviii, xlvi–vii.

[27] Ibid., lxi. A French translation made from the Latin at the same time is given as Document XVIII.

[28] *Forma subventionis pauperum, quae apud hyperas flandrorum urbem viget* (Ypres 1531), sig. Aii v, [Avi] v.

licit by natural equity insofar as it is a "remedy for necessity," for "the saving of life that would otherwise be endangered."[29] Where there is no longer any need, there is no longer any reason why begging should be licit. Thus, if charity is administered publicly, begging in the streets, begging from door to door, can be outlawed.[30] The regulations deride those who rail against the new law "and complain that their liberty to beg has been taken away from them, as if they have been deprived of their right." Liberty is not a licence to do what you will, but is subject to reason, and beggars under the new scheme have enough for modesty and for their needs—if not for their character.[31] In addition to these general provisions, however, the *Forma* devotes five sections to the problem of beggars from outside. It establishes the principle that native or "internal" inhabitants, "those who together with us are members of one political body," are to be preferred to foreigners or "externals," on the grounds that it is impossible to satisfy the needs of all and that the reforms would go to ruin if this were attempted.[32] Pilgrims are to be admitted into the city, but not allowed to beg, as previously. Rather, they are to be supplied according to their needs, as are travellers and the sick likewise. "But we do not let in those strangers who come to live in this city with a great flock of children purely for the pursuit of alms; except those whom we are persuaded to accept into the company of our own poor by the necessity of a just cause, or a most pitiable calamity (such as those that befall as a result of war, shipwreck, fire or other public dangers)."[33]

The mendicant orders at Ypres protested vigorously against the new reforms. While the public organisation of the collection and distribution of alms certainly threatened the status and revenues of these orders, it seems overly cynical to put their opposition down purely to self-interest.[34] The reforms were approved by the Sorbonne under the explicit condition that the mendicant orders be permitted to continue to beg, and the spiritual value of begging out of choice was recognised in the *Forma*.[35] Rather, the orders protested against what they saw as dangers to the practice of charity and the succour of the poor. This protest included, as a key element, an objection to the provisions with regard to strangers. Yes, it might be reasonable to purge the city of condemned thieves and vagabonds, but all peaceful migrants should be received as a profit to the city:

---

[29] *Forma subventionis pauperum,* sig. [Av] r, *De causis mendicationis.*

[30] Ibid., sig. [Bv] r-v, *Qua ratione publica mendicatio antiquanda.*

[31] Ibid., sig. [Avi] r, *De pauperibus morosis.*

[32] Ibid., sig. [Bvii] v, *Exteris et internis egenis qualiter benefacienda*; sig. Ciiii r, *Qualiter politiae prospicienda.*

[33] Ibid., sig. [Bvii] v, *Quibus casibus advenae ad inhabitandum civitatem admittendi.*

[34] As does Nolf, *Réforme,* l–lx.

[35] Ibid., doc. XVII, p. 122; *Forma subventionis pauperum,* sig. [Av] r.

it is unreasonable to fear that one cannot provide for all of them.[36] This common protest was repeated specifically by the prior of the Ypres Dominicans, to the effect that the *Forma* contains things "which seem to accord little with the sacred laws: such as keeping the poor away from the gates and forbidding them air and water (as the saying goes) like public enemies, and not permitting them even to present themselves to the eyes of the pious, or ejecting them if they have entered with a dreadful retinue and whirlwind; so that imploring the faith of God and man they cry out with that saying of the poet, 'What land so barbarous is this that we are barred the hospitality [*hospitium*] of the shore?'"[37] This is precisely the same quotation from Virgil's *Aeneid* that Vitoria would use in asserting the *ius communicandi* between all men and the consequent indefensibility of the Indians' trying to keep the Europeans out without just cause.[38] The important point for our purposes is that within the Dominican tradition it had already been applied to Europeans themselves, in the context of the migration of the poor.

A more dramatic form of the arguments for and against the practice of public begging occurs in a pair of speeches written by the indigent humanist scholar Christianus Cellarius, published in 1530 and 1531, respectively. The earlier is entitled *Oration in favour of the poor, that they be permitted to beg.* The latter, a retraction—under precisely what pressure we do not know, since the author is very obscure—is entitled *Oration against mendicancy, for the new relief of the poor.* Both addressed the case of foreign beggars. The *Oration in favour* pleaded for the admission of those who have been driven from their country by floods and earthquakes, tyranny and war "which has spread far and wide across Europe." "Do you want all these to go back to their country? What country? ... Are you so fierce that you begrudge us this common air? ... What savagery is this, to refuse to share [*communicare*] one's country with another? ... It certainly seems profoundly iniquitous to me to want to separate anyone from the common fellowship of men. Why do we not rather ... think this whole world our common country? ... Why do we get into so many squabbles over the empty names of regions?"[39] But Cellarius's reply to his own text in the *Oration against* provided an answer based on the necessary separation of the nations. Taking the "hard case" of a woman driven out of her own country by force, begging at your door, he asks what we should say to her and suggests the following:

---

[36] Ibid., doc. VIII, p. 64.

[37] Ibid., doc. XXIV, p. 150. The reference is to Virgil, *Aeneid* I. 539–540.

[38] Vitoria, *De Indis*, 3.1, tr. Pagden and Lawrance, p. 278.

[39] Christianus Cellarius, *Oratio pro pauperibus, ut eis liceat mendicare* (Antwerp 1530), sig. [Bi] v.

I do not command you to go back to your own country, woman, since you have none [*quandoquidem nulla est*]. I would rather encourage you if you can to find food by manual labour.... But you say that you cannot. Do you therefore need shelter? it will be provided. Are you sick? you will be healed. Are you hungry? food will not be denied. Pardon us that we give you hospitality rather than a home. Forgive us that we supply you with food for a few days rather than your whole life. We cannot do as much as we want.... You are a traveller, therefore we will treat you as a traveller, and it belongs to a traveller not to stay long in the same place. Do not be indignant that we give more to our own citizens than to you, since we are more obliged to them.... Why therefore do you wail so tragically as if we begrudge this common air. Do you so confuse the law of nature and of nations? who think that there is no difference between native and alien, Christian and pagan, as long as they are human.[40]

As we shall see, Soto's text is designed to provide an answer not merely to the pragmatics of the legislation, but also, and more, to these essentially juridical considerations.

Soto's juridical handling of mendicancy recognises two principal subjects of rights: the individual on the one hand and the *respublica* or "commonwealth" on the other. From the point of view of the individual, mendicancy involves the intersection of two rights: the right to freedom of movement and the right to the means of living. From the point of view of the commonwealth, the rights in question are the rights of territorial states vis-à-vis other territorial states, and the right of the public power to promote the internal common good. Because the rights of individuals dominate the treatise, I shall begin with the nature of the human individual as a juridical subject or a subject of rights.

The fundamental individual human right, for Soto, is the right to stay alive—more formally, to "preserve one's being" (*ius se conservandi*). The formula, and the primacy, of self-preservation are ultimately due to Thomas Aquinas's handling of natural law. Aquinas had argued that "the order of the precepts of natural law follows the order of natural inclinations. For firstly there is in man the inclination to his good in accordance with nature, in which he has something in common with all substances: insofar as every substance desires the preservation of its own being in accordance with nature; and in accordance with this inclination, there pertain to natural law all things by which the life of man is preserved, and

---

[40] Id., *Oratio contra mendicitatem pro nova pauperum subventione* (Antwerp 1531), sig. [b v] v.

the contrary is hindered."[41] This is natural *law*. When we come to natural *right*, we find Aquinas rather surprisingly adopting Ulpian's dictum that the *ius naturale* is something common to all animals, including man—surprisingly, because natural *law* (being a work of reason) is a law of human, that is, rational, nature alone.[42] Natural right includes all things that are "equated to" another thing absolutely speaking: for example, the female to the male for the purposes of generation, the parent to the child for the purposes of education, and so forth.[43] There is no mention here of a right of preserving oneself, nor is there indeed any hint of this "subjective" and "active" formulation of rights—the right that a subject has of doing *x*—even though the natural law is specifically formulated in this way as a law of natural actions. Right in Aquinas is instead formulated "objectively" as the equality, "equation," or commensuration of one thing to another that makes it the object of justice. However, to cut a very long story short, Soto, while preserving this objective sense of right, also uses the subjective sense which gives rights of action to individuals, and he takes over from Aquinas's discussion of natural *law* his most fundamental natural *right*, the right of preserving one's own being. He mentions this right several times in his major work *On justice and right* and it always figures as the right that overrides every other right. This right is more "innate" than any other—that is, more intimately connected with one's very nature than any other—and it can never be "trumped."[44]

In several phrasings of this right, Soto appears to attribute it to animals as well as human beings ("all things" are said to have this right innate in them).[45] This is consonant with his adoption, through Aquinas, of Ulpian's notion of a natural *ius* common to all animate beings. However, all such phrasings are limited to a natural right *of acting*. When it comes to right *over* things or persons, animals have no right at all, not even any natural right. They are not capable of injury, and restitution is never due to them but to their owner.[46] This is because they are not capable of owning their actions, which is what for the entire Thomist tradition grounds

---

[41] Aquinas, *ST* 1a2ae, q. 94, a. 2.

[42] The tensions in Aquinas's account are excellently brought out in M. B. Crowe, "St. Thomas and Ulpian's natural law," in A. Maurer ed., *St. Thomas Aquinas 1274–1974. Commemorative studies* (Toronto: Pontifical Institute of Medieval Studies 1974), 261–82.

[43] Aquinas, *ST* 2a2ae, q. 57, a. 3.

[44] I have discussed Soto's handling of natural law and natural right in *Liberty, right and nature*, ch. 4; see also Merio Scattola, "Naturrecht als Rechtstheorie: Die Systematisierung der «res scolastica» in der Naturrechtslehre des Domingo de Soto," in F. Grunert and K. Seelmann eds., *Die Ordnung der Praxis. Neue Studien zur Spanischen Spätscholastik* (Tübingen: Niemeyer 2001), 21–46.

[45] Domingo de Soto, *De iustitia et iure* (Salamanca 1556), lib. IV, q. 2, a. 2 and q. 7, a. 1, cf. q. 4, a. 1; Brett, *Liberty, right and nature*, p. 152.

[46] Soto, *De iustitia et iure*, lib. IV, q. 1, a. 2.

ownership or *dominium* over anything else.[47] Ownership of one's actions depends on being able, through reason and will, to command them. This in turn presupposes cognisance and volition of an end for the sake of which those acts are commanded. Thus, to own one's actions, and to act towards an end, come to the same thing in this tradition; and this is nothing other than human liberty. Animals are not said to be capable of either of these, for an animal is driven by natural instinct, and it does not properly *use* anything because it cannot apply one thing for the sake of another. As a consequence, humans do, but animals do not, have ownership of other things and occasionally other persons, as well as various other rights over both things and persons. Soto is keen to insist that not every right over something or someone is full-blown *dominium*.[48] But insofar as all other rights—for example usufruct in a thing, or paternal rights over a child—have the same foundation in human liberty or *dominium* of one's actions, they are extensions of the same juridical phenomenon from which animals are excluded.

There are some things over which man naturally has *dominium*. Man is naturally the owner, in private, of his actions and also of his honour and fame.[49] He is also naturally the owner, in common, of all the things of the earth—the lands, seas, rivers, woods, fish, beasts, birds. This *dominium* is said to be a necessary consequence of the simple fact of his natural life—he needs to use these things in order to stay alive.[50] Here we see an apparent tension in Soto's argument: *Dominium* is supposed to be founded on liberty, otherwise animals would have it. But the *dominium* of the earth in common is explicitly said to have "natural life" as its title.[51] Why then does it not follow in the same way upon the lives of animals? Why is it sufficient for cattle (*pecudes*—Soto's example) simply to have *potestas*, or

---

[47] See K. Seelmann, "Selbstherrschaft, Herrschaft über die Dinge und individuelle Rechte in der spanischen Spätscholastik," in M. Kaufmann and R. Schnepf eds., *Politische Metaphysik. Die Entstehung Moderner Rechtskonzeptionen in der Spanischen Scholastik* (Frankfurt: Peter Lang 2007), 43–57.

[48] Soto, *De iustitia et iure*, lib. IV, q. 1, a. 1.

[49] Ibid., q. 2, a. 3, and q. 3, a. 1.

[50] Ibid., q. 2, a. 1: "For insofar as man is bodily, he is owed those things that are necessary for his life. It was on this reasoning that Aristotle concluded that all things are for the sake of man. And therefore, just as man's limbs and natural potentials are owed to his nature even if it was by a miracle that God created men, just so, that [original] grant of *dominium* over things was a kind of consequence of natural right, as something owed to human nature, supposing its existence, which God had freely conferred upon him at his creation."

[51] Ibid., q. 1, a. 1: "The title of the natural *dominium* that man has in the things of the earth, is his natural life, which cannot be preserved without them, by reason of which God and nature gave to man, together with the desire of preserving himself, the right of using necessary sustenance."

power, over the grass, and not *dominium*? The answer lies in what he has said before, that, although a cow may be eating its grass to stay alive, it is doing this out of natural instinct: it does not have the purpose of staying alive and so it cannot properly be said to be *using* that grass in order to stay alive. Use is a free act. Thus its natural power over the grass will suffice for it to pursue its natural instincts. But a human being does not eat his or her lunch (let's say) instinctively, but purposively, and this involves an appropriation of that lunch that it would be an injury to interfere with. The natural life of a human being is qualitatively different from that of a cow, and *dominium* is consequent upon the one but not the other. Thus human natural *dominium* over the things of the earth is a function both of necessity and of liberty: neither will suffice by itself. Soto underlines this point by arguing that other rational creatures—angels and demons— do not have this *dominium* because, although they have liberty, that is, *dominium* of their actions, they are not embodied and therefore have no need of things.[52]

Human beings' having *dominium*, then, is intimately connected with their ability to reason towards an end. It is this same ability that generates, beyond natural right, the *ius gentium*—normally translated the "law of nations," as we have seen, but in this context Soto is talking about right, not about law. The difference between natural *ius* and the *ius gentium* is that while the former signals what is naturally commensurate with something else, the *ius gentium* signals what humans have reasoned to be commensurate given the ends that humans have and given the circumstances in which they find themselves.[53] This reasoning is natural reasoning; it does not require any created legislator, and it can be done by individual human beings on their own. "Establishing the *ius gentium* does not require all human beings to gather together into one place: because reason teaches it to individuals of itself."[54] The upshot is a consensus, precisely because the reasoning is natural; however, precisely because it depends on consensus, the *ius gentium* is positive, not natural. Under this *ius gentium*, human beings agreed to divide up their common *dominium* over the

---

[52] Ibid., q. 1, a. 2.

[53] Ibid., q. 1, a. 3: "to judge of things in order towards an end and under certain circumstances does not belong to all animals, but peculiarly to man in virtue of his reason, whose office it is to bring one thing together with another. Therefore the right that is established by this relational reasoning is called the *ius gentium*." See Scattola, "Naturrecht als Rechtstheorie," pp. 37–39; idem, "Before and after natural law," in T. J. Hochstrasser and P. Schröder eds., *Early modern natural law theories* (Dordrecht: Kluwer 2003), 1–30, at p. 11.

[54] Soto, *De iustitia et iure*, lib. III, q. 1, a. 3. This point is made even more emphatically at lib. IV, q. 3, a. 1, arguing that the things laid down in the law of nations "do not need a prince, nor any gathering of a commonwealth. For the law of nations differs from civil law for this reason, viz. that reason itself teaches it to individual men separately."

earth. In other words, what they had because they were *capable* of use, they divided up *the better* to use in the circumstances in which they found themselves. Those circumstances are the circumstances of fallen man, in which the earth no longer bears fruits spontaneously and natural innocence has been lost.

How did the division of the common happen? Here Soto relies on the famous passage in the *Institutes* to the effect that what belongs to no one falls by natural reason to the one who first occupies it.[55] According to Soto, natural reason in this context means the natural reasoning of individuals in the circumstances following the Fall, and this right therefore belongs to the *ius gentium*, relying on human consensus or agreement, rather than the *ius naturale*. The division of *dominia* under the *ius gentium* happened immediately after the Fall: thus, Soto says, Cain built a city, Noah's children dispersed to the different regions and islands of the globe, and Abraham and Lot agreed to go their separate ways. It is therefore clear that it is not just division in general that is a matter of the *ius gentium*, but the specific division whereby different nations came to possess different regions.[56] However, many things remained in common, because the *dominium* of them could not be divided up: the place of the city, roads or routes (*itinera*), air, water, shores and harbours, fish, wild animals, birds.[57] Again, this time in the related discussion of what constitutes theft, Soto argues from the *Institutes* that the gems that one finds on the seashore even now fall to the one who finds them—because "the shores remained in common under the *ius gentium*"—and "the judgement of the *ius naturale* is the same in respect of the veins of gold and other metals which are in the bowels of the earth."[58] Does that mean, then, that Spaniards who go to America in search of gold are the rightful owners, under the *ius gen-*

---

[55] Inst. 2. 1, *de rerum divisione*.

[56] Soto, *De iustitia et iure*, lib. IV, q. 3, a. 1, 3rd conclusion. Soto here argued against Cajetan, who had asserted that the specific division of territories is a matter of *ius civile*: "... two things. Firstly, that one thing belongs to one person, and another to another. Secondly, that this field is this man's and that field is that man's. With regard to the first, property stems from the *ius gentium*. For it is reason that dictates it.... With regard to the second, it stems from positive law: since before this thing is appropriated to this man and that to that, it makes no difference if it happens the other way round. For positive law is defined, from *Ethics* V, as that which is initially indifferent" (*Secunda secundae cum commentariis Cardinalis Caietani* (Lyon 1552), on q. 66, a. 2, fo. 107r; "66" is misprinted in Soto as "99").

[57] Soto, *De iustitia et iure*, lib. IV, q. 3, a. 1, 4th conclusion: *puta locus, ut ait illic Aristoteles nempe civitas, itinera* (etc.). The reference to Aristotle is odd; it ought to be a reference to Aristotle's critique of Plato's *Republic* in Book II of the *Politics*, which Soto has just been discussing in support of *divisio rerum*. But I cannot see which passage Soto is pointing to. The meaning seems clear, however: the space of the city is public space that cannot be divided.

[58] Soto, *De iustitia et iure*, lib. V, q. 3, a. 3.

tium, of any that they find? No: "the reply is that under this very *ius*, this is not at all licit, unless the inhabitants were to consent, or they held those finds for derelict: for the regions were divided under the *ius gentium*: and therefore although such things are in common to the peoples of that region, strangers cannot seize those things if the inhabitants are unwilling. For the French are not able, for this reason, to come into (*penetrare*) our lands, nor we into theirs."[59] This little passage adds a very important qualification to the topic of "division of *dominium*," one that was recognised by contemporaries.[60] Vitoria had held that "if gold in the ground or pearls in the sea or anything else in the rivers has not been appropriated, they will belong by the *ius gentium* to the first taker," explicitly in the context of Spanish activity in the Indies.[61] But in Soto's view, the division of the regions divides all the resources of those regions as well. For Soto, then, we live in a world of geographically separate political entities with a more restricted right of interpenetration than Vitoria had theorised. And yet this is the world in which there exists, according to Soto, a transregional right to beg. Who has that right and how is it founded?

Soto began the *Deliberation in the cause of the poor* with a discussion of what in sixteenth-century England were called "sturdy beggars," that is, people who travelled around living by begging, but who were yet strong enough to work. This category goes back to Roman law, in the Code,[62] and the Spanish legislation that Soto cites in addition largely repeats the Roman legal attitude: that these people are not to be tolerated; they are "vagabonds" or vagrants and are to be forced to work if they will not do it willingly. Soto's attitude is wholly typical: in the post-Fall condition of mankind, which, as we have seen, is the condition of the *ius gentium*, man must labour to earn his keep ("in the sweat of thy brow ..." etc.). Natural reason confirms Scripture: "For he whose own goods do not provide him with the wherewithal to live, has no right to seek the goods of others, unless he does a service to those others in his turn, either by his art, or some other work, or business." Thus, no one has a right to beg for another's goods if he is capable of earning those goods. In addition to

---

[59] Ibid. The passage is quoted by A.R.D. Pagden, *Lords of all the world. Ideologies of empire in Spain, Britain and France, c. 1500–c. 1800* (New Haven: Yale University Press 1995), p. 52, and Cavallar, *Rights of strangers*, p. 111.

[60] Soto's departure from Vitoria on this point was recognised by the Louvain Jesuit Leonard Lessius, *De iustitia et iure caeterisque virtutibus cardinalibus* (3rd ed., Antwerp 1612; first published Louvain 1605), lib. II, cap. 5, dub. xii, fo. 51, col. 1, who follows Soto and points out (implicitly) the inconsistency in Vitoria's position: Vitoria allows the prince of the commonwealth for the sake of the common good to prohibit hunting, that is, the "occupation" of wild animals; so why not the "occupation" of deposits of precious metals?

[61] Francisco de Vitoria, *De Indis*, 3. 1, tr. Pagden and Lawrance, p. 280.

[62] C. 11. 26, *De mendicantibus validis*.

this, no one has a right to travel in an aimless way. To travel around for no reason—no necessity, no convenience, and no utility—is vicious because it signals that the person in question has nothing to do: he is otiose or idle (and the devil finds work for idle hands). Travel that is not *to* anywhere, or *for* something, defeats the final causality—the purposiveness—of the *ius gentium* and of the division of *dominia*, and indeed of *dominium* in general, which is as we have seen the marker of distinctively human life. As such it is inherently criminal: such people, Soto explicitly tells us, "live against natural law."[63] And in an interesting passage from *On justice and right*, Soto (like Vitoria) rejected the original Aristotelian category of natural slaves, but allowed it a degree of validity in the case of those who deliberately choose a wandering lifestyle, which he connects with criminality: "Where ... Aristotle says that just as we can hunt animals, so we can make war against those human beings who are natural slaves: we should give him a hearing just to this extent, that we can drive off or subject by force those who roam around straggling in the manner of wild beasts, keeping none of the pacts of the nations, but trying to get their hands on other people's goods wherever they go."[64] Because they are not travelling between cities, to or for something, they effectively take themselves out of the human world and travel instead the borderline between city and nature, in the physical but not political space of animals.

Vagabondage or vagrancy, then, is by definition outlawed. By contrast, those who travel because of some business or other convenience, or out of necessity, have a perfect right to do so. The non-sturdy beggar falls into the latter class, and thus, unlike the Ypres *Forma*, Soto avoids the language of *vagare* for the movement of those who are truly poor. These are people who "go forth" (*exire*) or "go through the world" (*per orbem discurrere*) because they genuinely cannot support themselves in their own locality —for whatever reason. Soto takes care to guard against too stringent a definition of the sturdy beggar:

> ... for someone to be a legitimate pauper it is not necessary that he be sick. For it is enough, that he be either advanced in years, or weak, or is in the grip of any other impediment which means that

[63] Domingo de Soto, *In causa pauperum deliberatio* (using the edition of Salamanca 1566, in which the *Deliberatio* is printed together with the *Relectio de ratione tegendi et detegendi secretum* as a second volume to his commentary on bk. IV of the *Sentences*), cap. III (*De vagabundis*), fo. 100.

[64] Soto, *De iustitia et iure*, lib. IV, q. 2, a. 2. It is not entirely correct, then, to say that the Dominicans universally rejected any justification of war on the grounds of natural slavery, as argued in R. Tuck, *The rights of war and peace* (Oxford: Oxford University Press 1999), p. 70. Indeed, Soto's suggestion here is similar to the "beyond the pale" conception of the enemies of human society that Tuck attributes, as an entirely different way of thinking, to the humanist tradition and to Alberico Gentili (ibid., pp. 34–40).

he is not equal to the amount of labour that he would need to provide for himself and his own ... It is also relevant here, that there are many who from time to time are capable of some sort of work, but not continually, or often.... And there are moreover others who, even though they are sturdy, nevertheless have the right to beg. Namely, those who cannot find work, or people to hire them. And if they cannot find them in their birthplace, then they can go forth to look for it wherever (*quocunque*).[65]

The right to beg, then, is the consequence of the necessity of finding a livelihood. As such it is an extension of the natural right of self-preservation.[66] Nevertheless, Soto made it clear—and this is critically important—that the necessity that is relieved by begging, and generates the right to beg, is not the same as extreme necessity. In extreme necessity, where death is imminent (although you do not have to be actually at death's door), you may licitly take something that belongs to another without begging or asking permission, because, as Aquinas himself had taught, the law of property cannot prejudice the natural law of self-preservation to which the goods of the earth were originally ordained in common.[67] The corollary of this is that in extreme necessity, the rich are under a specific duty of charity to give *to that person*, even from goods that are not superfluous to their status, on pain of mortal sin.[68] The right by which a person takes that thing is a natural right. But the necessity of

[65] Soto, *In causa pauperum deliberatio*, cap. IX, fo. 111.

[66] See the analysis in K. Deuringer, *Probleme der Caritas in der Schule von Salamanca* (Freiburg: Herder 1959), esp. p. 65: "unmittelbare Folgerung aus dem Naturrecht auf Existenz."

[67] Soto, *De iustitia et iure*, lib. V, q. 3, a. 4 (*Utrum ei qui egestate premitur furari liceat*), 3rd conclusion: "In extreme need, viz. where it is evident and urgent, then one who is in that dire condition may licitly help himself from the goods of others: whether he takes them by stealth, or openly. We have already often stated this conclusion: because so innate in man is the right of preserving himself, that everything else cedes to it."

[68] Domingo de Soto, *Commentarium* in II.II. q. 32, a. 5, nn. 18–32, ed. in Deuringer, *Probleme der Caritas*, pp. 146–49; cf. the more truncated discussion in *In causa pauperum deliberatio*, cap. IV (*De advenis mendicantibus*), fo. 102. Soto stresses that this is a duty of charity, not justice, unlike Vitoria who had gone further and argued that while in grave need the duty is one of charity, in extreme need it is one of justice (Deuringer, *Probleme der Caritas*, p. 34). But in Soto, too, there is an intimate connection between the discussion of the rights of the poor to take, in extreme necessity, and the duty of the rich, in such circumstances, to give: "And it is argued by reason. For the pauper in extreme necessity can by natural law take that which is necessary for sustaining his life; therefore whoever may be is bound to give it to him. The consequence is proved: because otherwise there would be a just war on both sides, if it were licit for me to defend my goods and the other to seize them" (Soto, *Comm.* in II.II. q. 32, a. 5, n. 21, ed. Deuringer, p. 147). This piece of reasoning is entirely done in terms of justice, suggesting that extreme need blurs the boundaries between justice and charity; see Garrán Martínez, *Prohibición*, p. 95.

a full human life is much broader than this: "because not only those who are in an extreme of need, but even outside that, human beings still suffer needs, for the relief of which they have the right to beg."[69] The right to beg, then, is not directly a natural right. It is a right to ask for and to live off the goods of others—*aliena bona*—instead of living off your own. It has as its title a necessity that is not a natural necessity but one that arises in the circumstances of divided *dominia*.[70] It is a practice that presupposes both private goods and the spaces that remain public, and it is to the sense of "public" that Soto turned next.

As we have seen, Soto argues that anyone who cannot make a living at home "can go forth to look for it wherever." Public means public *to everyone*. According to Soto, it is illegitimate to draw a distinction between foreign beggars and native beggars. The only legitimate distinction is between sturdy or false beggars and true beggars. He claimed moreover (somewhat dubiously) that this is the only distinction that *has* been drawn in any legislation on the subject of beggars, going back to Roman times.[71] This means that it is illicit to send foreign beggars back home to be maintained by their native community, and it is illicit to prevent them from leaving it. If you genuinely are a mendicant, genuinely cannot support yourself, then it makes no difference where you beg and the right transcends all limits of place. Soto first argued this for internal borders within the confines of one realm.

> Paupers who are truly in need cannot be expelled from any place within the realm; but are either to be permitted to beg, or supported in some other way, just like the native inhabitants.... First reason. No one unless he is an enemy or assailant of the commonwealth, or is guilty of some crime or dreadful deed, can be kept out of any town. And the reason is ready to hand. For since by the law of nature and of nations roads and cities lie open to everyone regardless, no one, unless for some fault of his own, can be deprived of the right of staying where he wants.[72]

As we saw, the city-spaces and routes are cited in *On justice and right* as some of the things that have stayed in common after the division of things under the *ius gentium*, and are therefore open for the harmless use of all: this is the *ius peregrinandi* or the right of travel that Vitoria had used as one

---

[69] Soto, *In causa pauperum deliberatio*, cap. IV, fo. 103.
[70] The connection between private property and the right to beg is well brought out in Flynn, *Sacred charity*, p. 96.
[71] Ibid., cap. V (*Quo obiectionibus responditur*), fo. 105.
[72] Ibid., cap. IV, fo. 102.

of his justifications for Spanish activity in the Indies.[73] Although Soto is, for the moment, arguing the case *within* one realm, it is clear that for Soto as for Vitoria the right to travel is a natural right that applies to foreigners as much as to citizens of the commonwealth.[74] On top of this argument from freedom of movement, Soto added another rationale: the differing economic situation of different areas within one realm—one may (and indeed will) be poor, another rich. These different areas are interconnected like the parts of one body, and it is licit for a citizen—who is a citizen of the whole body and not just, or even in the first instance, of his native town or province—to go from one to the other in search of necessities.[75] This (as we said before) is not just extreme necessity, for instance, if there is famine or plague—this was his objection to the provisions of the 1544 law—but all that is needed for a human life, which goes beyond bare necessities.

However, Soto then extended the argument further: all Christendom also forms one body in the relevant sense.

> When I just now seemed to judge that one realm alone is one body, I was speaking (as St Paul says) "by way of indulgence." For I would add that under the law of Christ, paupers of one realm have open access to another. For when the Apostle instructed the Corinthians that we are all members of one body, he was not reducing the metaphor to the straits of one realm. Rather (he says) we are all with one spirit baptised into one body. It is not the case, therefore, that one realm alone is one body: rather all we Christians everywhere are regenerated by one baptism into one body.

But in fact this unity does not stop at Christendom, either: "And indeed if the matter is referred higher, to natural law, the human race is united by

---

[73] Vitoria, *On the American Indians*, 3. 1, 22; tr. Pagden and Lawrance, p. 278.

[74] Cf. ibid., cap. III, fo. 99: "there is a big difference between vagabond men and those who, since they are true paupers, go through (*discurrere*) the world begging. For concerning the first kind of men, it is provided not only by the particular laws of the realm, but by a much more ancient one, which is written among the common laws, and equally by the most ancient law, divine and natural, that they should not be permitted in the commonwealth with impunity. But I cannot see that the others, sc. strangers and travellers ... are prohibited by any law, wherever among the nations they wander. And indeed, if we listen to what both the Gospel and natural reason suggest, this does not appear to be fair and good either."

[75] On the necessary interconnectedness of cities within a realm, compare Soto's discussion of the "common good" of legislation in *De iustitia et iure*, lib. I, q. 1, a. 2: "in any commonwealth, for example in one whole realm, all laws are to be referred to the end of the whole. Not that particular laws are not be allowed to individual cities according to their status, but that all cities should be joined together with each other as the members of one body."

the closest bond in its very nature, so that, unless they were our enemies, or we feared some detriment to the faith from them, it would not be rightful to eject even infidel beggars from our commonwealth."[76] This extraordinary passage makes it clear that under natural law, there is no juridical difference between a Madrileño begging in Madrid, a Castilian begging in Madrid, an Aragonese begging in Madrid, an Italian begging in Madrid, and a peaceable, non-proselytising Turk begging in Madrid. The human race, even if it is regionally divided, is nevertheless interconnected to the extent that neither internal nor external borders of the realm can function to exclude a true mendicant. Since Soto shared with the entire Thomist tradition the premise that civil law cannot contradict natural law and remain legitimate, the consequences for internal legislation are plain.

It is in facing the objections to this chapter that Soto made his stress on *right* so very evident. Thus, for example, it is objected from Scripture that Paul enjoined the Galatians to do good to their own before others.

> To this one should reply. Firstly that Paul enjoins us to good deeds not only towards the members of our own households, but towards everyone, whatever their nation or status. He only teaches that, where resources do not allow for more, we begin from those who are closer to us.... Besides which we reply—and this is something that should be noted with attention on this passage—that it is one thing for someone to be more obliged to his own than to others (which is all that Paul was saying), and quite another for those others and outsiders to be deprived of the right that they have to seek alms from all mortals, especially among Christians. Which indeed is never licit.[77]

Again, it does not follow from the greater duty to one's own, that a beggar loses "the right that he has, saving the liberty of whomever, to beg both wherever and from whomever: and moving him by his prayers to pity."[78] Soto added that "neither should it be feared from beggars, that because of their number any province, or certainly any city, should ever have less of its own goods"—expressed even more clearly in the Spanish: "nor did any land [*tierra*] ever become impoverished because of a large number of foreign beggars."[79]

---

[76] Soto, *Deliberatio in causa pauperum*, cap. IV, fo. 103. It is worth noticing that the particular sentence about natural right and infidel beggars does not appear in the Spanish version: presumably it was too radical for general readers to stomach, and would have weakened his case.

[77] Ibid., cap. V, fo. 105.

[78] Ibid., fo. 106.

[79] Santolaria Sierra ed., *El gran debate sobre los pobres*, p. 71.

All this applies only to those who are genuinely in need: real mendicants. What about the rights to travel on the part of non-paupers? As we saw, the Spanish poor law tended to lump in pilgrims—Latin *peregrini*, the same word as for "travellers"—with mendicants, containing as it did a clause restricting the movement of pilgrims to Santiago. Soto devoted a whole chapter to the rights of those visiting Santiago. Here Soto's views are plain:

> ... it is not fitting to decide anything just because of one or other person who perhaps is a vagabond under his pilgrim's garb ... especially since pilgrims are foreigners.... We could give offence to other realms if we constrain pilgrims, like cattle, to follow set paths that are fenced in.... And indeed if some of them should be seized by a desire to visit your highness's court, or other major cities of the realm, would it not be uncivil and moreover inhuman to forbid them the roads or alms? I think that without doubt they would then have an action against us for a violation of the *ius gentium*. Although it would be licit, in that case, to set them a time within which they must return to their own country.[80]

—The reason being that if they just stay there under the pretext of pilgrimage, they are in fact behaving as vagabonds. Thus Soto's case is, I think, still clear: everyone has the right to travel, but that travel must be purposive, otherwise it does not count as travel but vagabondage. The other kind of non-purposive travel that Soto invoked is the movement of cattle, and it too can licitly be constrained. As we shall see, however, Soto made it clear elsewhere that the constraint of a delinquent human being is very different from the constraint of an animal.

I want to turn now from the rights of individuals to the rights of the commonwealth and its prince to legislate for the common good. We have seen how Soto insisted that the right to travel "cannot be taken away without fault" on the part of the individual. The force of this insistence is brought into relief if we compare the response on the part of Juan de Robles to this very point. "Every day free men lose thousands of liberties, without fault, but not without cause"—including liberties held under the law of nature. Robles deployed the familiar organic metaphor. All the members of a body, with their natural functions, are ordained to the good of the whole, and if that good demands, must cease from their functions or even be destroyed; "just so," he continued, "all us men who live within one political community, even though each of us possesses

---

[80] Soto, *Deliberatio in causa pauperum*, cap. IX [recte VI] (*De peregrinis ad divum Iacobum*), fo. 106.

liberty in our estate, if it is necessary for the good of the community that we lose our liberties and lives, it is just that they should be lost."[81] Soto's contrasting position accords well with the caveats he attached to the organic metaphor in *On justice and right*: "a limb does not have a being distinct from that of the whole; nor in any way is it for the sake of itself, but for the sake of the whole; nor of itself can it sustain either right or injury. But a man, albeit he is a part of the commonwealth, is nevertheless a subject existing for the sake of himself, and is therefore of himself capable of sustaining injury, which the commonwealth cannot visit upon him."[82] Nevertheless, Soto in that work still accepted the body metaphor in the context of the scope of the law: "all citizens are parts of the city, therefore the law that is laid upon them should form them towards the common good of the whole political community; like the parts of one body which are ordered towards the service of the whole."[83] Just as for his colleague Vitoria, the power of the prince to legislate for the common good extends to ensuring not merely the bodily, but also the moral well-being of his subjects: "all civil laws ... are to be instituted for the good of the soul, in which our felicity is in question; and it is for this reason that Aristotle ... said that the city is brought into being for the sake of living, but persists in being for the sake of living well.... For by the reason that man is born to felicity, by that same reason he is a civil animal."[84]

In the *Deliberation*, in his chapter in response to the sixth point of contention (that officials shall reform the hospitals so that the poor are fed and cared for there, rather than begging at the doors of houses), Soto relied on these foundational premises to argue that the prince can, in principle, outlaw the practice of begging in this specific form.[85]

> First conclusion. The prince, who holds the power of the commonwealth, has the right and the authority to prohibit beggars from asking from house to house.... For the prince (as Aristotle says, *Ethics* II) being by natural and divine law head of the commonwealth to this end, that he make the citizens good, can impose anything so long as it is a work of virtue, and prohibit those things that are vices and sins. And for the needy, as long as they are in need, it

---

[81] Juan de Robles, *De la orden que en algunos pueblos de España se ha puesto en la limosna* (1545), ed. in Santolaria Sierra, *El gran debate sobre los pobres*, at p. 179.

[82] Soto, *De iustitia et iure*, lib. V, q. 1, a. 7.

[83] Ibid., lib. I, q. 1, a. 2.

[84] Ibid., lib. I, q. 2, a. 1.

[85] As emphasised in A. Martínez Casado ed., *La causa de los pobres* (Salamanca: Editorial San Esteban 2006), pp. 27–36. The precision is important here, however, because Soto stresses that begging is a much wider phenomenon than purely begging from door to door: *Deliberatio in causa pauperum*, cap. XII, fo. 124.

is no sin to seek their daily bread from door to door; but as soon as those necessities are provided for them, they cannot, without fault, seek what belongs to another on the pretext of poverty.[86]

Because the right to beg from door to door within a commonwealth is not a natural right, but follows from need, take away that need and you can take away the right to beg in that manner; but *only* if you take away that need. Soto thinks that if the prince could provide abundantly, fully, and with certainty for the needs of the poor, this would be a glory to a Christian commonwealth. It would turn the commonwealth genuinely into a community of friends, like the one that we find in the Acts of the Apostles, where people genuinely loved their neighbours as themselves—for people are lying if they are rich and claim that some poor person is truly their friend.

However, the operative words here are "abundantly, fully and with certainty." Again it is crucial here that what beggars are begging for is not what they need to stay alive. People do not have to beg for that. They are begging instead for the means of livelihood. And therefore it is not enough to take away the right to beg and simply to provide them with a bare minimum of subsistence, a meagre weekly ration of grain and vegetables. Soto says that taking away the right to beg is just like taking away any other right: you become liable, not simply in charity but in *justice*, to restitution of all that is lost with the loss of that right. "Viz. that whoever deprives beggars of the right to ask ... becomes their debtor in the matter of relieving their misery and providing for their needs.... whoever deprives of a person of their right, is liable to them for their loss."[87] Thus, practically or morally speaking—his second conclusion—the prince cannot prohibit begging from door to door. This is because no prince can ever ensure that there is sufficient charitable provision for the poor so that all these needs are made up. The rich may certainly sometimes give to charitable foundations and hospitals, but since they cannot morally be compelled to charity except in the case of relieving extreme necessity (if there is a famine, for example), they will never give enough. Especially, Soto suggests, in Spain, where people don't think like that. Perhaps at Ypres or in Germany it could be made to work, where people are more civic-minded (*magis politici*).[88] He therefore concluded that "just as I was saying earlier ... that it is not possible, with such laws [i.e., the poor laws] to provide for native paupers abundantly so that there is no longer any need, and therefore any right, for them to leave their home and beg

---

[86] Soto, *Deliberatio in causa pauperum*, cap. XI, fo. 118.
[87] Ibid., fo. 119.
[88] Ibid., cap. XII, fo. 126; "gente más política" in the Spanish, Santolaria ed., p. 110.

elsewhere, so neither does it seem to be possible with such laws to provide for and relieve them in such a way that they no longer have any right to beg from door to door."[89]

Soto added a further point against keeping beggars from going out to beg: "that a pauper can, by begging, store up a bit of money by which he can change his estate." Soto criticised those who denounce paupers who beg even though they have got a few coins stitched up in their clothing. This is, according to Soto, perfectly legitimate. "For just as everyone has the right to change his status and rank for the better through other licit arts and contracts, so too a pauper could, from alms, accumulate a little store of money sufficient for him either to clothe and adorn himself more appropriately, so he could then offer his service to someone well-born or noble, or to equip himself with the tools and workshop of his craft: or perhaps set up a little business or trade, from which he could earn his living. But those who are shut up are excluded from this right."[90] For Soto's opponent Robles, this idea—that you can improve your status by begging—was outrageous. But in fact what it does is cleverly to turn on its head a point that had been first made by Cardinal Cajetan in the practice of the *giving* of alms.[91] According to Aquinas, you are bound to give as charity everything that is superfluous to maintaining your status. As Cajetan noted, this would mean that no one could ever store up the money needed to *change* their status; and this must, he says, be licit, at least in certain circumstances. Soto was only applying this same principle to the *receivers* of alms, the poor.

Soto's *Deliberation* is important because it brings into a European context issues that are largely elsewhere dealt with in the context of overseas expansion and the laws of war. As we have seen, Vitoria's perspective—some might say idealistic—allowed for an extremely wide-ranging interpenetration of states by inhabitants of other states; but since he only discussed it in the context of penetration of the Indies by Spaniards, he was seen at the time, and has been since, as offering only a pretext for imperial expansion. Thus the Jesuit Luis de Molina, among others, argued in direct opposition to Vitoria that any sovereign state must be able to close its borders and its goods to inhabitants of other states, unless they are in extreme need.[92] I shall return to this contemporary critique

---

[89] Ibid., cap. XI, fo. 120.

[90] Ibid.

[91] Cajetan's crucial contribution to the debate on charity in the School of Salamanca is discussed extensively in Deuringer, *Probleme der Caritas*, pp. 12–20, esp. 16–18.

[92] Luis de Molina, *De iustitia et iure*, tract. II, disp. 105, ed. in M. Fraga Iribarne, *Luis de Molina y el derecho de la guerra* (Madrid: CSIC 1947), p. 337.

later.[93] Soto's position was less vulnerable to it, in that he accepted and indeed welcomed the firm reality of divided commonwealths that can exclude others from helping themselves to their resources. However, he nevertheless argued that those states cannot close their borders to legitimate travellers: those who come for business or for other convenience or who come in a human need that is still not extreme need, what we today might call economic migrants. Those who come for business or other convenience cannot stay indefinitely. But those who come for need *can* stay indefinitely, and are no different from indigenous beggars in this respect. They cannot just help themselves to the resources of others, but they have a right to beg for a share of them. In such cases, the distinction between citizen and foreigner, inside and outside the state, simply does not apply.

However, if the borders of the commonwealth are necessarily porous in respect of the universal human community, the borders of that broader community are sealed tight against any other kind of nature. There is a world of difference between a cow, which simply cannot suffer injustice, and even a vagabond or a criminal; and while at a metaphorical level there is some passage between those two worlds, as we have seen, politically speaking there is none. Discussing whether it is licit to kill criminals in the fifth book of *On justice and right*, Soto employed the familiar quotation from Psalm 48 of the Vulgate to describe the transgressor of the law. "And man, when he was in honour, did not understand; he has been compared with the senseless beasts, and he has been made like to them." Just as for Locke over a century later, the criminal who transgresses the law of reason loses his human juridical status and "degenerates to the meanness and servitude of an animal. And for this it is licit to kill him as it is a beast."[94] But this does not mean, for Soto, that the criminal literally acquires instead the juridical status of an animal and may therefore be destroyed by a private individual, in Locke's words "as a *Lyon* or a *Tyger*."[95] Because, as Soto saw it, "even if human beings who have degenerated from their nature are compared to animals, they differ, however, in that beasts are by their nature such; and therefore anyone can kill wild ones without any injustice, and tame ones without injustice to them, although possibly to their owner; but a sinner (*peccator*), since he is not by nature cattle (*pecus*), must not be killed except by public judgement."[96] He is "corrupt humanity," but he is still by nature human, still inside the human

---

[93] See below, ch. 8, p. 201.
[94] Soto, *De iustitia et iure*, lib. V, q. 1, a. 2, ad. 3.
[95] John Locke, *Two treatises of government*, ed. P. Laslett (Cambridge: Cambridge University Press 1988), *Second treatise* § 11, p. 274.
[96] Soto, *De iustitia et iure*, lib. V, q. 1, a. 3.

community; and therefore he may only be killed by the public power whose duty it is to protect that community.[97]

We have seen, then, how Soto intervened within contemporary debates over the implications of natural law and the *ius gentium* to create a distinctive conception of political space that is both regionally divided and yet global. It is designed to protect the regional interests of native inhabitants as well as the trans-regional interests of the universal human community. As a specifically juridical theory of this space, however, it rests on a conception of human beings as sole possessors both of divided domains and the right to travel between them, and it excludes both animals and any human beings who behave like them. I turn now to explore in more detail how this foundational antithesis between animal and human agency was constructed.

[97] Ibid.: "For the killing of harmful men is not in itself good, but only insofar as it is related to the common good."

CHAPTER TWO

CONSTRUCTING HUMAN AGENCY

In the last chapter, we saw how Soto's essentially Thomist view of a human being's juridical status was premised upon Aquinas's understanding of human agency. The critical dimension that I want to highlight now is that this human agency is *free* agency. It is freedom, or *dominium* over my own actions, which makes me different from all other animals; and it is the foundation of the world of the moral, the juridical, and the political, which are all continuous with one another and from which animals—and a fortiori all other natural agents—are excluded. But over the century with which we are concerned, the idea that human beings are essentially and ineradicably free to control their own actions came under severe pressure from new and irreconcilable theological differences over the freedom of the human will, differences that therefore implicitly pressured the primary threshold of political space. If only free agents are capable of the political, then what makes a free agent ought, in principle, to have a profound impact on defining "the sphere of the city." But what I shall seek to show is the ways in which theologians of all different confessions, whatever their views on the necessitation of the human will in respect of sin and grace, managed to rework the distinction between human and animal agency in order to preserve their understanding of the city and its government. The commonwealth was salvaged for human beings, whatever the wreckage of their fortunes elsewhere.

I shall start with the controversy over human free will that erupted within Catholic circles, and begin with a few words more about Aquinas's own position. Aquinas held that *dominium* over one's own actions is exclusively human because it involves the operation of both the intellect and the will.[1] Crucially, however, he argued that it is the intellect that is the cause of this human freedom, even though its primary *subject* is the will.[2] It is the free operation of the intellect, discerning the rationale of the good and the bad in things, which permits the human will the act of choice, of *free will*—*liberum arbitrium*—and so permits the human being as a whole the moral self-direction towards an end that is nothing other than human freedom.[3] By contrast, an animal does not act from choice, or freely. This is because, although it has some judgement, this is not the free judgement of reason that would enable it to think in terms of the good and the bad; as a consequence, its appetite necessarily desires whatever it instinctively recognises as something to be pursued or avoided. Aquinas accepted, following Aristotle's analysis in Book III of the *Nicomachean Ethics*, that an animal (and a child) acts spontaneously or voluntarily—that is, from an internal principle of its own nature—unless it is compelled by an external principle, force, what the scholastics call "the violent."[4] But spontaneous or voluntary actions (which Aquinas and the entire Catholic scholastic following him take to be the same thing) are not to be confused with willed actions.[5] Nor are any "actions of a man" (*actiones hominis*) that he shares with animals to be confused with "*human* actions" (*actiones humanae*, emphasis mine).[6] They are not free and therefore can-

---

[1] Aquinas, *ST* 1a2ae, q. 1, a.1.

[2] Ibid., q. 17, a. 1, ad 2.

[3] Ibid., *Pars prima* (1a), q. 83 a. 1; q. 82, aa. 2 and 4. I follow the conventional translation of *liberum arbitrium* as "free will," even though "free judgement" is more accurate and makes better sense of Aquinas's arguments.

[4] Aristotle, *Nicomachean Ethics*, bk. III, ch. 2, 1111b7–10, cf. Thomas Aquinas, *Sententia libri ethicorum*, in *Opera omnia iussu Leonis XIII P.M. edita*, tom. XLVIII, vol. 1 (Rome: Ad Sanctae Sabinae 1969), Lib. III, Lectio 4, p. 130: *hoc enim dicimus esse voluntarium quod quis sponte et proprio motu operatur*; *ST* 1a2ae, q. 6, a. 5, for "the violent" as opposed to "the voluntary."

[5] Aristotle had argued in the passage above that "both children and animals have a share in the voluntary [*to hekousion*]," but not in "choice" [*prohairesis*]. There is no unproblematic Latin (or English) equivalent for *to hekousion*; *voluntarium* is unhappy because of its etymological link with *voluntas*, the will, which of course animals do not have and children do not properly exercise because they as yet lack reason. Aquinas explains that the term "voluntary" can be stretched to cover the agency of things that do not have will because their actions somehow participate in the rationale of willed action, insofar as they act of themselves towards some kind of end: *ST* 1a2ae, q. 6, a. 2.

[6] Aquinas, *ST* 1a2ae, q. 1, a. 1.

not bear a moral qualification. Throughout the opening questions of the *Prima secundae* of his *Summa*, Aquinas consistently deployed this antithesis between human agency and the agency of animals. The one is free, the other necessitated; the one is moral, the other is not.[7]

The consequence of this position in terms of the natural *dominium* of human beings over animals becomes apparent in the *Secunda secundae*, as we saw with Soto in the previous chapter. Through the reason that gives him *dominium* over his own actions, man is made in the image of God; and in the first book of Genesis God said, "Let us make man in our image and likeness, and let him be over the fish of the sea, the birds of the air" and every other living thing.[8] Aristotle too, in the first book of the *Politics*, had said that all things were made for the sake of man, for the uses to which he can put them.[9] This teleological argument is not at odds with the argument from Genesis, because as we saw in the last chapter, *dominium* in Aquinas's handling is an essentially teleological concept. The primary *dominium* is the ability to direct one's own actions towards an end, and the ability to use other things—to ordain one thing towards another— is an immediate function of it. Because man has *dominium* of his own actions, therefore he has *dominium* over everything else. Animals that do not have *dominium* of their own actions, cannot have *dominium* of anything else.

Aristotle and God made for a rock-solid combination on the question of natural human *dominium* over animals, and no one in the Catholic scholastic ever seriously challenged it. Worries about the partial recalcitrance of animals after the Fall really just served to prove their point. But the root of this position, the sharp antithesis between animal and human agency in terms of internal *dominium* or freedom, *was* open to question. Interestingly enough, the first person in our period to throw a spanner in the Thomist works was Francisco de Vitoria himself, in a lecture entitled "On that to which man is obliged, when first he comes to the use of reason."[10] It belongs to the group of lectures given between 1535 and

---

[7] Interestingly, however, Aquinas's language is more nuanced in others of his works, in which he is prepared to concede animals and their appetites a certain "participation in" or "likeness of" freedom, or even that animals are free, purely in the sense of physical motion: Aquinas, *Summa contra gentiles*, II. 48, n. 3: *Sunt igitur animalia irrationalia quodammodo liberi quidem motus sive actionis*. See the discussion of these passages in R. Pasnau, *Thomas Aquinas on human nature* (Cambridge: Cambridge University Press 2002), pp. 213–14.

[8] Aquinas, *ST* 2a2ae, q. 66, a. 1, cf. q. 64, a. 1.

[9] Aristotle, *Politics*, bk. I, ch. 8, 1256b15–20.

[10] *De eo ad quod homo tenetur dum primum venit ad usum rationis*. There is no English translation of this *relectio*; I use the parallel-text Latin-German edition of Ulrich Horst, Heinz-Gerhard Justenhoven, and Joachim Stüben, *Francisco de Vitoria, Vorlesungen* (2 vols., Stuttgart-Berlin-Köln: Kohlhammer 1997), vol. II, pp. 92–187. The text is briefly discussed in R.

1540, which includes the much more famous lecture "On the American Indians," and it engages with a famous and controversial thesis of Aquinas's to the effect that as soon as man comes to the use of reason, he is obliged to turn himself towards God. The moral self-direction of rational, that is, free, that is, *human* agency is necessarily in the direction of God; otherwise it is mortal sin.[11] Vitoria's two-pronged discussion centres around two sets of human beings who appear to throw Aquinas's understanding of human agency into doubt. The first are children, dreamers, and the insane, who would seem to be both human and free but whose actions do not bear a moral qualification; the second are barbarians, who would seem to be both human and free but may have no knowledge of God. That they *are* both human and free and therefore capable of the political is, as we have seen, the famous argument of the lecture "On the American Indians." But if their actions are not properly moral actions, this threatens the continuity between the moral and the political that is at the heart of both Aquinas's and Vitoria's theology of law and of the human city.

Vitoria's solution to the problem of the first set of beings is easier than his solution to the second. For Vitoria, the use of reason is the moral use involved in directing oneself to the good or to the bad. It is thus intimately connected with the cognitive acquisition of the precepts of natural law.[12] But, he proposed, this moral use does not exhaust the sphere of human reason. The cognition of an insane person, for example, is not the same as simply the sensual perception of animals, and indeed there can be some madmen who are skilled in the arts; but this kind of reasoning nevertheless does not give the madman free will, and therefore his agency

---

Schnepf, "Zwischen Gnadenlehre und Willensfreiheit. Skizze der Problemlage zu Beginn der Schule von Salamanca," in Kaufmann and Schnepf eds., *Politische Metaphysik*, pp. 23–42.

[11] The problematic is laid out by Vitoria's Dominican near-contemporary Martín de Ledesma, *Secunda quartae* (Coimbra 1560), q. 71, a. 1, fo. 548, col. 1: "And St Thomas (on [*Sentences* bk. IV] dist. 42, a. 5 ad 6 and 7, and in his *Questions on evil* q. 5 a. 2 ad 8 and q. 7 a. 10 ad 8) confirms this opinion, i.e. that it is not possible for someone to die solely in venial or original sin. And … the whole difficulty lies in the fact that St Thomas asserts that when someone comes to the use of reason, he is bound to turn himself towards God. And the holy doctor is only saying that when someone comes to the first moment of the use of reason he is bound to think of his salvation, because he can come to the use of reason and not know God. But if he comes to the use of reason and knows what is evil, even if he does not know God, but still he knows what is good and what is evil, he is bound to turn himself towards God; and if he does this he will achieve grace, but if he does not he will sin mortally."

[12] Cf. above, ch. 1, n. 3. For the connection between the present relection and Vitoria's broader handling of natural law, see the discussion in Daniel Deckers, *Gerechtigkeit und Recht. Eine historisch-kritische Untersuchung der Gerechtigkeitslehre des Francisco de Vitoria (1483–1546)* (Freiburg: Herder 1992), pp. 110–14.

does not bear a moral qualification. Thus Vitoria opened a gap between the bare use of reason and the moral use involved in free will.[13] Secondly, he opened another gap, this time between freedom and free will. Children, madmen, and people in their dreams are capable of free acts of the will that are distinct from animal appetites, even though none of them can be said to have the moral use of reason that makes for free will. Unlike animals, they are not naturally necessitated to act from an internal principle of their own; and thus we must conclude that there is a freedom distinct from mere spontaneity that is nevertheless not the same as the freedom involved in acting from free will. There can be a will that is free, *libera voluntas*, without free will, *liberum arbitrium*.[14]

Thus, while staying true to an authentically Thomist, intellectualist position on free will, Vitoria nevertheless used beings that are not animals but are yet not central cases of the human—let us call them, in the unfriendly world of the sixteenth century, "para-human"—to break open Aquinas's iron links between humanity, freedom, and morality. What then of the barbarians? Are they, too, para-human—that is, not quite natural agents but not properly moral agents either? Mid-way through his discussion, Vitoria essayed the proposition that someone who does not know God simply does not have the use of reason, even if he "understands well" about other matters.[15] But "because this appears paradoxical and will not please all ears," Vitoria chose rather to stay with his initial premise, that that there could be a person, brought up in a barbarian land, who had the use of reason but for a brief time no knowledge of God. Such a person would nevertheless be capable of morally good acts by definition, since the use of reason is a moral use, as we have seen.[16] It would not be necessary for the agent himself to refer his acts to God for them to be good, because they are related to God by God himself.[17] Likewise, such a person would be capable of sin. This is so even though Vitoria insisted that sin involves breaking God's law, not simply acting against reason: if there were no God, there could be no moral sin, although there could be the kind of sin that occurs in nature and in art.[18] But how could a person break God's law if he did not know God? The

---

[13] Vitoria, *De eo ad quod homo tenetur*, pp. 104, 122; also p. 154.

[14] Ibid., p. 104–107.

[15] Ibid., p. 156.

[16] Ibid., pp. 140, 146.

[17] Ibid., p. 148, just as "the slave, who performs his task in the way that his master set it for him, acts in a virtual sense for his master and towards the end, which his master ordained."

[18] Ibid., pp. 158–59, 160. Vitoria holds this position explicitly against Gregory of Rimini, who had famously argued that even if there were no God, "there would still be sin and moral evil."

answer lay in the Thomist thesis of natural illumination, by which human beings know what is wrong even if they do not know why it is wrong or if it is the result of a prohibition or not.[19] It is therefore not necessary formally to know that the law is God's law in order to be able to break it and to sin. As we might expect from the author of "On the American Indians," then, barbarians even with their barbarous education turn out to be fully human and not para-human agents.

Despite resolving the question of the barbarians, Vitoria's handling of the freedom of children, the insane, and dreamers proved unsettling for his fellow Thomists. By denying the complete coincidence of the free, the rational, and the moral, he had opened a fissure in the Thomist position that later Thomists found hard to reject altogether. Thus his fellow Dominican Martín de Ledesma, on this same Thomist question of whether the use of reason demands that man direct all his actions towards God, briefly distinguished from moral reasoning not only the reason involved in art—building a house—but also the reason involved in governing a commonwealth.[20] Again, the Mercedarian friar Francisco Zumel, whom we shall meet again very shortly, associated with Vitoria's argument (the force of which he could not bring himself altogether to deny) the thesis that not only a liberty in respect of works of art, but also a liberty "in naturals," can be separated off from the moral use of reason involved in free will: "as is clear in the insane, who judge that this is better than that in things of art, and in natural things too they judge that it is better to save than to destroy themselves."[21] In both authors, then, we find the suggestion—albeit very tentative—of a sphere of natural reason and a sphere of natural freedom that does not coincide with the sphere of the moral.

For a further development of Vitoria's ideas in this relection, however, we need to turn not to subsequent Thomists but to the renowned Spanish Jesuit theologian Luis de Molina (1536–1600) in his celebrated work *The concord of free-will with the gifts of divine grace*, first published in 1588. The impetus for this was the controversial theology of free will, in which

[19] Ibid., p. 160.

[20] Ledesma, *Secunda quartae*, q. 71, a. 1, fo. 548, col. 1: "one should note, that it could be that someone has the use of reason to build a house (for example) but does not recognise good or evil ... and such a person does not have the use of reason; and [even] if he had the use of reason to govern a commonwealth, if he does not recognise good and evil he does not sin: because this is what it is to have the use of reason, viz. to know how to act well and badly, i.e. what it is to act well or badly."

[21] Francisco Zumel, *De Deo eiusque operibus. Commentaria in primam partem Sanctae Thomae* (Salamanca 1590), Tomus primus, q. 14, a. 13, disp. 2, Appendix, fo. 412, col. 2; cf. Zumel, *Variarum disputationum tomi tres* (Lyon 1609), Tomus secundus [on the *Prima secundae* of Aquinas], disc. 3, sect. 6, fo. 116–24.

the dispute with the Lutherans and the Calvinists centred around their thesis of the necessitation of the will to sin in fallen man. However, Molina's defence of the latitude of human liberty in respect of divine grace provoked so much opposition from Dominicans and others who held to the more restricted Thomist view that the controversy soon came to be as much between Catholics themselves. Most famously (or notoriously, perhaps), Molina developed the idea of *scientia media*, "middle knowledge," to explain God's foreknowledge of human actions in a way that is compatible with human liberty or autonomy. Molina argued that God knows these future actions through a special kind of knowledge—*scientia media*—whereby what God foreknows is not the actions themselves that result from the human will, but what any individual human will shall will in any particular set of circumstances.[22] The success of this conception among Jesuit theologians can be judged from the relieved remark of Rodrigo de Arriaga (1592–1667), working in Prague in the middle of the next century: "even if this subject once seemed very difficult (for the infallibility of divine predestination can scarcely be reconciled with our liberty), now however the matter is very simple: for middle knowledge, which Father Luis de Molina first shed light upon, has solved this knot in such a way that nothing further can be desired."[23] However, the corollary of *scientia media*—and what we are more principally concerned with here—was a thesis on the liberty of the human will, even in acts of spiritual merit. Molina posited that the will of God works "with" rather than "in" the will of man, thus giving the human will an independent causal role in respect of grace.[24] Human freedom, therefore, is rooted in the will rather than in the intellect as it was for the Thomists, and it is in developing this position that Molina pushed Vitoria's ideas about *libera voluntas* to their limit and beyond.

After reviewing the arguments of "the heretics" in the first disputation of the *Concordia*, Molina began in Disputation 2 to develop his own position, opening with a discussion of the sense of the term "liberty." In one sense, he said, liberty is opposed to servitude, and this is not what we are talking about here.[25] Right at the start, then, he marked off liberty in a juridical sense from liberty in the sense he is interested in, liberty of

---

[22] See W. L. Craig, *The problem of divine foreknowledge and future contingents from Aristotle to Suárez* (Leiden: Brill 1988), pp. 169–206.

[23] Rodrigo de Arriaga, *Disputationes theologicae in primam partem S. Thomae* (Antwerp 1643), disp. 33, fo. 371, col. 1.

[24] In seeing Molina's position in terms of causality I follow the insightful account in J. Schmutz, "La doctrine médiévale des causes et la théologie de la nature pure," *Revue Thomiste* 101 (2001), 217–64.

[25] Luis de Molina, *Liberi arbitrii Concordia cum gratiae donis, divina praescientia, providentia, praedestinatione et reprobationes* (3rd ed., Antwerp 1609), disp. 2, p. 7, cols. 1–2.

agency. This is so even though, as we shall see, he still kept the classic locution of "*dominium* over one's own actions," which might be thought precisely to slide between the two. In chapter 4 we shall see how other Jesuits handle that ambiguity in the term *dominium*. For the present, Molina argued that in a second sense, the word "liberty" derives from the Latin word *libet*, "as one pleases."[26] This is the relevant sense; but here again we need to distinguish. In one sub-sense, everything that acts spontaneously, from an internal principle and not external force, can be said to act freely or as it pleases. This is *liberty from coercion*. But, against the heretics (and this is the common Jesuit inheritance from Aquinas), this is not enough for free will, because children, madmen, and even animals can act spontaneously or voluntarily, in the sense of not being externally coerced. All the Jesuits in fact cautioned against calling voluntary acts free acts, even if there was patristic authority behind it. Thus Francisco Suárez (1548–1617), the great systematiser of Jesuit theology and philosophy, cautioned his readership in his theological *Opuscula* of 1600: "I shall not, however, neglect to draw it to your attention that in this age one should avoid that manner of speaking ... lest in our manner of speaking we should agree with the heretics of this age"—the heretics who think, as we shall see, that the rationale of the voluntary coincides with that of the free.[27]

Thus we need to isolate a second sub-sense, in which liberty is opposed to necessity: that is, and here again this definition is common to all the Jesuits, liberty properly speaking is the liberty by which an agent, even when everything necessary for an action is in place, nevertheless has the power to act or not to act.[28] This is *liberty of contradiction*. This makes an agent a *free agent* as opposed to a *natural agent*—one that operates necessarily. Freedom, this possibility of acting or not acting, requires the judgement of reason, as Aquinas had said. But, in contrast to Aquinas, Molina insisted—and again this is a position common to Suárez and later to Arriaga[29]—that this does not mean that the operation of reason is itself free, as opposed to the necessitated judgement that we find in animals. For these Jesuits, freedom is purely in and of a will that can act or not act. It is in this context, of locating freedom purely in the will, that Molina referred directly to Vitoria's discussion and concurred with his conclusion. Children and the insane do not, in fact, simply act spontaneously;

---

[26] Ibid., p. 8, col. 1.
[27] Francisco Suárez, *De concursu, motione et auxilio Dei*, lib. I, cap. 1, in *Varia opuscula theologica* (Lyon 1600), p. 3; cf. his discussion of the distinction between the voluntary and the free in *Tractatus de voluntario et involuntario*, in Francisco Suárez, *Ad primam secundae D. Thomae tractatus quinque theologici* (Lyon 1628), disp. 1, sect. 3.
[28] Cf. Suárez, *De concursu, motione et auxilio Dei*, lib. I, cap. 1, p. 3.
[29] Ibid., cap. 1; Arriaga, *Disputationes theologicae in primam secundae Divi Thomae*, tom. I (Antwerp 1644), disp. 5, sect. 3, cf. disp. 2, sect. 1.

they are at least to some extent free in the sense of having a will that can act or not act. To have this will, Molina insisted, does not presuppose the kind of complex judgement of reason that is necessary for moral action; all it needs is the cognisance of a good of some sort—not necessarily a *moral* good—on the part of the agent.[30] But for Molina as opposed to Vitoria, this gives such agents not simply *libera voluntas*, but *liberum arbitrium*, free will, even if their "use" of it is not sufficient for morality.[31]

It is only much further on in the *Concordia* that the radical consequences of this move become apparent, based on thinning down the cognitive conditions on freedom. On the grounds of their different cognitive abilities, Vitoria had wanted to place children, the insane, and dreamers—para-human agents—in a middle ground of freedom between irrational animals that operate only spontaneously, not freely, and fully rational human agents who operate from free will. But in Molina, there is no such middle ground: what we have is rather a sliding-scale, a difference of degree; and animals are not off that scale, but at the bottom of it.[32] In Disputation 47 of the *Concordia*, which is about the source of contingency in actions, Molina clearly asserted that "although we must not countenance in brute animals even that freedom that, in Disputation 2, we claimed to exist in insane people and in children … nonetheless it seems highly likely that in brute animals there is a certain trace of freedom with regard to some of their movements, so that it is within their power to move in one direction or another"—can act or not act, the liberty of contradiction.[33] Thus, a range of animal actions, for example wandering in one direction rather than another, are genuinely free (and thus, when Molina finally got round to the real subject of Disputation 47, a source of contingency). Molina cautioned that this is only the case so long as they have not cognised a good (or a bad) that is sufficient to necessitate their appetite—for example, a stick bearing down upon them will certainly necessitate their appetite, and their resultant flight or cowering will not be a free action.[34]

[30] Molina, *Concordia*, pp. 8–9.

[31] See A. Aichele, "Moral und Seelenheil. Luis de Molinas Lehre von den zwei Freiheiten zwischen Augustin und Aristoteles," in Kaufmann and Schnepf eds., *Politische Metaphysik*, 59–83, at p. 74.

[32] See T. Pink, "Suarez, Hobbes and the scholastic tradition in action theory," in T. Pink and M.W.F. Stone eds., *The will and human action. From antiquity to the present day* (London: Routledge 2004), 127–53, at pp. 137–38. Pink's study appreciates the crucial role of the animal/human contrast in all these authors.

[33] Luis de Molina, *On divine foreknowledge (Part IV of the Concordia)*, tr. with introduction and notes by Alfred J. Freddoso (Ithaca NY: Cornell University Press 1988), p. 89.

[34] Ibid.; the qualification, "not sufficient to necessitate the appetite," comes a little further on at pp. 92–93.

Molina considered why this is so from the point of view of his Thomist opponent, Francisco Zumel, who, while not entirely rejecting the force of Vitoria's position (as we have seen), nevertheless in his central argument followed Aquinas in locating freedom in the free judgement of reason.[35] From this point of view, animal action is not free because an animal does not cognise the shade or food freely in terms of end or good, nor can it relate means and ends. It simply goes for, or avoids, what is in front of it. Its action is not properly end-directed, then, and therefore not free. But Molina rejected this Thomist, and strongly intellectualist, understanding of freedom. "The proper response," he said, is to deny that free activity requires such complex moral deliberation in terms of end or good. *Human beings* do not deliberate every step of the way, and still they act freely; so why not animals?[36] What is needed for a free action of the appetitive faculty is merely some cognition of a good that is not vehement enough to necessitate the appetite, whether rational or irrational.[37] This goes for animals, human beings, and angels. What makes the difference is which cognitions are so vehement as to necessitate the appetite. Molina held that in rationals—angels and sane adult human beings, even if they are sensual—the only thing that can necessitate the appetite is the clear cognition of God that the saints in heaven enjoy.[38] All human beings on earth, then, are absolutely free to act and not act, the contrary of necessitation; while animals, for whom the cognition of a desirable object or the fear of a stick would be sufficient to necessitate the appetite, have only a trace of this freedom. Children and the insane are apparently somewhere in between.

To sum up, then, Molina made freedom, understood as the possession of free will, not something that marks human beings off from animals, but rather a question of degree. Now Molina never explicitly said that animals have a trace of free will, just that they have a trace of freedom. Perhaps the former bald assertion would be too daring even for someone of the theological audacity of Molina. But that they have a trace of free will is in fact what he was saying, and he underlined this by asserting that they "have a trace of freedom ... or (what is the same thing) ... [an] innate trace of *dominium* over their own actions."[39] As we saw, in the Thomist tradition, to have *dominium* over one's own actions just is to have free will. To extend to animals *dominium* over one's own actions is contrary to the

---

[35] Ibid., pp. 89–90.
[36] Ibid., pp. 90–92. Aquinas himself had conceded that "it is not necessary for someone who goes along a road to think of his destination at every step": *ST* 1a2ae, q. 1, a. 6.
[37] Ibid., pp. 92–93.
[38] Molina, *Concordia*, disp. 2, p. 9.
[39] Id., *On divine foreknowledge*, pp. 91–92.

whole theology of humanity as made in the image of God, and to the consequence of that, that animals are objects of human *dominium* rather than subjects of *dominium* in themselves. Such an assertion, Zumel remarked, "is not safe";[40] and it is noteworthy that in his juridical treatise *On justice and right*, Molina took the absolutely standard Thomist line that animals do not have *dominium* over their own actions, and therefore they cannot have *dominium* over anything else.[41] But here in his work on freedom, the line between dominative and non-dominative subjects is blurred. Instead of animal agency functioning as the antithesis of human agency, as it does for the Thomists, animal agency itself becomes a case of the para-human.

Molina's position on animals was vigorously combated by his Thomist opponents; but it was also rejected even by those within his own Society who defended his position on free will. Thus Francisco Suárez, while opposing the constitutive role in freedom that the Thomists ascribed to the intellect, nevertheless argued that the act of the intellect, cognising a moral good, is the antecedent condition or "root" of free will.[42] He did allow that children and the insane have a kind of "indifference" and exercise a kind of judgement with respect to various kinds of non-moral goods.[43] But his almost exact contemporary and close partner in dialogue Juan de Salas (1553–1612) went beyond Zumel in rejecting the distinction between freedom and free will that Vitoria had tried to make, consequently denying that children have any more freedom than animals.[44] For these seventeenth-century Jesuits, a free act, a non-necessitated act, is an act performed from free will; the animal appetite is necessitated, which makes their actions only spontaneous, not free. But it should be noticed that while they reaffirmed the Thomist equation of free and moral actions, not all of them accepted the conditions on end-directedness that for Aquinas and the Thomists were part of the same equation. Suárez stayed within the compass of Thomism in arguing that animals do not act for the sake of an end in the formal sense, because they cannot grasp the

[40] Zumel, *De Deo eiusque operibus*, Tomus primus, q. 14, a. 13, disp. 2, Appendix, fo. 412, col. 2.

[41] Luis de Molina, *De iustitia et iure* (Mainz 1614), tract. 2, disp. 3, n. 6.

[42] Suárez, *De voluntario et involuntario*, disp. 2, sect. 2, n. 15: "man has free will, for this freedom arises from reason ... because reason can attain to the universal rationale of the good and the bad." For Suárez's theory in relation to Aquinas's intellectualism, see Pink, "Action theory," and T. Rinaldi, "L'azione volontaria e la libertà nel pensiero di F. Suárez," in *Francisco Suárez. Der ist der Mann* (Valencia: Edicep 2004), 307–22.

[43] See E. Gemmeke, *Die Metaphysik des sittlich Guten bei Franz Suarez* (Freiburg: Herder 1965), pp. 177–78.

[44] Juan de Salas, *In primam secundae divi Thomae*, tom. I (Barcelona 1609), tract. 1, disp. 4, sect. 1, fo. 28–36. For the relationship between Salas and Suárez, see V. Ordoñez, "Juan de Salas junto a Suárez," *Revista española de teología* 13 (1953), 159–213.

formal rationale of the good.[45] But Juan de Salas and Rodrigo de Arriaga argued clearly that animals, too, act for the sake of an end properly speaking.[46] They insisted that the cognitive capacities of beasts allow them both to recognise their proximate ends as goods, and to relate means to ends in a limited way. The acts of their sensual appetites, in wanting those goods, are therefore properly end-directed: even if this is not in a *moral* sense, because they are not free. Thus, whereas for Aquinas a properly end-directed action is a free and a moral action, here again the Jesuit discourse questioned the coincidence of these terms, and thus the absolute human-animal dichotomy on which the opening of the *Prima secundae* turns.

In sum, then, by breaking down the conflated dichotomy in Aquinas between all aspects of human agency and all aspects of animal agency, these Jesuit authors really changed Aquinas's question. What makes something a human act is a question that makes sense in the moral context of the *Prima secundae* because *everything* about human agency means that it carries a moral qualification, as distinct from *everything* about animal agency, which does not. But on the Jesuits' tight analysis of freedom as fundamentally a liberty of contradiction situated in the will, there can be a human act (one proceeding from intellect and will) that is nevertheless not a free, and therefore not a moral, act; Suárez instanced the necessary love of God on the part of the saints in heaven.[47] And, as we have just seen, there can be an end-directed act that is neither human nor free. The important question to them was not what makes a human act, but what makes a *moral* as distinct from a natural act.[48] As we shall see when we come to examine their more overtly political thought in subsequent chapters, that distinction constitutes the fundamental "threshold of the state."

One of the reasons, perhaps, why later Jesuits drew back from Molina's position on the continuity between animal and human action is that it

---

[45] Suárez, *Tractatus de ultimo fine hominis*, in *Tractatus quinque*, disp. 1, sect. 1, n. 9.

[46] Juan de Salas, *In primam secundae*, tract. 1, disp. 4, sect. 4, fo. 47–49; Arriaga, *Disputationes theologicae in primam partem*, disp. 46, sect. 4, fo. 474; cf. the extensive discussion in Rodrigo de Arriaga, *Cursus philosophicus* (Antwerp 1632), disp. 8 physica, sect. 6, subsect. 2 (*Quid de brutis*), fo. 355–57. See Dennis Des Chene, *Physiologia: Natural philosophy in late Aristotelian and Cartesian thought* (Ithaca and London: Cornell University Press 1996), pp. 198–99.

[47] Francisco Suárez, *Tractatus de bonitate et malitia humanorum actuum*, in *Tractatus quinque*, disp. 1, sect. 1, n. 8; cf. his appreciation of the conflation of the human and the moral in Aquinas, ibid., n. 3, n. 11.

[48] Thus, Arriaga, having argued that the appetites of animals are end-directed, argues that so too are the acts of the sensual appetite in man; the question of whether these acts are *human* acts, however, is really just a *quaestio de nomine* (Arriaga, *Disputationes theologicae in primam partem*, disp. 46, sect. 5, fo. 477). Cf. Suárez, *De ultimo fine hominis*, disp. 2, sect. 2, n. 9 on necessary acts of the will: the controversy over whether they are *human* acts "pertains to the manner of speaking."

goes dangerously close—though from the opposite direction—to the accusation they threw at "heretics" of any stripe, but especially Calvinists: that they turn human beings into animals because of their doctrine of the necessitation of the will to sin in fallen man. Lutheranism, they conceded, was less extreme than Calvinism from this point of view.[49] They saw this moderation as pure inconsistency rather than any theological, let alone philosophical, virtue: Molina insisted that Luther's position was not merely bad theology but bad philosophy, and indeed one of the strengths of the Jesuit position in the controversy is the continuity it yielded between the philosophical and the theological treatment of free will. Nevertheless, Jesuits recognised the distinctive characteristics of the Lutheran position. Luther had indeed denied free will to human beings, but this allowed him to concede them some freedom of choice "in inferior things" that in his view did not amount to *liberum arbitrium*.[50] Subsequent Lutheran theology, in the handling of Philip Melanchthon and those who followed him, allowed that although the fallen will was unfree with respect to the inner obedience of the heart to the law of God, it was nevertheless free, in the sense of free to do or not to do, in respect of "externals" or "civils": the exterior works of natural and civil law, the domain of "philosophy" as distinct from "Gospel."[51] The Lutheran controversialist Martin Chemnitz (1522–1586) laid particular stress on this distinction as solving the problems of free will: "that necessary and most useful distinction between the internal works of the law and external practices, by which external discipline and civil justice is attributed to free will."[52] He insisted that fallen man still has the substance of his intellect and will intact—otherwise he would be an animal—and that his action is different from the motions of those things that either act purely naturally or are impelled by external violence. The question lay, however, in what things are still subject to the will; and this he limited to external actions. "And this is that which we commonly say, that men who are not reborn

[49] Thus, for example, Molina in the opening of his *Concordia* (lib. I, disp. I, p. 7) conceded that Luther allows the human will some "cooperation" and "activity" insofar as the will commands external actions.

[50] See R. Saarinen, *Weakness of will in Renaissance and Reformation thought. From Petrarch to Leibniz* (Oxford: Oxford University Press, forthcoming), ch. 3.2.

[51] S. Kusukawa, *The transformation of natural philosophy* (Cambridge: Cambridge University Press 1995), ch. 2; Philip Melanchthon, *Philosophiae moralis epitome* (N.P. 1538), p. 35: "Therefore it must be opined without any doubt whatsoever, that the human will is in some way free, that is, that it can obey the judgement of reason, pursue or avoid things offered to it, and command the inferior members and forces in external actions.... there is in men some choice and some liberty, by which they may command to themselves the duties of the law."

[52] Martin Chemnitz, *Loci theologici*, ed. Polycarp Leyser (Frankfurt/Wittemberg 1653), *Sextus locus de libero arbitrio*, p. 170, col. 1.

can in some sense carry out external discipline: That is, perform external honest works that are consonant with the law of God, and avoid their contrary crimes." "The whole of political government," he went on, "testifies to this."[53]

As suggested, the Jesuits universally (and with varying degrees of subtlety) regarded this split between the liberty of the will in internals and externals as totally incoherent.[54] However, it was still better than Calvinism, which in their eyes allowed no sphere of freedom for the will at all. It was thus "the religion of beasts," as the notorious title of the French Jesuit Théophile Raynaud had it; and those who say that animals have liberty—so Molina?!—are themselves animal.[55] However, the work implicitly attacked not only Calvinists but also the very individual on whose behalf it is apparently set up as an "appeal": the Thomist theologian Domingo Bañez (1528–1604) and his doctrine of God's "physical pre-motion" of the will in acts of spiritual merit, a motion that the human will has no liberty to resist.[56] The terminology of "physical" in this context was itself controversial. The sense of "physical," in the philosophical and theological language of the Jesuits, does not reduce to "material" (although it includes this). Rather, its sense is of what is "real" contradistinguished against what is the work "of reason" (i.e., dependent for its being upon the operation of the intellect), and of what is "natural" contradistinguished against what is "moral."[57] In the question of causality, these distinctions operated to detach the Aristotelian "final cause"—the causality of the end—from the other three types of Aristotelian cause (material, formal and efficient).[58] Final causality was increasingly understood only as a "metaphorical" kind of causality, because the causal activity of the end operates not on the substance or nature of the thing itself but only on the intellect

---

[53] Martin Chemnitz, *Examen concilii Tridentini* (Frankfurt 1574), fo. 129 cols. 1 and 2.

[54] For one of the more subtle accounts, see Rodrigo de Arriaga, *Disputationes theologicae in primam secundae,* tom. I, disp. 5, sect. 6, fo. 41–42.

[55] A. Rivière [Théophile Raynaud], *Calvinismus bestiarum religio* (Lyon 1630), p. 46: "anyone who says that they [sc. the beasts] are devoid of the necessity that is in opposition to liberty, or allows that they are free, is cattle [*pecus*], is a beast, and unworthy of being included among the number of men."

[56] See W. Hübener, "Praedeterminatio physica," in J. Ritter and K. Gründer eds., *Historisches Wörterbuch der Philosophie* (Basel: Schwabe 1989), Bd. 7, cols. 1216–25; this article has a rich bibliography of primary sources for the dispute in both Catholic and Protestant circles, to which I am much indebted in what follows.

[57] See Sven Knebel, *Wille, Würfel und Wahrscheinlichkeit. Das System der moralischen Notwendigkeit in der Jesuiten-scholastik 1550–1700* (Hamburg: Felix Meiner Verlag 2000), pp. 487–91. For an example of the equation of the physical and the natural in contradistinction to the moral, see Suárez, *De bonitate et malitia humanorum actuum,* disp. 1, sect. 2, passim.

[58] See the extensive discussion in Des Chene, *Physiologia,* ch. 6: "Finality and final causes."

that cognises it as an end and the will that wants it. Unlike Aristotle, therefore, the Jesuits tended to restrict the final cause to the sphere of moral agency, as a kind of cause that operates only on free agents and leaves the agent's will free to pursue it or not. By contrast, "physical" causality included everything that naturally or really acts upon the substance, without involving any capability for freedom it may have. Thus, an action that is physically or naturally caused cannot be a free action. In consequence, the Thomist position, that God physically "pre-moves" a free agent in such a way as to preserve its nature as a free, rather than a natural agent, was just a self-contradiction—not the profound mystery of faith that the Thomists wanted.[59]

The angry exchanges between Calvinists and Arminians on the freedom of the will in the early part of the seventeenth century paralleled, at least to some extent, the arguments between Jesuits and Thomists. They shared much of the terminology, partly simply because of the contiguity of the debates, partly because of the Aristotelian foundations underlying much of the argument on all sides, and partly because the metaphysical categories of the Catholic controversy were being imported into the Protestant milieu at just the same time that Jacob Arminius (ca. 1560–1609) was developing his explosive stance on predestination and human free will. It is highly probable that Arminius himself had read Molina on "middle knowledge," although contemporaries were more likely to accuse him of indebtedness to Suárez or to the Italian Jesuit controversialist Robert Bellarmine.[60] Again, however, we are in this context less interested in predestination taken broadly than in concomitant understandings of causality and agency. Here it is important that at Arminius's university of Leiden in Holland, just as at the Lutheran universities of Helmstedt and Wittenberg in Germany (and indeed partly prompted by developments at those universities), the Jesuit metaphysics of Pedro da Fonseca and Suárez were beginning to be introduced into the philosophical curriculum in the closing years of the sixteenth century and the beginning of the seventeenth.[61] The precise relations between these aspects of the

---

[59] Suárez, *De concursu, motione et auxilio Dei*, lib. I, cap. 4. Bañez was in fact initially reluctant to accept the terminology of "physical" pre-motion, precisely because it plays into his opponents' hands.

[60] Eef Dekker, "Was Arminius a Molinist?", *Sixteenth Century Journal* 27/2 (1996), 337–52, at pp. 349–50.

[61] For context of this development at the German Lutheran universities, see W. Sparn, "Die Schulphilosophie in den lutherischen Territorien," in *Grundrisse der Geschichte der Philosophie. Die Philosophie des 17. Jahrhunderts,* Bd. IV: *Das heilige Römische Reich,* eds. H. Holzhey and W. Schmidt-Biggemann (Basel: Schwabe 2001), 475–97, at pp. 487–93. For the university of Leiden, and the mutual implication of the Arminian controversy and the introduction of Jesuit metaphysics, see P. Dibon, "Die Republik der Vereinigten

intellectual context are complex. Nevertheless, the polemics between Arminians and Calvinists in Holland and England over human free will were recognisably conducted in the same kind of language as we have been tracing in Catholic circles. I do not wish to underplay the different inflections of the debate in the Protestant controversy, nor indeed the differences within that controversy in the varying contexts in which it arose. The Dutch debate, in particular, was marked by the political strategy of the Dutch Calvinists to link Arminianism with the heresy of Socinianism.[62] However, the common currency of the free will debate brought with it certain shared assumptions that can be masked by too strenuous a focus on division and discord. I shall return to these at the end.

Meanwhile, on the point about natural versus moral agency, Calvin himself had fought against the charge that his theology deprived fallen human beings of distinctively human agency. The motion of the holy spirit, he insisted, does not take away human action; human beings do not receive their conversion like a stone receives an impulse from one who throws it. "That simile is beside the point.... For who is so foolish, that he would be so bold as to think the motion of a man no different from the throwing of a stone? Nor does anything like this follow from our teaching."[63] However, Calvin here considered only the case of something moved purely by external force, or violence. Jesuits could easily concur that human beings are not like stones in this sense. As we have seen, the key category for their polemic is not the violent but the spontaneous or voluntary. By arguing that human liberty or free will meant a freedom from coercion, not from necessitation, and rejecting the familiar language of free will as *dominium* over one's own actions, Calvin could seem vulnerable, in the post-Jesuit controversial arena, to the charge of turning human beings into *animals*. Animals too are or can be free from coercion, as we have seen. So how are humans different, if they do not have free will in the vulgar sense?

Later Calvinists took care to answer this question in their response to the Arminians. Samuel Rutherford, in his explicit attack on Arminian theology as Jesuitical, the *Exercitationes apologeticae pro divina gratia* of 1651, gently took issue with Calvin for describing human freedom solely as the absence of coercion.[64] Later Calvinists do preserve the equation that the Jesuits decry, between the voluntary and the free. However, they dis-

---

Niederlande," in ibid., Bd. II: *Frankreich und Niederlande*, ed. J.-P. Schobinger (Basel: Schwabe 1993), 42–85, at pp. 50–51.

[62] See S. Mortimer, *Reason and religion in the English Revolution: The challenge of Socinianism* (Cambridge: Cambridge University Press 2009).

[63] Calvin, *Institutes*, bk. II, ch. 5, n. 14.

[64] Samuel Rutherford, *Exercitationes apologeticae pro divina gratia* (Franeker 1651), exercitatio I, cap. 1, n. 6, p. 6.

tinguish, as the Jesuits do not, between the voluntary and the spontaneous, and this is what enables them to keep for creatures capable of the
voluntary—human beings—a freedom that is distinct from mere spontaneity, or freedom from coercion. As Rutherford proclaimed: "Our
theologians assert that the nature of liberty, arising from the judgement
of practical reason, is immunity from coercion and also from natural
necessity";[65] "the will, as free, has both an objective and an internal indifference, and by this liberty is formally distinct from non-coercion, from
spontaneity, and from all other natural causes."[66] Nonetheless, they still
wanted to insist that there is a certain sense in which the fallen human
will *is* necessitated, even while it is free; it does not have the "pure indifference" of the Arminians and Jesuits, which Rutherford described as
chimerical. Thus, what they strove to resist was the way that the Arminians and the Jesuits deployed the contrast between the moral and the
natural (or physical) as a contrast between the free and the necessitated,
which implicitly assimilated all necessitation to the natural necessitation
that contradicts freedom.[67] For the Calvinists, the voluntary, and therefore the free, was compatible with necessitation to act, as long as we understand necessitation correctly.

The French Calvinist Pierre du Moulin, in his *Anatomy of Arminianisme* (translated into English in 1620), gives us a clear account of human
liberty in this sense. In chapter 32, "Of Free-will," du Moulin began by
asserting that "a liberty from constraint, and from physicall necessity hath
remained to the will" after the Fall; for "if by an external principle, by a
naturall and immutable law, it should be necessarily determined to one
thing, it were not a will, but *either* a violent impulsion, *or* a natural inclination and propension, destitute of knowledge and judgement, such as
is the inclination of heavy things to the center of the world."[68] (We may
imagine stones again.) Thus, two things are involved in human liberty:

---

[65] Ibid., n. 7, p. 7.

[66] Ibid., n. 9, p. 9. "Objective indifference" is an indifference based in the object proposed
to the will by the intellect, in the sense that the will is not necessitated by the nature of
that object. "Internal indifference" is the indifference that the will has of itself, "vital, elective," by which it can actively will or not will a particular thing. This "dual indifference"
is designed to counter the Arminian response that "objective indifference" is equally a
feature of natural causality, and hence argues nothing for liberty: ibid., n. 8, p. 9. For the
contrast in Catholic discourse, see Knebel, *Wille, Würfel und Wahrscheinlichkeit*, p. 204.

[67] For an example of the Arminian deployment of this contrast, cf. *The Arminian Confession of 1621*, parallel-text edition by Mark A. Ellis (Eugene, Ore.: Pickwick Publications
2005), ch. 6, n. 5, p. 62, on the quality of divine providence: God perfects some things "as
if by a physical action," others "as if by a moral or ethical action," according to the different nature and faculties of things that have been impressed upon them at creation.

[68] Pierre du Moulin, *The anatomy of Arminianisme* (London 1620), ch. 32, n. 1, p. 282, emphasis mine.

liberty from coercion, and liberty from "physicall or natural necessity." These two are not the same, but they coincide in having their source external to the agent, in a law of nature here apparently clearly understood in the new sense of the laws of physics or physical causality. This emphasis on the externality of what takes away human freedom was critical to the line du Moulin wanted to hold against the Arminians. As the Dutch Calvinist Anton de Waal (Walaeus) complained in his defence of du Moulin's *Anatomy*, the Arminians think that a thing is free only if it is free from all necessitation, both external *and* internal (a position they shared with the Jesuits).[69] Du Moulin, by using the new concept of the laws of nature to move the kind of necessitation involved in natural inclination into the realm of external compulsion or "constraint" together with violence, cleared a space for an *internal* necessitation of the will to sin that does not take away liberty because it is not a form of compulsion: for "there is a kind of necessity which is voluntary; neither is liberty contrary to necessity, but to constraint or servitude."[70]

Du Moulin argued that this freedom from compulsion is essential to the will and inseparable from it. This differentiates human beings both from falling stones and from animals that act from natural inclination. Here du Moulin made the critical distinction between the voluntary and the spontaneous: "… everything which is voluntary is *spontaneous*, but not contrarily: For even cattell are moved of their own accord, and they have their *spontaneous* appetites and inclinations; but those are done voluntarily, which are done with some knowledge and reason."[71] Lack of knowledge and reason, then, characterises equally cattle and falling stones, thus making the agency of cows natural rather than free, on the stone side rather than the human side, even though cattle are clearly different from stones. All these passages bring out clearly the strong intellectualist tenor of the Calvinist distinction between the voluntary, or the free, and the spontaneous—the antithesis of Molina, of course, whose thinning-down of the cognitive content of freedom had enabled him to extend a trace of genuine freedom, not just spontaneity, to animals. On this basis du Mou-

---

[69] *Responsio Antoni Walaei ad censuram Ioannis Arnoldi Corvini, in cl. Viri, Petri Molinaei Anatomen Arminianismi* (Leiden 1625), cap. 3, p. 93; cf., for the Arminian position, Simon Episcopius, *Collegium disputationum theologicarum* (Dordrecht 1615), disp. 5, n. 5, p. 15. For the comparable position of the Jesuits, see Arriaga (arguing here with his Catholic opponents), *Disputationes theologicae in primam secundae,* tom. I, disp. 6, sect. 1, fo. 45, col. 2: "for whether the necessity that is brought to bear on the will is through something intrinsic or extrinsic, is entirely incidental, if equally it cannot resist either, and each equally precedes, in nature, our own activity."

[70] Du Moulin, *The anatomy of Arminianisme*, ch. 32, n. 16, p. 287; cf. n. 15, p. 286.

[71] Ibid., ch. 32, n. 7, p. 283.

lin went on to classify a range of human actions according to whether they are natural or voluntary. Some human actions "are merely naturall, as the contrary motion of the Arteries.... Which because they are not in our power, nor at mans pleasure, the will is neyther occupied about them, nor doe they fall within the compasse of Election or deliberation." As far as the circulation of your blood is concerned, then, you may as well be a cow. Other types of human action, however, do involve deliberation and the will, and are therefore free. These include actions such as taking a walk, which are partly natural and partly voluntary. But some other kinds of action are purely voluntary: "civill" actions, such as buying or selling, "for he that doth these things at the command of another, yet is willing to obey him that commandeth, and therefore is driven to doe it, not only by anothers will, but also by his owne"; and "civilly honest" actions, such as "when a heathen helps up him that is fallen, or sheweth the way to him that is out of it."[72] In this ethical and political sphere, then, du Moulin was careful to specify that the will of fallen man is entirely free to do or not to do. This is not the case with actions in respect of God's law, but not because the Fall has turned men into cattle. Unlike a cow eating some grass, man sins knowingly, and therefore voluntarily, even if necessarily.

Anton de Waal and the other theology professors of Leiden, in their 1626 *Censure* of the Arminian Confession, similarly defended the freedom of the will both from external coercion and from natural necessity, although they did not make the distinctive move that du Moulin did in classifying natural necessitation as a kind of external compulsion. Thus, the Dutch Calvinists held both that the sinful will necessarily sins, and that nonetheless it is free, because it determines itself to its course of action through its own internal tendency: "not by a necessity of nature, nor of external violence, but by its own inclination, from the corrupted dictate of reason." This phrase again brings out clearly the distinctive intellectualist tenor that we saw in du Moulin's account. What makes the difference between freedom and spontaneity is the dictate of reason, the free judgement or deliberation of the intellect. De Waal and his colleagues argued that the will is free to choose between any objects presented to the will by the intellect, as long as they do not have an obviously necessary connection with either well-being or destruction. In such cases as these, they held, we do not deliberate, but pursue or avoid them spontaneously rather than freely, "by a necessity of nature." So there is a small class of actions in which human agency loses its distinctive marker of deliberation and we act like animals. But in other cases, we pursue or

[72] Ibid., p. 285, nn. 10–12. For the meaning of "civilly honest" actions, see chapter 3, below, pp. 63–64.

avoid not spontaneously but according to the judgement of reason, and this is human free will. As for du Moulin, this is what makes human beings different from cattle, and it remains even in fallen man.[73]

What all these works demonstrate is the intellectual pressure on Calvinist theologians to provide a *philosophical* account of human agency that will distinguish human beings from animals and allow a space for "civil" government, government by command (rather than physical compulsion). In contrast to the Lutherans, these Calvinists reinstated the continuity between the philosophical and the theological that characterises the Jesuit position, even though this involved them in a difficult demonstration of how the philosophically free human will necessarily sins by a kind of necessitation different from natural necessitation.[74] And we see the same thing if we turn from the Calvinists' handling of human freedom to their handling of human *dominium* over the rest of creation. Now of course, having rejected the locution of *dominium* over one's own actions for human freedom, there was no such essential association between the two positions as we find in Catholic discourse. But if we look at the Dutch Calvinists' theological refutation of Arminianism, we find a similar insistence to the Catholics on the central role of internal human reason, and therefore freedom, in the external relations of man with creation. It is—just as for Calvin himself—these internal properties that make man in the image of God; his *dominium* over other creatures is only secondary. What they objected to in the Arminians is their notion that the image of God lies *primarily* in that external *dominium*, and that man's internal distinctiveness, his reason, is apparently purely instrumental to the exercise of it. This Arminian position is unparalleled in Catholic discourse; indeed, this is one point where the Dutch Calvinists seem genuinely justified in associating Arminianism with Socinianism.[75]

The political implications of this coincidence between the parties are brought out in the most uncompromising way by Thomas Hobbes's han-

---

[73] Antonius Walaeus et al., *Censura in confessionem* (Leiden 1626), Censura in cap. VII, sect. 2, pp. 105, 104.

[74] This provoked a disgusted response from de Waal's Arminan opponent Simon Episcopius: "Whatever is antecedently necessary, is necessary in one way only, and that is, that it cannot be otherwise; and this of his, that he denies that it is an absolute and natural necessity, is nothing other than a *sophon pharmakon*." [Simon Episcopius], *Apologia pro confessione* (N.P. 1630), p. 82r; the reference is to Euripides, *Phoenician Women*, 472: "the unjust argument ... needs clever medicine."

[75] Nicolaus Bodecherus, *Sociniano-Remonstratismus* (Leiden 1624), pp. 31–33; cf. *The Arminian Confession*, cap. V, n. 5, p. 56, col. 1, and Simon Episcopius, *Collegium disputationum theologicarum in Academia Lugdunensi privatim institutarum* (Dordrecht 1618), disp. V, theses iii and v (pp. 14–15).

dling of human freedom, especially in the debates that he had with "the Great Arminian," Bishop John Bramhall, published between 1654 and 1656.[76] It is not new to point to the affinities between Hobbes's position on the freedom of the will and the theology of Calvinism, nor to the affinities between Bramhall's position and the theology of the Jesuits, especially Suárez.[77] Hobbes himself, in *The questions concerning liberty, necessity and chance* of 1656, protested his allegiance to the theology of Luther and Calvin:[78] freedom means freedom from coercion, not freedom from necessitation or—perish the thought—*dominium* over one's own actions. The human will is causally necessitated, but yet the man who acts willingly acts freely: liberty and necessitation are compatible. Bramhall objected that Hobbes had thereby turned a theological thesis about the necessitation of the fallen will to sin into a philosophical thesis about natural causal necessitation, the equivalent of the Stoics' fate.[79] But what we have seen is that in doing so, he paralleled in some sense what contemporary Calvinists had been doing themselves. They too had "philosophised" Calvin's original thesis about freedom from coercion. But, in the contrary direction to Hobbes, they had developed it into a thesis about freedom from natural necessity in order to avoid their opponents' charge of turning human beings into animals. While not assimilating either human beings or animals to stones that are thrown, that is, impelled by external violence, they nevertheless assimilated animal agency more to the action of a falling stone, which falls "by a natural inclination or propension," in du Moulin's words, "without reason or judgement," or "judgement and deliberation."

When we turn to Hobbes, we see that he kept the category of "necessity of nature," its association with falling stones and with the absence of the deliberation that precedes a free act. Thus he said in *De cive* that we shun death "by a certain necessity of nature, not less than that by which a stone falls downwards." In such cases we cannot will otherwise, and such action cannot therefore be the object of vituperation.[80] The difference

---

[76] A detailed account can be found in Nicholas D. Jackson, *Hobbes, Bramhall and the politics of liberty and necessity* (Cambridge: Cambridge University Press 2007). See also J. Overhoff, *Hobbes's theory of the will* (Lanham: Rowman & Littlefield 2000), ch. 4.

[77] See L. Damrosch, "Hobbes as reformation theologian," *Journal of the History of Ideas* 40 (1979), 339–52, and the editor's introduction in V. Chappell ed., *Hobbes and Bramhall on liberty and necessity* (Cambridge: Cambridge University Press 1999), xi, xv; discussed in Skinner, *Hobbes and republican liberty*, pp. 24–27, 33–34. Jackson, *Politics of liberty and necessity*, pp. 97–99, highlights the controversy between Jesuits and Jansenists being disputed in Paris at the time of Hobbes's first exchanges with Bramhall in 1645.

[78] Thomas Hobbes, *The questions concerning liberty, necessity and chance* (London 1656), p. 235; in Chappell ed., *Hobbes and Bramhall on liberty and necessity*, pp. 80–81, para. 20.

[79] Jackson, *Politics of liberty and necessity*, p. 280.

[80] Thomas Hobbes, *De cive*, ed. H. Warrender (Oxford: Clarendon 1987), cap. I, sect. VI, p. 94.

with the Calvinists is that they associated this necessity of nature with the spontaneity that characterises animal action, as opposed to the voluntariness of human action. But for Hobbes, such necessity is what characterises stones *as distinct from* animals: spontaneity and the voluntary are almost exactly coincident, and the line is drawn not between humans and animals but between animates and inanimates. So in *The Elements of Law* Hobbes wrote that the estate of natural right or natural liberty is that in which every individual is "free to do, and undo, and deliberate as long as he listeth; every member being obedient to the will of the whole man; that liberty being nothing else but his natural power, without which he is no better than an inanimate creature, not able to help himself."[81] We need to add a caveat here, because in chapter 9 of *De cive*, and chapter 21 of *Leviathan*, Hobbes offers a "definition" of liberty "in the proper signification" as the absence of impediments to motion. In these contexts, Hobbes drew the line rather between anything that has the power to move and anything that does not. This included some inanimates—like water—on the same side as all animates, and might seem to deprive his conflation of human and animal agency of its point. But I am going to defer considering liberty in this sense just as Hobbes does in *De cive* and *Leviathan*, where it figures not in the sections entitled *Libertas* and *Of Man*, respectively, but in those entitled *Imperium* and *Of Common-Wealth*. It is deployed to handle questions of human freedom in the specific context of being commanded by the will of another.[82] That is, it does its work in a specifically *political* context; and it cannot unproblematically be taken out of this context to form part of an account of Hobbes's theory of *natural* human liberty.[83]

For the moment, then, it is sufficient to point out that even once the new definition of liberty "in the proper signification" is fully in place, in *Leviathan*, Hobbes did not feel that he had no more need, in the section *Of Man*, to make the point about human and animal action being equally voluntary. On the contrary, while this position is in fact severely understated in the earlier two works, in *Leviathan* Hobbes threw it in his reader's face. Thus he emphatically declared that deliberation, the "alternate

---

[81] Thomas Hobbes, *The elements of law*, ed. F. Tönnies (London: Frank Cass 1969), part II, ch. 1, p. 116.

[82] As brought out in Skinner, *Hobbes and republican liberty*, esp. ch. 5: Hobbes is replying to a "republican" rhetoric that takes subjection to the will of another as slavery, the antithesis of freedom.

[83] It might be objected that "liberty in the proper signification" figures in chapter 14 of *Leviathan*, that is, in the section *Of Man*. However, the very brief mention of this sense of liberty does not actually do much work in this chapter, save only to make the point that its absence does not entail a corresponding absence of the liberty to act at will. For a full discussion, see below, ch. 6, pp. 159–60.

Succession of Appetites, Aversions, Hopes and Fears," "is no less in other living Creatures than in Man." "And Beasts that have *Deliberation*, must necessarily also have *Will*."[84] But the coincidence between the voluntary and the spontaneous, the human and the animal, is most explicit in Hobbes's exchanges with Bramhall, and it is highly probable that the polemical emphasis in *Leviathan* is a result of the debate that he held with the bishop in the presence of the earl of Newcastle in the spring of 1645.[85] Certainly, the works that were finally published in the mid-1650s are saturated with the contrast (or otherwise) between animal and human. Bramhall had started off his important-sounding *Discourse of liberty and necessity* by distinguishing between liberty, which involves election or choice, and spontaneity, which does not. "A spontaneity," he said, "may consist with determination to one, as we see in children, fools, madmen, brute beasts, whose fancies are determined to those things which they act spontaneously, as the bees make honey, the spiders webs. But none of these have a liberty of election, which is an act of judgement and under-standing."[86] Hobbes's counter, in his own record of the debate, was to show that all these "spontaneous" actions do indeed involve choice: "horses, dogs and other brute beasts do demur oftentimes upon the way they are to take.... Fools and madmen manifestly deliberate no less than the wisest man, though they make not so good a choice."[87] Although he left a small space for a spontaneity that does not involve deliberation—the actions of children before they understand pain, like our purely spontaneous avoid-ance of death in *De cive*—most human and animal actions are equally de-liberate and therefore equally voluntary and equally free.

Given this position, it is no surprise to find Hobbes also rejecting Bramhall's defence of the standard position on natural human superiority over animals. In a rejection of the Aristotelian teleology repeated ad nau-seam in these discussions, Hobbes held that there is no natural difference between the killing of a man and the killing of an animal. "He takes it ill that I compare the murthering of men with the slaughtering of brute

---

[84] Hobbes, *Leviathan*, p. 44. There is an interesting congruence between Hobbes's view of the appetites and that of some of the later Jesuits mentioned above, in that they both allow the appetite, and therefore animals, to pursue a good (or avoid an evil) formally recognised as such. The difference is, of course, that the Jesuits think that the appetite is necessitated and the will is not, whereas Hobbes thinks that both are necessitated, indeed, are the same thing.

[85] See Skinner, *Hobbes and republican liberty*, pp. 130–31, for the impact of the debate on the theory of liberty in *Leviathan*.

[86] In Chappell ed., *Hobbes and Bramhall on liberty and necessity*, p. 2.

[87] Thomas Hobbes, *The treatise "Of liberty and necessity*," ed. ibid., pp. 18–19. This was origi-nally a private letter written by Hobbes to Newcastle, apparently in the summer of 1645, laying out his side of the argument. Its publication in 1654 was without Hobbes's knowledge.

beasts.... The Elements (saith he) are for the Plants, the Plants for the brute Beasts, and the brute Beasts for Man. I pray, when a Lyon eats a Man, and a Man eats an Oxe, why is the Oxe more made for the Man, than the Man for the Lyon?"[88] In parallel he rejected the thesis of natural human *dominium* over the animals. In a very funny passage, Hobbes "would ask the Bishop, in what consisteth the Dominion of man, over a Lion or a Bear." Consequently upon the Bishop's own thesis, it cannot consist in any kind of moral or political obligation on the part of lions and bears, since he has defined them as incapable of such.

> It resteth therefore that the dominion of man consists in this, that men are too hard for Lions and Bears, because though a Lion or Bear be stronger than a man, yet the strength, and art, and specially the Leaguing and Societies of men, are a greater power, than the ungoverned strength of unruly Beasts ... and for the same reason when a hungry Lion meeteth an unarmed man in a desert, the Lion hath the dominion over the man, if that of man over Lions, or over Sheep, or Oxen, may be called dominion which properly it cannot.... By this short passage of his, concerning Dominion and Obedience, I have no reason to expect a very shrewd answer from him, to my Leviathan."[89]

That is, if you really cannot understand that humans are no different from animals in terms of natural *dominium*, you cannot understand the specific character of human *political* dominion over other human agents.

Hobbes's final words here bring out the political significance of the theological discussion of human and animal freedom. The dividing line between human and animal agency, as the dividing line between free and necessary agency, is taken by all confessions to be the ultimate dividing line between the political and the non-political. Political government is government by law, and law is not physical violence, but a verbal or written directive that is comprehensible by reason, and backed up by a system of rewards and punishments that apparently demand a nature that can freely respond to them. Bramhall spoke very much in line with the Jesuits and the Arminians when he said that "this very persuasion that there is no true liberty is able to overthrow all societies and commonwealths in the world. The laws are unjust which prohibit that which a man cannot possibly shun.... It is to no more purpose to admonish men of understanding than fools, children or madmen if all things be necessary. Praises and dispraises, rewards and punishments, are as vain as they are undeserved

---

[88] Hobbes, *The questions concerning liberty, necessity and chance,* p. 141.
[89] Ibid., p. 142.

if there be no liberty."[90] As we have seen, however, whatever their differing views on the necessitation of the fallen will, Lutherans, Calvinists, and Thomists all equally agreed that the human will is free in the sphere of the political: "the whole of political government testifies to this," as Chemnitz declared. All confessions allowed the will sufficient liberty to follow the law and to respond to reward and punishment. The philosophy of human free will, then, was profoundly implicated in a certain common definition of the city. In refusing to distinguish between madmen, children, animals, and sane adult human beings in terms of liberty, Hobbes was doing, and knowingly, something politically very different from everyone else, something only the Jesuit Molina had even come close to. Like Molina's position, that of Hobbes is theologically "not safe," not even from a Calvinist point of view, because it threatens the boundary not just of human being but of the spheres that are taken to be coincident with that being: the moral, the political, the juridical. Where Molina had recoiled from this consequence, however, it is all part of Hobbes's design to draw the line differently.

[90] Chappell ed., *Hobbes and Bramhall on liberty and necessity*, p. 4. Compare Episcopius in reply to the Censure of the Arminian Confession, *Apologia pro confessione* (N.P. 1630), *Examen Censurae capitis* VII, pp. 81r–82v, arguing that if you follow the Calvinists' position, a law can no more be passed upon the will than upon the sensual appetite (given that both are necessitated), and that this furthermore overthrows all religion, which is based on reward and punishment.

CHAPTER THREE

NATURAL LAW

We have seen, then, that for almost all of our authors the construction of human being as free being coincides with the construction of the subject of law. Government by law is not the application of external force (violence), nor is it the harnessing or engendering of passion or appetite (natural inclination)—even if, as we shall explore in chapter 6, it cannot separate itself entirely from these physical dimensions of government. Rather, it works by commanding choice, and it demands a subject capable of choice: free in the sense of the last chapter. That choice is not simply between material objects or courses of action, but between those things understood as in some way good or bad. The concomitant of a natural capacity to choose in this sense is some kind of natural principle or principles of choice, which is provided for our authors by the notion of a natural law. The endless controversies over this contentious notion (what sense of "natural"? what sense of "law"?) are of interest to us in this chapter insofar as they develop in juridical terms the boundary line between the human and the animal, and thus delineate a legal space in which human agency and human freedom can themselves acquire a juridical qualification.

I turn first to the Protestant milieu, where the story about natural law really begins with Philip Melanchthon's project of reforming the university curriculum in the wake of the Lutheran reformation.[1] Luther's own theology, with its fundamental distinction between Law and Gospel, *Gesetz* and *Evangelium*, had left little room for what he called "philosophy," or the use of natural reason. Together with the early Melanchthon, he had denigrated philosophy as the vain pretensions of human reason to know and to do what belongs only to God. But Melanchthon came to change his mind on the place of natural reason; not only in respect of a reformed natural philosophy, but also in respect of a reformed ethics. He continued to accept the distinction between Law and Gospel. But he placed them both within an overarching structure of God's law, the *lex Dei*, which contains the entirety of God's legislative will towards his creatures.[2] And it was this within this overarching structure that Melanchthon was able to find a place for moral philosophy, which he understood precisely as natural law: "Philosophy ... teaches nothing of the remission of sins, nor does it teach in what way God might approve the unworthy.... But moral philosophy is a part of divine law. For it is the law of nature itself, as understood and explained by the most ingenious men.... And it is certain that the law of nature is truly the law of God concerning those virtues that reason understands."[3] Melanchthon argued that despite the corrupting effects of sin upon human nature, there nevertheless remained in fallen man what he called "natural notions" of the good, which he sometimes described as rays of divine wisdom, obscured but not entirely blotted out by the Fall. From these natural notions the entirety of natural law, that is, moral philosophy, can be deduced; the Ten Commandments, made known through revelation rather than through nature, serve to renew and reinforce this natural knowledge, containing as they do the same essential principles.[4]

The corollary of the space that Melanchthon found for natural law within Luther's domain of *Gesetz* is that natural law, understood as moral philosophy, is in a broad sense a *civil* philosophy: because in governing our external actions alone, what it governs is our relations with others, that is, the sphere of politics.[5] Melanchthon repeatedly calls the external

---

[1] See Kusukawa, *Transformation*, ch. 2: "Law and Gospel." As John Witte points out, the later Luther had found a place for natural laws governing various institutions such as marriage, property, and worship: J. Witte, *Law and Protestantism. The legal teachings of the Lutheran Reformation* (Cambridge: Cambridge University Press 2002), pp. 92–93. However, he had not systematically and philosophically elaborated this space, as Melanchthon was to do.

[2] M. Scattola, *Das Naturrecht vor dem Naturrecht. Zur Geschichte des «ius naturae» im 16. Jahrhundert* (Tübingen: Niemeyer 1999), pp. 38–48.

[3] Melanchthon, *Philosophiae moralis epitome*, pp. 2–3.

[4] Scattola, *Naturrecht*, pp. 43–45, 47.

[5] See Kusukawa, *Transformation*, p. 71: "for Melanchthon, ethics *was* political" (emphasis in the original).

actions that are the domain of natural law "civil actions." It is in this sense that we must understand his high regard for Roman, that is, civil law, which he called (following Ulpian) a "true philosophy."[6] This sphere he filled out further with the authority both of Cicero and of Aristotle: Cicero with his fundamental conception of *officium*, "office" or duty, a function that one fulfils in the social context in which all human beings find themselves; Aristotle with his conception of justice as the virtue that respects the other's good.[7] Melanchthon's commentaries on Aristotle's ethical and political works were a concrete delineation of this new civil philosophy, one that was to be extremely influential not merely for the Lutheran tradition but also for the Calvinist.[8] This is not to say that Calvinist works of ethics and politics coincided entirely in the framework established by Melanchthon. His handling had been dictated, as we saw, by the Lutheran distinction between Law and Gospel, a distinction that was alien to Calvinist thinking, which emphasised far more the continuity between the two.[9] In parallel, Calvinists did not conceive of the same sharp split between the internal and the external actions of human beings (the split that also distinguished the Lutheran and the Calvinist positions on free will). The early Melanchthon had gone so far as to gloss this domain of external actions as "the corporeal life."[10] But the later Melanchthon modified his earlier position,[11] and in turn we saw du Moulin describing such actions as "when a heathen helps up him that is fallen, or sheweth the way to him that is out of it" as "civilly honest" in Melanchthon's sense:[12] a "natural and political good," as de Waal put it in his own treatment of Aristotle's *Ethics*.[13] Like Melanchthon, too, Calvinist philosophers and jurists treated the contents of the Decalogue as part of this ethics of natural reason.[14]

---

[6] R. Stintzing, *Geschichte der deutschen Rechtswissenschaft. Erste Abteilung* (Munich-Leipzig: Oldenbourg 1880), p. 286.

[7] See Jill Kraye, "Melanchthon's *Ethics* commentaries and textbooks," in idem, *Classical traditions in Renaissance philosophy* (Aldershot: Ashgate 2002), ch. VII.

[8] C. Strohm, "Melanchthon-Rezeption in der Ethik des frühen Calvinismus," in G. Frank and H. J. Selderhuis eds., *Melanchthon und der Calvinismus* (Stuttgart-Bad Canstatt: Frommann-Holzboog 2005), 135–57.

[9] Ibid., pp. 149–50.

[10] Kusukawa, *Transformation*, p. 66.

[11] Strohm, "Melanchthon-Rezeption," p. 151.

[12] Above, ch. 2, p. 55.

[13] Antonius Walaeus, *Compendium Ethicae Aristotelis ad normam Christianae veritatis revocatum* (Leiden 1644), p. 106: *bonum naturale et politicum*. The context is his defence of the freedom of the will in this sphere, argued equally, as we have seen, by Melanchthon and du Moulin.

[14] Strohm, "Melanchthon-Rezeption," pp. 151–52; D. Wyduckel, "Recht und Gesetz im Bereich des Reformierten Protestantismus," in C. Strohm ed., *Martin Bucer und das Recht* (Geneva: Droz 2002), 1–28, p. 7. Kraye, "Melanchthon's *Ethics* commentaries," p. 12, suggests how this assimilation of the principles of Scripture and natural reason was instru-

All of this had a critical impact on the genres of natural law in Protestant circles. There are two systematic treatises on natural law by the Lutherans Johannes Oldendorp and Niels Hemmingsen, both close associates of Melanchthon himself.[15] But otherwise we shall find our material either in commentaries or other works of civil law by both Lutheran and Calvinist jurists, or in a variety of legally informed meditations upon Aristotle's *Nicomachean Ethics* and (especially) *Politics*. Some of these latter are direct commentaries, others are treatises taking elements of the text as a basis—or at least a partial basis—but radically reworking them in the contemporary intellectual and political context. The role that specifically theological concerns and affiliations played in this enterprise is, however, debated. One of the most famous examples, the *Politica methodice digesta* of Johannes Althusius, leading light of the Calvinist *Hochschule* of Herborn and syndic of Emden, has been read both as an essentially secular treatise and as an expression of a specifically Calvinist *politica Christiana*.[16] Moreover, the *politica* genre extended to include works that deliberately sought to detach the polity (at least as concerns its immediate function) from spiritual salvation. The most prominent of these is the 1615 treatise *De republica* by Henning Arnisaeus, a philosopher at the Lutheran university of Helmstedt.[17] But even if they differ radically in intent and in political conclusions, Althusius's and Arnisaeus's works are both part of a broader "political" conversation, enmeshed in an overlapping web of reference that prevents their being considered as "closed 'systems.'"[18] Crucially for our purposes, both of them make extensive use of law and of natural law.[19]

One of the key elements of that shared intellectual matrix was humanist jurisprudence. Althusius himself wrote two works of civil jurisprudence

---

mental in allowing a natural law politics to develop in relative independence from theology; cf. H. Dreitzel, *Absolutismus und ständische Verfassung in Deutschland* (Mainz: Philipp von Zabern 1992), p. 19.

[15] Johannes Oldendorp, *Eisagōgē juris naturalis sive elementaria introductio juris naturae gentium et civilis* [ca. 1538–40], printed in *Tractatus universi iuris* (Lyon 1549), vol. I; Nicolaus Hemmingius, *De lege naturae apodictica methodus* [1562] (Wittemberg 1577). See Witte, *Law and Protestantism*, pp. 139–40 on Hemmingsen and pp. 154–68 on Oldendorp.

[16] See the nuanced discussion in C. Strohm, *Calvinismus und Recht* (Tübingen: Mohr Siebeck 2008), pp. 189–99, 225–26. R. von Friedeburg and M. J. Seidler, "The Holy Roman Empire of the German Nation," in H. A. Lloyd, G. Burgess, and S. Hodgson eds., *European political thought 1450–1700* (New Haven: Yale University Press 2007), 103–72, see the work as an example of *politica Christiana*, but with the caveat that this is a fluid category.

[17] The classic study is Horst Dreitzel, *Protestantischer Aristotelismus und absoluter Staat* (Wiesbaden: Franz Steiner 1970).

[18] The phrase is von Friedeburg's and Seidler's, "Holy Roman Empire," p. 129.

[19] See Dreitzel, *Protestantischer Aristotelismus*, pp. 155–56, for law and natural law in Arnisaeus: he rejected the natural law account of the state, but not the use of legal reasoning and natural law principles per se.

as well as his political treatises;[20] less well known now, but highly influential in his time, the Dutch humanist and jurist Hubert van Giffen wrote both a *Politics* and an *Ethics* commentary as well as a series of important legal commentaries.[21] Both Althusius and van Giffen emphasised the central role of method in the law, an emphasis that went back to Melanchthon's immediate circle: there was a critical synergy between the humanist project of reforming civil law jurisprudence into a science—*ius in artem redigere*—and the Lutheran and Calvinist reform of the sphere of ethical and political philosophy.[22] Moreover, humanist jurisprudence had from the beginning been characterised by its own engagement with philosophical ethics.[23] This among other factors explains the attraction of the new confessions to humanist lawyers, many of the most distinguished of whom—men like Matthaeus Wesembeck or Hugues Doneau—were themselves Lutheran or Calvinist.[24] But they were not all, and indeed one of the most influential for their writings, François Connan, though a friend of Calvin's, was a Catholic. The work of these jurists cannot be simplistically reduced to their confessional affiliation, and this in turn defies any reductively theological handling of the crossover between their works and those of Lutheran and Calvinist ethical and political philosophers. Our object in this section, therefore, is not "Protestant natural law," per se, but a reframing of the space of natural law in the context of particular genres of philosophical and juridical literature, a reframing that is inflected by theology but combines the broad inheritance of Melanchthon's ethical philosophy with that of humanist jurisprudence.

The central aspect of this reframing, as I have suggested, is *alterity*: natural law as a sphere of behaviour towards others. This perspective immediately posed the question of what kinds of behaviours towards others count as law. In the first title of the Digest of Roman law, *De iustitia et iure* ("On justice and right") the jurist Ulpian had defined the sphere of natural law as the other-relating behaviours that are common to all animals. Natural law, he stated (D. 1.1.1.3–4), is "what nature taught all animals: for that law is not peculiar to the human race, but is common to all animals....

---

[20] See Strohm, *Calvinismus und Recht*, pp. 199–224, for the relationship between humanist jurisprudence and theological commitments in Althusius's juridical works.

[21] Details of van Giffen's career can be found in Stintzing, *Geschichte*, Abt. I pp. 406–407.

[22] Wyduckel, "Recht und Gesetz," pp. 2, 12–14.

[23] Strohm, *Calvinismus und Recht*, p. 31.

[24] As Strohm stresses, however, confessional affiliation is not always easy to determine: ibid., pp. 13–22, considering the cases of Wesembeck and the brothers Scipio and Alberico Gentili. Van Giffen is another example: originally a Calvinist, he converted to Lutheranism before ultimately converting again to Catholicism as he ended his career at the Jesuit university of Ingolstadt. Strohm's "Einleitung" generally represents a subtle treatment of the problem of "confessionalism" in relation to law.

From this stem the conjunction of male and female, which we call marriage, the procreation of children, their upbringing: for we see that the other animals too, even wild ones, are judged expert in this law." From the beginning, however, almost all Lutheran and Calvinist jurists and theologians rejected his authority.[25] Law demands reason, and this by definition excludes animals that act only from instinct. So Oldendorp declared, in what will now be a tediously familiar way, that "if you give law or right to brute animals, you necessarily also give them reason; and in consequence you make men of beasts, and beasts of men"; "in animals there is no reason, and therefore no law." Oldendorp went on to remark that "this definition [of Ulpian's] is more about natural inclination or affect, than right or law."[26] Now Melanchthon himself had in fact given a positive role to natural affections in our behaviour towards others. He called them by the Greek term, *storgai phusikai*, and held that they "move us without respect to profit [*utilitas*] and pleasure, as a father loves his children not for the sake of his own profit."[27] *Storgē* more generally was an inherited Stoic notion of a natural love towards others.[28] It figures in the political philosophical literature, for example in the chapter on families in Henning Arnisaeus's *De republica*,[29] and even in Thomas Hobbes's *The elements of law*.[30] Several jurists similarly acknowledged a positive, other-related sense of affection, and a community of inclinations between animals and human beings, while at the same time holding that there is no community of *law*, because this lies in reason alone.[31] In his first work

[25] An exception is Konrad Lagus, a jurist belonging to Melanchthon's immediate circle, who solved the problem of Ulpian by distinguishing between a *ius naturale primarium*, the uncorrupted instincts common to both human beings and animals, and a *ius naturale secundarium*, a law of reason necessary to correct the corruption of human instinct brought about by the Fall. See Stintzing, *Geschichte*, Abt. I, pp. 300–303.

[26] Oldendorp, *Eisagōgē*, fo. 47, n. 8; 47v, n. 10.

[27] Melanchthon, *Philosophiae moralis epitome*, pp. 20, 41, contrasting this position with that of the Epicureans, who think that all affections are for the sake of utility and pleasure; the contrast between Stoics and Epicureans on natural affection was an ancient philosophical *topos*.

[28] Natural family affection was attributed to the Stoics by Diogenes Laertius, *Lives of the philosophers*, VII. 120. I owe this reference, with thanks, to David Sedley.

[29] Henning Arnisaeus, *De republica seu relectionis politicae libri duo* (Frankfurt 1615), lib. I, cap. 1, sect. 11, n. 3.

[30] Hobbes, *The elements of law*, Part I, ch. 9, p. 44.

[31] Scattola, *Naturrecht*, pp. 161–78 (*Num ius naturale cadat in bruta animantia?*) distinguishes three strands of opinion within humanist jurisprudence on the subject: a first, which tried so far as possible to keep Ulpian's original meaning, even if this meant stretching the sense of *ius*; a second, which limited *ius* to rational beings, but allowed some metaphorical or analogical notion of *ius* in animals; and a third, which denied *ius* to animals altogether. As Scattola's detailed exposition shows, however, even the first group acknowledged a clear juridical boundary between human and animal nature.

of jurisprudence, Johannes Althusius allowed that in animals there were "certain inclinations and affections of justice, just as there are simulacra of the virtues; but I would not say that there is among them equity and law."[32] Matthaeus Wesembeck went so far as to argue that "natural law blossoms from natural inclinations," which "like *storgai phusikai* are embedded in all animals, or the common nature of men and beasts," even if they only have the nature of law in respect of the rational nature of human beings.[33]

However, not everyone shared such a positive evaluation of animal inclination. Another strand of thought joined hands with the humanist critique of Ulpian stemming from Lorenzo Valla, which denied any juridical community between human beings and animals on the grounds that animals are incapable of the social relations that are the domain of law. One of the key voices in developing this line of argument was the French humanist lawyer François Connan, who had been a student of Andrea Alciato's—and a fellow-student of Calvin's—at the University of Bourges.[34] Connan devoted the sixth chapter of his commentary on the first title of the Digest to a sustained attack on Ulpian's definition of natural law, offering a radically different construction of his own. "For," he said,

> … it appears absurd to link beasts with man in a society of law (*ius*), just because they may have certain adumbrations of it in procreation and in rearing young. For on that reasoning we ought to allow them to share in piety and temperance and in fact all the virtues, since they have some likeness of these things, and in my opinion a greater likeness than of right and justice … for the other virtues apply to men in themselves, but justice embraces those with whom one lives. But there can be no society of life among beasts either between themselves, or with man, and therefore no community of right at all…. For whatever they do, they do it for the sake of themselves; but justice offers all its reward to others.[35]

As we shall see more fully further on, it was Aristotle's understanding of justice in Book V of the *Nicomachean Ethics* that was at the basis of Connan's objection. On the Aristotelian account, justice alone among the vir-

---

[32] Johannes Althusius, *Iuris romani libri duo* (Basel 1586), lib. I, cap. 1, fo. 2.

[33] Matthaeus Wesenbecius, *Commentarius in institutionum iuris libros IIII*, I, 2, 1, cit. in Scattola, *Naturrecht*, p. 175, n. 174.

[34] For details of Connan's life and work, see Christoph Bergfeld, *Franciscus Connanus (1508–1551). Ein Systematiker des römischen Rechts* (Köln-Graz: Böhlau 1968).

[35] François Connan, *Commentariorum iuris civilis libri decem* (Lyon 1566), lib. I, cap. 6, n. 1.

tues is *ad alterum*, "with respect to another."[36] But for Connan, no animal action and no animal inclination counts as towards others in the necessary way. Connan was followed in his line of thinking by Hubert van Giffen[37] and by Henning Arnisaeus, whose *De republica* is indebted to both of them. In the course of asking after the naturalness of human society, Arnisaeus similarly rejected Ulpian's definition of natural law—*in bruta non cadit ius*—and put Connan's argument directly in the Ciceronian terminology of the *utile* and the *honestum*, what is profitable to oneself and what is morally right. "Brute animals, given over to their own desires, have no sense of the *honestum*, but only of the *utile*," and are therefore incapable of social relations with others.[38] For both authors, justice demands that one's own good may only be pursued within the limits of respecting the good of others.

In this context we can see just how innovative was Hugo Grotius, the first major Protestant natural lawyer of the seventeenth century, in his earlier work on natural law. In the unpublished *De iure praedae* of about 1604–1605, he revived—or, better, reconstructed—the idea of a *ius naturale* that was common to all animates. Part of the explanation for this lies in the use he made of alternative sources. Grotius was commissioned by the Dutch East India Company (the VOC) to construct a defence of aggressive Dutch commercial activity against the Portuguese in the East Indies—specifically, the Dutch seizure of a Portuguese carrack off the coast of present-day Malaysia—against the objections of some of the VOC shareholders who feared that such aggressive prosecution of Dutch commercial interests constituted a violation of the norms of just and pious behaviour.[39] To make the contrary case, Grotius stepped outside his broadly Protestant humanist juridical training at the University of Leiden and turned to the jurisprudence of his political opponents, in particular the notoriously free-thinking Spanish jurist Fernando Vázquez de Menchaca.[40] Vázquez, despite the humanist sophistication evinced in

[36] Aristotle, *Nicomachean Ethics* bk. V, 1130a2–3: "... justice alone of all the virtues seems to be the other's good, in that it is with respect to another."

[37] Van Giffen is discussed in this connection by Scattola, *Naturrecht*, pp. 175–76.

[38] Arnisaeus, *De republica*, lib. I, cap. 1, sect. 4, nn. 4 and 5. As we shall see below, the terminology of *utile* and *honestum* was very familiar to Connan himself, but he did not actually put the point about animals in these terms.

[39] For a detailed analysis of the context of the *De iure praedae*, see M. van Ittersum, *Profit and principle: Hugo Grotius, natural rights theories and the rise of Dutch power in the East Indies (1595–1615)* (Leiden: Brill 2006).

[40] I have discussed Fernando Vázquez more generally in *Liberty, right and nature*, ch. 5. For the tactical dimension of Grotius's use of his work, see van Ittersum, *Profit and principle*, pp. 327–28.

his *Illustrious Controversies* (first published in 1564), chose in the matter of law to stay with the quadripartite division of *ius* first advanced by the medieval lawyer Bartolus of Sassoferrato, which preserved Ulpian's sense of natural law.[41] Vázquez laid out this scheme in precisely the chapter on the freedom of the sea that Grotius plundered (although it was in fact a gift, since Vázquez did not scruple to say that the opinion of the Portuguese and of the Spanish, that they had acquired exclusive rights over passage to their respective Indies, was "insane").[42] For Vázquez, natural law, the first juridical stage and the one that marks a community between human beings and animals, is a law that is pure instinct, inclination, and appetite. It has no compulsive force—it is rather the natural behaviour of all animates, sanctioned by God.[43]

Despite borrowing Vázquez's juridical scheme, however, Grotius did not share his understanding of natural law. Rather, he reconstructed it to address the ethical concerns of the shareholders of the VOC, presented in the preface. Adopting the Aristotelian thesis that virtue is a mean, Grotius nevertheless chose to reject the Aristotelian conception of justice as the virtue that regards only the other's good. This view of justice, he suggested, had come to dominate the minds of good Dutch citizens. But in fact it could slide into the vice of insufficient regard for one's own good. For, contrary to prevailing opinion, justice does not regard only the other's good, but also one's own good, and the relevant virtue is the mean between the two.[44] The pursuit of self-interest, the *utile*, was thus not merely negatively just—that is, only within the confines of the *honestum*—but positively just, and it was so for all natures. Love of others, and the consequent regard for their good, was a secondary, and centrally human, corollary of this natural love of self.[45] In a sense, then, Grotius had revived a *ius naturae* that nature taught all animals—even though what he had reconstructed was a long way from Ulpian's original. Ulpian had suggested for natural law those natural affections that are towards others, whereas Grotius suggested precisely the one that is not. In his later work, the *De iure belli ac pacis*, first published in 1625 and revised in 1631, he reverted to a much more traditional framing, in the context of addressing exactly the contrary case—not people who think that justice prevents them from pursuing their self-interest, but people who think that justice *fails* in the

---

[41] For more detail on Bartolus's scheme of law see below, p. 76.

[42] Fernando Vázquez de Menchaca, *Controversiarum illustrium libri tres* (Frankfurt 1572), lib. II, cap. 89.

[43] Ibid., n. 24, and lib. I, cap. 10, n. 18; cap. 29, n. 14; cap. 35, n. 15.

[44] Hugo Grotius, *De iure praedae commentarius. Commentary on the law of prize and booty* (Oxford: Clarendon 1950), vol. II (collotype reproduction of the original manuscript), cap. 1, fo. 3; vol. I (translation), pp. 2–3.

[45] Ibid., cap. 2 (*Prolegomena*), fo. 5'–6'; vol. I, pp. 9–12.

face of the pursuit of self-interest.[46] The thrust, then, was to reassert a sphere of justice independent of the pursuit of self-interest, within which —but only within which—the pursuit of self-interest must operate if it is going to be just at all. That sphere is the sphere of natural sociability as a function of natural reason, adumbrated in the natural affections of animals.[47]

In sum, *alterity* (what would in the seventeenth century come to be theorised, and problematised, as "sociability") is the dominant mood of the humanist and Protestant handling of natural law. It is there even in Thomas Hobbes, whose natural law, like that of Melanchthon, coincides with moral philosophy and concerns the sphere of our actions in respect of others:"the conversation, and Society of man-kind."[48] As is well known, Hobbes insists that the natural inclination of both animals and human beings is always towards the self, explicitly characterised as the *utile* in *The elements of law*.[49] Nevertheless, natural law fundamentally tells you what to do in the presence of another, that is, "seek peace," if you can; and if you can't, go to war by all means. Accordingly, the precepts of natural law are the key social virtues of the traditional account.[50] But if we now turn to the Catholic scholastic tradition we find by contrast a very different framing of natural law, one that centres on individual *agency* and regulates the behaviour of individual agents in their aspect as beings of a particular

[46] Hugo Grotius, *De iure belli ac pacis*, lib. I, *Prolegomena*, n. 3. I have used the Amsterdam edition of 1720 by Jean Barbeyrac, which also contains the *Mare liberum*; this edition was the basis for his 1724 French translation, which was in turn translated into English in 1738 and is now published as *The rights of war and peace*, ed. R. Tuck (Indianapolis: Liberty Fund 2006).

[47] Ibid., nn. 6–7. I have discussed the respective juridical positions of utility and sociability in both works in "Natural right and civil community: The civil philosophy of Hugo Grotius," *Historical Journal* 45 (2002), 31–51.

[48] Hobbes, *Leviathan*, ch. 15, p. 110.

[49] Hobbes, *The elements of law*, Part I, ch. 14, p. 72.

[50] Id., *Leviathan*, pp. 92, 111. Whether natural law is *ad alterum* in the same sense as in the broader Protestant tradition is dubious, however; that tradition insists that justice is the virtue that is concerned with the other's good *rather than* one's own, as Grotius correctly analysed in *De iure praedae*. Perez Zagorin, *Hobbes and the law of nature* (Princeton: Princeton University Press 2009), p. 43, asserts that "despite their appeal to self-interest, they [the laws of nature] are genuine moral principles intended to facilitate peaceable social and other-regarding behaviour"; Sharon Lloyd, *Morality in the philosophy of Thomas Hobbes. Cases in the law of nature* (Cambridge: Cambridge University Press 2009), esp. ch. 3, argues more strongly that the ultimate good served by the laws of nature is not that of the individual but the common good of mankind. However, Hobbes's statement that a law of nature is a rule, found out by reason, "by which a man is forbidden to do, that, which is destructive of his life, or taketh away the means of preserving the same; and to omit, that, by which he thinketh it may be best preserved" (*Leviathan*, ch. 14, p. 91) seems hard to reconcile with this strong interpretation of other-regard.

kind. While authors in this tradition grapple equally with the question of animal behaviour in relation to law, they do not do so from the social perspective that characterises Protestant humanist Aristotelians and jurists. Their concerns centre not so much around the incapacity of animals to recognise others but on the incapacity of animals for obligation as opposed to necessitation.

Catholic scholastics did not have to work, as did Melanchthon and his followers, to vindicate a sphere of natural law within an inherited theological framework. It is an extension of the discussion of agency in Thomas Aquinas's *Prima secundae*, the opening of which we looked at in the previous chapter. Law figures here as one of two means—the other being grace—whereby God moves us to the good. Thus, like his theology of *dominium*, Aquinas's theology of law was premised upon the conception of reason directing an agent towards its end or good. The primary reason is that of God, directing all things to the ends that he has appointed for them: this is eternal law.[51] Creatures without reason act toward their end by the natural instincts that God has implanted in them at creation. This is the first mode of what Aquinas calls "participation" in the eternal law. It is important that human beings, too, participate in the eternal law in this mode, for they too have their natural instincts or inclinations towards what is good for them. There is some juridical space, then, that human beings and other beings occupy equally. However, in addition to this, creatures with reason participate in a second way, and this is through a rational appreciation of God's law. This second kind of participation is nothing other than natural law, by which human beings are enabled to direct *themselves* toward their own end or good.[52] Aquinas stresses the deep connection between the first kind of participation and the second. The order of the precepts of natural law follows the order of man's natural inclinations, because the good to which natural law directs is nothing other than the good towards which our inclinations tend.[53] Some of these inclinations are shared with animals (procreation, the rearing of young), others indeed with everything that is: the universal inclination of every created being towards its own self-preservation. However, it is clear in the *Prima secundae* that the inclinations themselves do not constitute natural law: the instinctual participation of animals in the eternal law is "not a law, except by similitude."[54]

---

[51] Aquinas, *ST* 1a2ae, q. 91, a. 1; q. 93, a. 1.

[52] Ibid., q. 93, a. 5; q. 91, a. 2.

[53] Ibid., q. 94, a. 2. See J. Porter, *Nature as reason. A Thomistic theory of the natural law* (Grand Rapids–Cambridge: Eerdmans 2005) for the importance of prerational nature in Thomist natural law.

[54] Ibid., q. 91, a. 2 ad 3.

Catholic theologians and lawyers in the sixteenth century hesitated over how to interpret the role that Aquinas gave to inclination in natural law. Domingo de Soto struggled hard to reconcile it with Aquinas's insistence upon rationality as the condition of properly law-governed behaviour, resulting in a complicated discussion that some critics have seen as simply confused. In the end, however, Soto could apparently see no solution to the problem of the regulatory role of natural inclinations other than to view those inclinations themselves as constitutive of natural law —at least partly so—and thus to acknowledge a community of natural law between animals and human beings.[55] Outside the Dominican tradition, other Catholic theorists too were sympathetic to giving natural inclination some kind of constitutive role in natural law. Tommaso Bozio, one of the original members of the Oratory, argued in his *De iure status* of 1600 not only for a single natural law that was common to both animals and human beings, but also for a law common to all beings.[56] Alberto Bolognetti also developed what we might term this radically Thomist interpretation of Ulpian.[57]

The Jesuits, however, universally found Aquinas's account of non-positive law—that is, eternal law and natural law—deeply problematic. Their difficulties centred around his concept of the eternal law as a law of both irrational and rational nature, and around his understanding of natural law insofar as it was rooted in non-rational inclination. Criticising Aquinas's use of one concept of law to cover the direction of both irrational and rational agency, Juan de Salas characterised Aquinas's understanding of law as "any rule prescribing a certain mode of acting, with a certain necessity, in order to arrive at some end."[58] But this definition is "extremely broad, and general," and by not specifying the nature of the necessitation, it in fact equivocates on the nature of the rule or law. Aquinas himself admits that the necessitation of natural inclination in irrational creatures is only a law by way of similitude. But then how can the eternal law, insofar as it governs through this kind of necessitation, be called a law? On this point, Gabriel Vázquez (whom we shall meet more fully later on) noted dryly, "the Thomists really labour."[59] But Jesuits with

---

[55] See my *Liberty, right and nature*, pp. 142–46, for a more detailed discussion of natural law in Soto.

[56] Tommaso Bozio, *De iure status* (Cologne 1625), lib. I, cap. 1, pp. 1–2.

[57] Alberto Bolognetti, *Tractatus de lege, iure et aequitate*, in *Tractatus illustrium iurisconsultorum* tom. I (Venice 1584), cap. iii, fo. 291, nn. 6–10.

[58] Juan de Salas, *Tractatus de legibus, in primam secundae S. Thomae* (Lyon 1611), tract. 14, disp. 1, sect. 4, n.11, fo. 5.

[59] Gabriel Vázquez, *Commentariorum ac disputationum in primam secundae S. Thomae* (I have used the Lyon 1631 edition; the commentary in its entirety was first published at Alcalá between 1598 and 1605), fo. 11 (commenting on q. 91, a. 1).

views on natural law as different as Salas, Vázquez, and Suárez, all agreed. Eternal law, insofar as it governs inanimate and irrational creatures, is either a completely different sense of law, or is only metaphorically a law. All law properly speaking involves an act of *imperium* or command (*praeceptum*) that obliges a creature possessed of free will to do or not to do something.[60] This is so whether this act is seen, as originally in Aquinas and in some of the Jesuits too, as an act of reason, or, in Suárez and others, as an act of a superior will.[61] Inanimates and irrationals, having no free will, cannot be commanded; they can only be necessitated, either through divine power or through their natural inclinations implanted by God. Suárez spelled this out clearly with the categories of the physical and the moral, the necessitated and the free, which we encountered in the previous chapter. Irrational and inanimate creatures "effect their motions not freely, but of the necessity of nature." For this reason they are not subject to law, "because the property of law is to impose a bond and a *moral* obligation; but only intellectual beings are capable of this, and even they, not in all their actions, but only in those that they do freely; for *all moral being depends upon freedom.*"[62] Or as Salas said: "Because natural necessity is not properly *obligation*, neither is eternal law, insofar as it governs irrational creatures, properly law."[63]

Law, then, belongs to a moral, not a physical universe, and the Jesuits used this sharp distinction—with which, as we saw in the last chapter, they replace Aquinas's distinction between the animal and the human— to break Aquinas's sequence between eternal and natural law. It follows

---

[60] Vázquez is seemingly the exception to the rule: he drew the ire of his fellow Jesuits for arguing that natural law is, primarily, rational nature itself, and only secondarily an act of *imperium* in the mind of God and an act of judgement (*iudicium*) in us. Nonetheless, it is clear from his commentary that it is only the act of *imperium* in the mind of God that properly constitutes natural *law*. Rational nature is better called natural *ius* than natural *lex*, and our judgement is more an application of natural law than natural law itself (ibid., disp. 150, cap. 3, fo. 5). See Harro Höpfl, *Jesuit political thought. The Society of Jesus and the state, c. 1540–1630* (Cambridge: Cambridge University Press 2004), ch. 11, pp. 268–69, although I disagree with the apparent implication that Vázquez's natural *ius* should be regarded as a "'not-quite' law": as a moral norm it has priority over any law.

[61] The two positions are clearly represented by Salas and Suárez, Salas arguing that if law only commands rational nature, it must itself be the work of reason, Suárez that the only thing capable of commanding (in the sense of imposing an obligation) is the will. Salas, *Tractatus de legibus*, tract. 13, disp. 1, sect. 6, fo. 10–11; Suárez, *De legibus ac Deo legislatore* (1612), ed. L. Pereña (6 vols., Madrid: CSIC 1971–81), lib. II, cap. 5–6.

[62] Suárez, *De legibus*, lib. II, cap. 2, nn. 10–11, emphasis mine. See P. Westerman, *The disintegration of natural law theory. Aquinas to Finnis* (Leiden: Brill 1998), pp. 80–89, and N. Breiskorn, "Lex aeterna," in Grunert and Seelmann eds., *Die Ordnung der Praxis*, 49–73, at pp. 62–63. On Suárez's critique of the Thomist analogical procedure as "metaphorical," see J.-F. Courtine, *Nature et empire de la loi. Études suaréziennes* (Paris: Vrin 1999), ch. 4, esp. p. 95.

[63] Salas, *Tractatus de legibus,* tract. 14, disp. 4, sect. 1, n.2, fo. 63, emphasis mine.

that they also either relegated or outright rejected Aquinas's account of the relationship between our necessary, natural inclinations, and the precepts of natural law. The intimate connection between the two in Aquinas cuts across the clear divide they wanted to make between the moral and the natural. So what then *does* give the content of natural law? The *content* of natural law lies in the necessary goodness or badness of certain actions in relation to human nature, a relation that can be found out by reason *even if*—as for the voluntarist Suárez—natural reason by itself is not sufficient to account for its formal nature as a law, that is, its capacity to impose an obligation. Accordingly, Salas, discussing Ulpian in the context of the correct division of laws, argued in a direct critique of Aquinas that "any command which is founded purely upon reason without any positive or arbitrary law should be called natural, *whether it commands things that are in accordance with natural inclination, or not.*"[64] Suárez was not so direct in his rejection of the inclinations as a basis for the commands of natural law. Nevertheless, he made it plain that Aquinas's categorisation of the precepts of natural law is only one among several, and he put it last with the qualification that we are not to think of these inclinations as "purely natural" but as "determined and elevated" by reason.[65]

If a broad consensus developed across confessions and professions on the exclusion of animals from the sphere of *ius*, and the consequent excision of Ulpian's *ius naturale*, this did not, however, solve all the problems associated with the topic of *divisio iuris*, "the division of law." In particular, getting clear on natural law and animals only served to muddy the question of the relationship between natural law and the *ius gentium*, the "law of nations." The central problem was that Ulpian, having defined natural law as "what nature taught all animals," went on to say that "the law of nations is that which human nations use. And it is easy to understand that this departs from natural law, because that law is common to all animals, while this is common only to human beings among themselves." Thus, the distinction between the *ius naturale* and the *ius gentium* depended on extending law to animals. But if animals are not judged to be capable of law, then what happens to that distinction? As we saw in chapter 1, a fragment of Gaius in the same title favoured the absorption of the law of nations into natural law.[66] But the most extensive text on the actual contents of the *ius gentium*, the celebrated *l. Ex hoc iure* of Hermogenianus (D. 1.1.5), did not seem necessarily to coincide with Gaius's definition of the *ius gentium* as natural reason: "Of this law of nations wars were brought

---

[64] Ibid. disp. 2, sect. 2, n.11, fo. 35, emphasis mine.
[65] Suárez, *De legibus*, lib. II, cap. 8, nn. 3–4.
[66] See above, ch. 1, p. 6.

in, peoples separated, kingdoms founded, properties distinguished, boundaries put on fields, buildings set in place, trade, buyings and sellings, lettings and hirings, and obligations instituted: except for some that were brought in by civil law." Neither did the parallel words in the *Institutes* (*Inst.* 1.2.1): "for at the demands of practice and human necessities, human nations established certain things for themselves: wars arose and there followed captivities and servitudes, which are contrary to natural law." These were not intuitively obviously the work of natural reason alone: they could look much more like positive institutions, possibly indeed of a dubious legality going by natural law alone. But if this was the nature of the *ius gentium*, then what served to distinguish it from the positive institutions of individual commonwealths, that is, civil law?

The heritage of medieval law and theology had been, broadly, to accept Ulpian's definition of the *ius naturale* and therefore to keep the *ius gentium* as a distinct species of law between natural and civil. We have already seen how Aquinas handled this in-between domain of *ius* in different parts of the *Summa*, making it either natural, but not natural like the *ius naturale*, or positive, but not positive like civil law. On the lawyers' side, as we saw earlier in this chapter, Bartolus had also accepted Ulpian's definition of natural law and had solved the problem of the *ius gentium* by dividing it into two, thus yielding a quadripartite division of the field of *ius*: natural law, the primary law of nations, the secondary law of nations, and civil law. The *ius gentium primaevum* is constituted by natural reason (Gaius). The *ius gentium secundarium* (Hermogenianus) was instituted by the nations—the *gentes*—not from pure natural reason and indeed sometimes contrary to it.[67] For both Aquinas and Bartolus, then, the *ius gentium* was part of an essentially temporal story about the development of human juridical relations, one that begins with a *ius* so immediate that it is shared with creatures that are not capable of any kind of reasoning.[68] The rejection of Ulpian's natural *ius* in the sixteenth century called the whole story into question, as both lawyers and theologians turned directly from the critique of Ulpian to ask about the nature of the *ius gentium*.[69] The extraordinary variety of responses shows the difficulty universally experienced in generating a replacement, a difficulty that crossed both confessional and professional divides because a solution was not given in either of the broad modes of understanding natural law that we examined above.

---

[67] Bartolus of Sassoferrato, *In universum ius civile commentaria* (Basel 1562), fo. 640, D.12.6.64.
[68] The importance of temporality in the medieval understanding of the *ius gentium*, and the impact of this on the later tradition, is suggested in Haggenmacher, *Grotius*, pp. 326, 343.
[69] The intimate connection between these two developments is brought out in Scattola, *Naturrecht*, p. 178.

We may take as our initial guide Juan de Salas's treatment of "the division of law," handled with his usual theological sophistication but also unusually well informed on juridical approaches to the problem. Having outlined his critique of Ulpian (and therefore also of Aquinas), Salas moved on to ask about the relationship between *ius naturale* and *ius gentium*, on the subject of which, he said, quoting an old saw, "there are as many opinions as you can count heads," *tot capita, quot sententiae*.[70] In a heroic effort, Salas sorted them into five basic positions. The first is that the law of nations, explicitly including the contents of the *l. Ex hoc iure* (wars, servitudes, division of property, kings ...), is natural law, and Salas attributed this to his fellow Jesuit Juan Azor and to the Spanish lawyer Fernando de Mendoza. The second is that the *ius gentium* is partly natural and partly positive, divided between a primary and a secondary law of nations. Defenders of this position are the lawyers Bartolus and Fernando Vázquez de Menchaca, who separate out the contents of the *l. Ex hoc iure* from the law of natural reason. The third position is that of François Connan, who posits a double natural *ius*, one related to the demands of natural reason, the other a function of human utility. The fourth is that the whole of the law of nations, taken in its proper sense, is positive, an opinion represented for Salas by the Dominicans Soto, Medina, and Bañez, and by the Jesuits Molina, Aragon, Miguel de Salón, and Gregory de Valentia. The fifth is the view taken by the Jesuit Gabriel Vázquez, that the *ius gentium* is not, in fact, a law at all, but simply a series of juridical permissions.[71] Salas's categorisation covers only Catholic lawyers and theologians. But we can use it, with a small shuffling of the order, to cover the entire range of solutions offered to the problem.

Let us take first, then, his second position, which explicitly preserves the inherited notion of the *ius gentium* as part of a temporal story about mankind. According to this scenario, the *ius gentium* is divided into two, a primary law that is constituted by natural reason, and a secondary law that is a function of positive legislation. Fernando Vázquez, whom we met earlier in discussing natural law, was indeed the major sixteenth-century defender of this position. Following on from a natural law common to all animals, Vázquez posited a *ius gentium primaevum* that is common to all human beings by their nature, because it is constituted by natural reason. He went on from here to elucidate the *ius gentium secundarium*. This law, he argued, cannot be explained by any appeal to the *gentes* taken universally, precisely because it is not natural. It must, then, have been originally the civil law of different commonwealths, which subsequently spread across the entire human race.

---

[70] Salas, *Tractatus de legibus*, tract. 14, disp. 2, sect. 2, n.12, fo. 35, col. 2.
[71] Ibid., fo. 35–38.

The secondary law of nations is that which did not emerge simultaneously with the human race, but which with the decline of the ages is found to be practised by most of those peoples that are governed by customs and laws, and do not live a life in the woods in the mode and manner of wild beasts ... and this law in the beginning was purely a civil law, not a law of nations ... although afterwards it was gradually or in succession accepted also by all or most of the peoples ... and so this secondary law of nations is said to be not so much natural, as positive, and so it is not fixed or immutable.[72]

There is, however, a contradiction in Vázquez's position. From the *l. Ex hoc iure*, Vázquez held that civil societies—*regna* broadly speaking—are a *function* of the secondary law of nations, as much as are wars, servitudes, and private properties.[73] But if that is the case, how can the secondary law of nations be *originally* civil?

The young Hugo Grotius, whom we saw earlier had adopted Vázquez's juridical scheme for the purposes of justifying Dutch activity in the East Indies, avoided this problem. The *ius gentium primaevum* was equally for him a *ius* that is constituted by natural reason, even if—and here he was closer to Vitoria and Soto—it rests on consensus in accordance with the voluntarist framework of the *De iure praedae*.[74] This *ius*, unlike the *ius naturae*, tells us that the goods of others are to be respected: the principle of sociability that other humanist and Protestant natural lawyers had taken as the natural foundation of all *ius*. As to the *ius gentium secundarium*, here Grotius shared Vázquez's insight that it cannot be originally the positive law of the *gentes* taken universally as a pre-civic body of some kind. Just as for Vázquez, the positivity of the secondary law of nations is a function of already-constituted cities. However, differently from Vázquez, Grotius placed the juridical origin of cities not in the secondary law of nations itself but in a new pre-civic source of *ius*, the will of the individual. This in turn gives rise to the commonwealth or *civitas*, and hence to *ius civile*. We shall examine these crucial moves in the next two chapters. For the moment, the point is that the *ius gentium secundarium* can in this way be situated without tension in a post-civic domain, and it is a law that is specifically between commonwealths rather than *inter homines* or even *inter gentes*.[75] Grotius kept this sphere of *ius* in his later work, the *De iure belli*; but by this time he had jettisoned the four-stage theory altogether, just as he had jettisoned a law common to all animals. Thus, the *ius gentium* as constituted by the will of all nations is now the law of

---

[72] Vázquez, *Illustrium controversiarum libri tres*, lib. II, cap. 89, nn. 25–26.

[73] Ibid., lib. I, cap. 41, n. 30.

[74] Grotius, *De iure praedae*, cap. 2, fo. 6': *Ius gentium primarium*; vol. I, p. 12.

[75] Ibid., fo. 12': *Ius gentium secundarium*; vol. I, p. 26.

nations simply speaking;[76] all other human relations outside the city are governed by natural law. However, Grotius still admitted here some sense of temporal development, this time through a distinction *within* natural law between that which flows immediately from nature and that which is a consequence of the establishment of property.[77]

The move to replace the Bartolist scheme for one that sees the development within the *ius gentium* as occurring *within* natural law can be traced back to the early sixteenth century and the work of the German humanist jurist Ulrich Zasius. Zasius posited that the law of nations constitutes a unified domain of law, which is, however, subject to variation as human life develops and its usages and customs change.[78] We find an essentially similar position (but without the focus on customary usage) in one of the early Lutheran jurists from Melanchthon's circle, Melchior Kling, who in his 1542 commentary on the *Institutes* divided natural law into two: a *ius naturale primaevum*, innate notions naturally written upon human minds, and a *ius naturale secundarium*, which was instituted at the demands of human necessity and requires a degree of discursive reasoning.[79] This secondary law of nature is none other than the *ius gentium*. Johannes Oldendorp argued slightly differently that the *ius gentium* does not constitute a separate domain of law. The *ius gentium*, "if we are speaking properly, is partly referred to natural law, and partly to human. Of itself it does not constitute a third species."[80] As natural law, it is the law of natural reason, and this includes the contents of the *l. Ex hoc iure*.[81] However, there is nevertheless an order in its precepts, between the *precepta summa* and the more particular commands that we work out through a mixture of natural reason and the political "argumentation" we engage in to produce purely positive law.[82]

The holder of the third position on Salas's list, François Connan, equally criticised the Bartolist distinction between *ius gentium primaevum* and

---

[76] Grotius, *De iure belli*, lib. I, cap. 1, sect. 14, n. 1.

[77] Ibid., lib. II, cap. 8, sect. 1, n. 1; lib. I, cap. 1, sect. 10, n. 7.

[78] See Susan Longfeld Karr, "Nature, self and history in the works of Guillaume Budé, Andrea Alciati, and Ulrich Zasius," unpublished Ph.D. thesis (Chicago 2009), pp. 202–203.

[79] Melchior Kling, *In quattuor Institutionum libros enarrationes* (Lyon 1566), pp. 4–5. Confusingly, the division between primary and secondary natural law could also be used by jurists to refer to the distinction between Ulpian's natural law, common to all animals, and the law of natural reason, that is, the *ius gentium* (or the *ius gentium primaevum*, for those who continued to use that terminology). See Scattola, *Naturrecht*, pp. 181–86.

[80] Oldendorp, *Eisagōgē*, fo. 48v, n. 13. Oldendorp goes on to say, however, that nothing prevents us talking of it as a third species in "a looser and popular way," for the sake of teaching.

[81] Ibid., fo. 49v, n. 2.

[82] Ibid., n. 3; positive law is "posited by a kind of political and civil argumentation for the purpose of extending natural law": ibid., fo. 48v, n. 12.

secundarium and argued instead for two elements within natural law. But, unlike the German jurists, he posited a sharp disjunction in principle between the two components, concomitantly with a rejection of a developmental relationship between them. This break between the two has led to his position being assimilated to that of Fernando Vázquez, but Salas was right to distinguish between them.[83] Connan's argument turned on a fundamental, and highly innovative, revision of the whole sphere of *ius*. Having established that Ulpian's triadic structure, based on the inclusion of animals within juridical community, must be dismissed, Connan referred instead to the bipartite structure advanced by Paulus at D.1.1.11. "'Law,' he [Paulus] says, 'has many senses. In one way, certainly, that which is always equitable and good is called law (*ius*), as in natural law. In another way, that which is useful to all or most within any city is called law, as in civil law.' In which it is most of all to be noted," Connan continued, "that he placed the rationale of the equitable and the good in natural law, and utility in civil law. And this we shall hold on to with all our might because it contains the essence of everything that we are going to say."[84] He went on to relate the bipartite division of *ius* in Paulus to the bipartite division of what is right (*to dikaion*) set down in Book V of Aristotle's *Nicomachean Ethics*. Aristotle had argued that right in its true sense is political right (*dikaion politikon*), which obtains between those who are free and equal and share the same law. Political right he had then subdivided into natural (*phusikon*) and "legal" (*nomikon*, in Latin *legitimum*): natural, "that which is everywhere the same"; legal, that which is originally indifferent and has its origin in agreement (*sunthēkē*) and utility (*to sumpheron*).

Connan solved the problem of how natural *ius* could be a subset of political *ius* by arguing, on the authority of Cicero, that the Greek term *politikon*—"political"—must stretch more broadly than the Latin term *civile*, or "civil."[85] *Politikon* refers to the natural sociability that characterises all mankind as distinct from other animals, not to being "shut up within the walls of cities." The principle of this sociability is right reason, *recta ratio*, which is in Ciceronian fashion the natural law of all human beings. Connan explicitly invoked the notion of a world city to characterise this natural and universal society of all human beings.[86] However,

---

[83] Haggenmacher, *Grotius*, pp. 341–43, suggests that Connan's second kind of *ius*—the *ius gentium*—is purely positive, assimilating his position to that of Fernando Vázquez. As I read it, it is crucial to Connan's argument that the *ius gentium* is a kind of natural law, albeit one that is based on a different principle from the first kind of *ius naturale*. That different principle—utility—characterises civil law as well, however, which does indeed bring him closer to Vázquez.

[84] Connan, *Commentariorum*, lib. I, cap. 6, n. 2.

[85] Ibid.

[86] Ibid., n. 3.

the law of this world city, the *ius naturale*, has a "twofold nature" (*bipartita ratio*): one, which is "everywhere the same," and reduces to the immutable principle of equity, "Do not to another that which you would not have done to yourself"; a second, which is "regulatory of those utilities that are necessary to the sustenance of life." The first is called the *ius naturale* "truly and properly"; the second, "which has to do with utility," will "not ineptly be called the *ius gentium*."[87] To this latter belong all the things traditionally held to belong to the secondary law of nations: "property, kingdoms, wars, servitudes, manumissions, contracts and other things of this sort." This *ius* is introduced not so much by nature as by human judgement, "and yet it is a part of natural *ius*." Its constitutions can be changed, but this does not mean that they are civil rather than natural.[88] Somewhat confusingly, Connan explained this by separating out the two principles that Aristotle had laid down as the source of *dikaion nomikon*, that is, agreement and utility. Connan argued that the institutions of civil law are constituted by the agreement of citizens, but those of the *ius gentium* are "thought up" for the convenience of all men.[89]

Connan's analysis caused something of a storm among both Protestant and Catholic theologians and jurists. Salas tells us that only Connan holds this opinion. But his influence is everywhere, for example in the work of Johannes Althusius, to whose Aristotelianism and Ramist methodological principles it clearly appealed. In his early *Iuris Romani libri duo* of 1586, Althusius, having quoted the opening of the Digest to the effect that "law is the science of the good and the equitable" (*aequum*), posited that "all that is equitable is twofold: natural, or legal" (*legitimum*).[90] Natural is what right reason has taught all men, but this *aequum naturale* is double: primary, which is immediately apprehended as just and is immutable; secondary, which is discursively judged to be just, and is mutable. The latter "is called the *ius gentium*." This, Althusius went on, "principally has regard to the utility and the necessity of human society, and hence it is often subject to change.... Of this law (*ex hoc iure*) judgements, wars, captivities, servitudes, obligations etc. have come forth." He thus blended elements of the two-stage idea with the twofold-nature thesis of Connan, who is cited for the view that the primary *aequum naturale* contains the distinction between the honest and the shameful and is thus not to be derived from natural inclinations, which are "vicious and depraved."[91] In his mature

[87] Ibid.

[88] Ibid., nn. 5–6.

[89] Ibid., n. 6.

[90] Johannes Althusius, *Iuris Romani libri duo*, lib. I, cap. 1, p. 1. The distinction between *ius naturale* and *ius legitimum* occurs not only in the Latin Aristotle but in the Roman law, at Inst. 2.1.14.

[91] Ibid., p. 2.

work of jurisprudence, the *Dicaeologica* of 1617, Althusius referred to these ideas within a new framework of his own, in which all *ius* has as its principle the utility and necessity of human social life. It divides into "common" (natural) and "proper" to a particular place (civil).[92] The *ius gentium* falls under the former, following broadly the same kind of reasoning as in the earlier work.[93]

The final stage in the process of the naturalisation, and hence "detemporalisation," of the *ius gentium* was simply to equate it with natural law *tout court*, the first of Salas's possible positions. Two important later Protestant jurists moved in this direction. In his celebrated *Commentaries* on the civil law, first published in 1589, the distinguished French Calvinist exile Hugues Doneau (Hugo Donellus) derived both from the same principle, although he still allowed for some temporal development between the two.[94] In his tract concerning the division of *ius* of 1586, Hubert van Giffen went further: the *ius gentium* coincides with the *ius naturale*, and the correct division is not into "primary" and "secondary" but into "pure" and "mixed."[95] But this move cannot be exclusively associated with Protestant jurisprudence. It is there in Catholic jurisprudence as well, and from the same point in time. The Spanish lawyer Fernando de Mendoza, whom Salas mentions, published his commentary on the title *De pactis* in the Code in 1586. Here he argued that all of those things traditionally attributed to the *ius gentium* in fact belong to the *ius naturale*: the two terms are convertible. Like van Giffen, Mendoza held this view partly in opposition to Connan, basing himself on what he saw as the correct interpretation of Aristotle. However, Mendoza still allowed a variation in the logical conclusions of the *ius naturale* (i.e., the *ius gentium*) according to time.[96]

All these authors held back, therefore, from the absolutely simple equation between natural law and the law of nations. This final development occurred, however, with two Protestant authors, Alberico Gentili in his *De iure belli* of 1598 and Thomas Hobbes in his *De cive* of 1642, and in

---

[92] Johannes Althusius, *Dicaeologicae libri tres*, repr. of Frankfurt 1649 (Aalen: Scientia Verlag 1967), lib. I, cap. 13, nn. 6–8, p. 36. For human social life and the importance of place, see below, ch. 8, pp. 215–19. See also J. Witte, *The Reformation of rights. Law, religion, and human rights in early modern Calvinism* (Cambridge: Cambridge University Press 2007), pp. 156–65.

[93] Althusius, *Dicaeologicae*, lib. I, cap. 13, nn. 18–20, pp. 37–38.

[94] Haggenmacher, *Grotius*, p. 352.

[95] Scattola, *Naturrecht*, pp. 187–90. Compare van Giffen's critique of Connan in his commentary on the *Nicomachean Ethics*: *Commentarii in decem libros ethicorum Aristotelis ad Nicomachum* (Frankfurt 1608), p. 406, *De divisione iuris*.

[96] Ferdinandus de Mendoza, *Disputationum iuris civilis in difficiliores leges ff. de pactis libri tres* (Alcalá 1586), lib. III, cap. 1, q. 1, nn. 4–18, fo. 509–27; critique of Connan at n. 5, interpretation of Aristotle at nn. 10, 12.

the handling of the latter it did away with the entire inherited notion of the *ius gentium* as a diverse range of institutions covering both private individuals and public bodies (things such as buying and selling on the one hand, and war on the other).[97] If natural law and the law of nations are straightforwardly the same, the *ius gentium* becomes simply the *ius inter homines* of Gaius's definition, with the implication that the actions of states can be perceived analogically with, or even implicitly assimilated to, the actions of individuals prior to any civil laws.[98] Gentili, an Italian Protestant exile who held the chair of civil law at Oxford, used Gaius's formula to describe the *ius gentium* and equated it with the law of nature, explicitly in the context of actions between states. He described it, however, in terms that were very close to Melanchthon's as a "particle of divine law" left to man after the Fall.[99] The really radical development of this line of thought is to be found in the work of Hobbes, who argued explicitly that the *ius gentium* is natural law applied to *civitates*, commonwealths or states, "because cities once established take on the personal properties of men."[100] As part of this conception he took issue, mildly, with the common phrase *ius gentium*. The law of nations in the sense that he has described it is a law, *lex*, not a right, *ius*, which he had in the immediately preceding section defined as two very different things, a "bond" (*vinculum*) and a "liberty" (*libertas*).[101] Paradoxically, this brought him closer to certain developments within the Catholic scholastic tradition, whose authors were characterised by Salas as holding the converse position, that the *ius gentium* is purely positive.

Salas associated this position, the fourth on his list, with both Dominican and Jesuit authors. This bare categorisation, however, masks important differences. We have already seen how Vitoria and Soto had begun to

[97] See J. Schröder, "Die Entstehung des modernen Völkerrechtsbegriffs im Naturrecht der frühen Neuzeit," *Jahrbuch für Recht und Ethik* 8 (2000), 47–71.

[98] As David Armitage points out, however, it is too strong to argue from there to the position that individuals were reciprocally perceived to have the characteristics of states, as Tuck wants in his *Rights of war and peace*. See D. Armitage, "Hobbes and the foundations of modern international thought," in A. S. Brett and J. Tully eds., *Rethinking the foundations of modern political thought* (Cambridge: Cambridge University Press 2006), 219–35, at p. 225.

[99] Alberico Gentili, *De iure belli libri tres* (Hanau 1598), lib. I, cap. 1, p. 3, p. 10.

[100] Hobbes, *De cive*, cap. XIV, sect. IV, pp. 207–208. But it is important to note both that the *ius gentium*, despite being applied to states as persons and not to individual persons, is the very same natural law that governs the latter, and that the analogy between the two types of person is not absolutely thoroughgoing. See N. Malcolm, "Hobbes's theory of international relations," in idem, *Aspects of Hobbes* (Oxford: Clarendon 2002), 432–56, in a critique of the caricature of Hobbesian international relations as unrestrained *Machtpolitik* that some of his interpreters have wished upon him.

[101] Ibid., sect. III, p. 207.

insist on the positivity of the *ius gentium*, without abandoning the idea that it is in some sense an exercise of natural reason. In the context of clearing up Aquinas's confusing statements, the upshot of their work had been to preserve the idea that the *ius gentium* is constituted by a process of natural reasoning, but nevertheless to distinguish it more decidedly from natural law by arguing that its status as law was a function of human consensus, not nature, and that therefore it was positive rather than natural law. The *ius gentium* kept its temporal position, however, as something subsequent to natural law and prior to civil law. Effectively, this Dominican solution, preserving both the temporality and the naturalness of the reasoning behind the *ius gentium*, is not so very far distant from the sort of approach we saw in the Lutheran jurist Melchior Kling. By contrast, a series of major Jesuits differ considerably in holding that the positivity of the *ius gentium* entails that it *cannot* be the product of natural reason, but must have its source in human arrangement of some kind.

This position is essentially clear already in the first treatise *De iustitia et iure* that we have from a Jesuit, Molina,[102] and Francisco Suárez explained the nub of the matter in the second book of his *De legibus* with his customary clarity.[103] The law of nations cannot be an exercise of natural reason, because if it were, it would be natural law. But, again, this cannot be the correct position to take, because the *ius gentium* involves things that are not intrinsically necessary to human nature, such as the division of property, servitudes, the practice of warfare, and other such things.[104] The conclusion must be, then, that the *ius gentium* as distinct from natural law cannot contain *any* precepts that are intrinsically necessary to a rational creature and thus discoverable by natural reason alone.[105] Rather, the source of the substantive content of the *ius gentium*, the basis for positive consensus, is not natural reason but customary usage.[106] Even so, Suárez did not deny a certain proximity between the operation of natural reason and the precepts of the *ius gentium*: they can be seen to have arisen at the *prompting* of natural reason—this is how he understood Soto and sought to accommodate Aquinas—and they are in accord with human nature. So, in the matter of the just power of making punitive war, Suárez wrote that "of the force of natural reason, it was not necessary that this power should be in the commonwealth that had been attacked; for human be-

---

[102] Molina, *De iustitia et iure*, tract. I, disp. 5, n. 4.

[103] Suárez, *De legibus*, lib. II, caps. 17 and 19.

[104] Ibid., cap. 17, n. 8.

[105] Ibid., n. 9 (in conclusion).

[106] For example, the immunity of ambassadors: Suárez, *De legibus*, lib. II, cap. 19, n. 7. See B. Tierney, "Vitoria and Suarez on *ius gentium*, natural law, and custom," in A. Perreau-Saussine and J. Murphy eds., *The nature of customary law* (Cambridge: Cambridge University Press 2007), 101–24.

ings could have instituted another mode of vengeance, or committed that power to a third prince as an arbiter with coercive power; but nevertheless because the mode that is now observed is easier and more in agreement with nature, therefore it was introduced, and is so just that it cannot rightfully be resisted."[107]

Salas himself agreed with Molina and Suárez that the law of nations is wholly positive. But (as it was in respect of the Dominicans) this agreement is too bare a conclusion as it stands, because it elides a key question: if the *ius gentium* is positive law, who is its legislator and in what capacity? Salas and Suárez both kept elements of Vitoria's conception of a world community that is lacking in Soto, for whom the reasoning involved in the *ius gentium* can be done by individuals alone. So, for Salas, the legislator is "all the nations," *omnes gentes*: "it is called the law of nations not precisely because all nations use it, but because they use it *as its authors*."[108] However, they are not its authors as single nations, but as forming one community:

> For all nations, insofar as they make up one community of the whole human race, can oblige individuals to those things that are useful to the whole human race, just as a city can oblige individuals to those things that are useful to the whole city, and a kingdom to those things that are suitable for the whole kingdom; and it is ascertained by tradition that they did wish to oblige [them] in this way to some things, and to have explained their will with nods, words, usage and habits, or other signs, particularly in the beginning of the world, when because of the small number of men and their mutual love, it was easy for all or the majority to agree in that will.[109]

The *ius gentium*, then, is a law that obligues individual human beings rather than states. By contrast, it is Suárez's well-recognised innovation to have made a distinction between two senses of the *ius gentium*: one, "the law that all peoples and the various nations [*omnes populi et gentes variae*] ought to keep between [*inter*] themselves"; two, "the law that individual cities, or kingdoms observe within [*intra*] themselves," but in which nevertheless all or almost all cities and kingdoms coincide.[110] The former is properly the law of nations, the latter a kind of universal civil law. Suárez went on to give the reason for the existence of the *ius gentium* in its proper sense. It lies in the fact that the human race "always has some kind of unity, not simply of a species, but also a quasi-political and moral

---

[107] Suárez, *De legibus*, lib. II, cap. 19, nn. 3, 8.
[108] Salas, *Tractatus de legibus*, tract. 14, disp. 2, sect. 3, n. 21, fo. 39, emphasis mine.
[109] Ibid.
[110] Suárez, *De legibus*, lib. II, cap. 19, n. 8.

unity.... So that even if every perfected city, commonwealth or kingdom, is in itself a perfect community, and being made up of its own members, nevertheless each of them is also a member in some sense of this universal community."[111] These communities are not wholly self-sufficient and therefore require a law to regulate their mutual actions. Thus, despite the similarities in language to Salas—and indeed to Vitoria—on the unity of the whole human race, Suárez differed profoundly in apparently perceiving the universal community to be made up not simply of individual human beings, nor even of *gentes*, but of commonwealths.[112] The *ius gentium* properly speaking, then, is a law between states, losing the distinctive temporal position that it still retained in some sense for Salas and that was central to the Dominicans.

I want to turn finally to the fifth of Salas's listed positions, that of the Jesuit Gabriel Vázquez. Vázquez (1549–1604) was one of the Society's most subtle and original intellects and Suárez's personal *bête noire*—at least in the matter of law, and a fortiori in the matter of the *ius gentium*. With characteristic intellectual enterprise, Vázquez handled the question of the relationship between natural law and the law of nations by stepping out of the confines of the Thomist debate entirely and looking instead to François Connan, the debt to whom is made plain from the opening chapter of the discussion that refutes the opinion of Ulpian.[113] Vázquez took over from Connan the idea of a two-fold natural *ius*, which he relates to a two-fold human nature: "firstly in itself and without qualification and outside any civil society and commonwealth, secondly insofar as man lives in a commonwealth with a common custom of life; and out of these two states two natural *iura* arise, i.e. natural simply-speaking, which is called 'primary' or 'primeval,' and the *ius gentium*, which is called secondary." The latter is natural, because it is common to all peoples and nations and could not be so if it were not judged to be suitable by natural reason. Vázquez further adopted from Connan the framing of the distinction in terms of the *honestum* and the *utile*. "The second thing to be noticed is what François Connan excellently noted [in] the first book of his commentary ... i.e. that *ius* is said in two ways, firstly the *ius* of justice, secondly that of utility." The first Vázquez equates to his own understanding of natural *ius* as nothing other than human nature itself, which is the primary rule of the just and the unjust and commands and forbids ac-

---

[111] Ibid., n. 9.

[112] I say "apparently" because the language in this chapter is not stable, shifting between *respublicae, populi, nationes*, and *gentes*.

[113] Vázquez, *Commentariorum ac disputationum in primam secundae S. Thomae*, tom. II, disp. 157, cap. 1, fo. 51–52.

cordingly. But the second "is that which is not the rule of the just and the unjust, virtue and sin, nor does it command anything in such a way that the contrary is a sin, but simply concedes a free faculty of using a thing as useful, or even as honourable: but in such a way that not to use it, or to use something else, is not morally wrong." The *ius gentium*, then, is not *ius* in the sense of a law, but only in the sense of "a licence or faculty," "for this is one of the significations of *ius*."[114] In sum, then, "the *ius gentium* is solely a law of permission and utility appropriate to human nature considered as within a civil community."[115]

As Salas remarked, this is not exactly what Connan had said. Connan had never argued explicitly that the second "nature" of natural *ius* was purely permissive.[116] Nor does Vázquez's view that the primary natural law is a law for individuals living a solitary life fit well with Connan's humanist-Aristotelian conception of both kinds of natural law as a subset of *politikon dikaion*, the *ius* that relates to human beings as seeking the company of others.[117] What Vázquez is doing rather is to map Connan's distinction within *ius* onto a distinction between *lex* and *ius*, which (as we shall see in the next chapter) is a marker of the Catholic scholastic tradition. His creative fusion of a scholastic and a legal-humanist inheritance produced a startlingly novel and, to contemporaries, threatening account of the *ius gentium*: that the law of nations is not a separate legislative domain, but a zone of permission left over from natural law. This removes all need to ask, as other Jesuits do, who is the legislator of the *ius gentium*. It does not *have* a legislator. It is just what people in civil communities may either do or not do within the bounds of conforming to natural law as the law of rational human nature. No one is legally obliged to go to war, for example, under the *ius gentium*; they only *may* do so. But if they do, then natural law dictates that no one should be killed without just cause, just as it dictates that no individual man should kill another without due cause. The clear implication is that all justice outside civil law reduces to the justice of individual solitary behaviour: the only *law* governing inter-state relations is natural law.

Both Suárez and Salas engaged in an extensive polemic against this way of thinking. Neither of them would accept that the *ius gentium* is purely permissive. Both insisted that the *ius gentium* is properly a law, and

---

[114] Ibid., cap. 3, nn. 15–16, fo. 53.

[115] Ibid., n. 17, fo. 54.

[116] However, his distinction between justice and liberty offered some support to Vázquez's interpretation: see below, ch. 4, p. 100.

[117] It has some resonances, however, with the account Connan gave as the best possible sense he could make of Ulpian's tripartite division of *ius*, before turning to offer his own bipartite analysis: *Commentariorum*, lib. I, cap. 3–5.

a positive law, as we have seen.[118] But we should not think that their apparent demolition of this view entirely won the day. Rodrigo de Arriaga, the brilliant Spanish Jesuit working in Prague in the middle of the seventeenth century, offered a sustained defence of Vázquez against the critiques of Salas and Suárez.[119] The latter, he objected, does not give any reason why the *ius gentium* cannot be a matter of pure faculty; he just takes it as given.[120] Salas does better in showing that the *ius* that is commonly divided into *naturale*, *gentium*, and *civile* is a *ius* in the sense of law. But this does not establish that this common division is the right way to think about it. "For," he said, although their position is clear, "I can scarcely however find any laws apart from the concessions that Father Vázquez and Connan posited."[121] He runs through the five major examples from Suárez and Salas: the receiving of ambassadors under conditions of immunity and security; contracts and commerce; the law of war; slavery; treaties of peace. "And to tell the truth, all of these things clearly seem to me either not to be true obligatory laws, to the extent that they belong to the *ius gentium*; or if they are obligatory, they are natural laws." So, considering the international practice by which the injured party (rather than any third party) vindicates by war the injury done, Arriaga argued that the law in this case is clearly natural law rather than any "law" of nations. "And when Father Suárez says that there could have been another resort in doubtful cases, i.e. constituting a judge as arbitrator with coercive power, this seems to me a contradiction in terms as far as the present question goes. For how will the other king be compelled to accept those judges, except by force of arms? But this is precisely to be able to make war. And therefore the power to make war stems from the law of nature itself."[122] Oddly, then, the closest equivalent to Hobbes's position is to be

---

[118] There is a brief treatment of the contrast with Vázquez in J. P. Doyle, "Francisco Suárez on the law of nations," in M. W. Janis and C. Evans eds., *Religion and international law* (The Hague-London: Nijhoff 1999), 103–20; see also M. Kremer, *Den Frieden verantworten. Politische Ethik bei Francisco Suárez (1548–1617)* (Stuttgart: Kohlhammer 2008), pp. 127–30.

[119] Rodrigo de Arriaga, *Disputationes theologicae in primam secundae S. Thomae*, tom. II (Antwerp 1644), disp. 7, sect. 8, subsect. 2, fo. 72.

[120] This is not quite fair; on Suárez's understanding, faculty or *ius dominativum* is always correlate with *ius praeceptivum* or law. That is, the area in which an individual man is in control or command (hence *ius dominativum*) is inseparable from the area in which he is commanded by the legislator, for both are united in their nature as *ius* and go together to make up any specific domain of *ius*, for example, the *ius naturale* or the *ius gentium*. It makes no sense, for him, to have the command as natural and the permission as "of nations." See further below, ch. 4, p. 96.

[121] Arriaga, *Disputationes theologicae in primam secundae*, tom. II, disp. 7, sect. 8, subsect. 2, n. 56, fo. 72.

[122] Ibid. n. 60, fo. 73.

found in this particular strand of Jesuit thinking that opposes any idea of a *law* of nations distinct from natural law, and simply gives nations a series of rights consistent with the law of nature, rights that Vázquez, at least, holds are natural.

To sum up, this fraught and multiplicitous debate is index enough of the general uncertainty over the *ius gentium* in the century with which we are concerned. But two things seem clear. One is the emergence of two new theses about the *ius gentium*: either that it is simply natural law, or that it is a positive law between states. The second is that these two new ideas contradict a persistent inherited way of thinking about the *ius gentium* as a temporal phenomenon, a distinct juridical stage of human civilisation. In the final chapter we shall consider the political implications of preserving or not what I shall call this temporally situated "world of the *gentes*." For the present we turn to the key juridical dynamic that sixteenth- and seventeenth-century natural law discourse introduces into the framework of law: the individual in possession of, and in pursuit of, his rights.

CHAPTER FOUR

NATURAL LIBERTY

We finished the last chapter by comparing Vázquez and Arriaga with Hobbes, two different theories that collapse the obligatory force of the *ius gentium* into natural law, resting partly on the difference between *ius* as a faculty of action and law as an obligatory rule. It is this distinction— somewhat the elephant in the room of the last chapter—that needs to come to the fore now if we are to understand the juridical dynamics that mark the domain of the *ius gentium*, leading ultimately to the formation of the commonwealth or state. As is very familiar, one of the key moves of sixteenth- and seventeenth-century natural jurisprudence is to insert the individual into this story, an individual who is not merely naturally free in the sense of the second chapter of this book, but naturally free in a juridical sense too. This is that "common liberty of all," in the scholastic tag,[1] which belongs, together with common property, to natural law: not

---

[1] It derives from Isidore of Seville, *Etymologies* V. 4, QUID SIT IVS NATVRALE. *Ius naturale [est] commune omnium nationum, et quod ubique instinctu naturae, non constitutione aliqua habetur; ut viri et feminae coniunctio, liberorum successio et educatio, communis omnium possessio, et omnium una libertas, adquisitio eorum quae caelo, terra marique capiuntur.* It was inserted into Gratian's *Decretum* at D. 1. c. 7, and from there became the common inheritance of the scholastic natural law tradition. The "common liberty of all" has its Roman legal source in Ulpian (D.1.1.4).

freedom from necessitation, which is an intrinsic property of the human agent, but freedom from subjection, which is a property relative to other human agents, if not to God. In this chapter I want to think about how that conceptual space is opened up in the different kinds of natural law theory we looked at in the last.

The thrust of my analysis in the last chapter was to suggest, I hope, a large degree of inter-confessional consensus on the relationship between natural law and reason while at the same time pointing to a broad contrast. Whereas natural law in legal humanist and Protestant discourse is a civil philosophy, a norm of sociability, natural law in the Jesuit scholastic is an extension of a natural philosophy of human agency, an individual rule of action. This explains a phenomenon that has often been noted, and sometimes related to the humanist inheritance (which is certainly true), that this Protestant jurisprudence tends not to make a sharp distinction between *ius* in the sense of law and *ius* in the sense of a subjective right.[2] While, therefore, for the sake of speaking English I have thus far generally been translating this fluid *ius* as "law," this is not really apt for any of the Protestant Aristotelians and humanist lawyers. The central sense is neither an individual right nor a commanding law, but an *inter*-subjective rightfulness or lawfulness, or the body of norms that governs a particular domain of such inter-subjectivity. This perspective means that there is no great pressure to draw the distinction between what I am commanded to do and what I do by my own right. By contrast, the perspective of individual agency that dominates the Catholic scholastic, following Aquinas, exerts severe pressure to distinguish between a rule of action with its source outside the agent and a right of action understood as a faculty of that agent itself. With that broad contrast in mind, I want to turn now to look at the juridical place of natural liberty, beginning this time with Catholic scholastic discourse.

As we saw in the first chapter, the distinction between law and subjective right was routinely in use among Catholic theologians when Domingo de Soto came to write his work *On justice and right* in the early 1550s. However, there was no clear consensus on how the latter should be properly understood. Soto had been prepared to concede a natural right of self-preservation to all animate creatures, and he was followed in this, for example, by Juan de Salas. Salas, having rejected any sense of *law* as common to animals, and consequently the role that Aquinas gave to natural inclinations in his understanding of natural law, was nevertheless prepared to allow that it might be correct to attribute to them some kind of *right*. Thus, continuing his critique of Aquinas on natural law, he proposed that "the division of law following the inclinations seems rather to

[2] See for example Wyduckel, "Recht und Jurisprudenz," p. 6.

belong to right taken as the faculty of doing something than to right taken as law, bidding or command: which alone is our subject here." For, he wrote, in a metaphorical or analogical sense "one should concede to animals—yes, and even to inanimates—right in the sense of 'what is right,' or a kind of faculty of doing something, the use of which it would be an injustice to interfere with. For they demand, as if by their own right, the things that are naturally due and proportioned to them, so that they may exist in a good state, and be preserved, and serve the uses of men for whose conveniences they are brought forth."[3] However, together with Soto (and Molina, as we saw in chapter 2) he also insisted that "beasts, since they can have no *dominium*, therefore can have no right either in a thing or to a thing; otherwise there would be injury done them, if they were hindered ... which is false."[4] Just like Soto, then, while Salas conceded to animals a right of natural agency, he would not concede them any right in or over other things, including themselves: for all such rights are a function of *dominium*, which for all the later Catholic scholastics is exclusively the preserve of rational nature, that is, a nature that is free from necessitation or has *dominium* over its own actions. The corollary, as we saw in the first chapter, is that *all* rational nature has *dominium* over its own actions; there is no such thing as a natural slave in the sense of natural chattel.

This position on *dominium* is authentically Thomist. However, the way that Salas ran it together with a negative argument about right as the obverse of injury is not. This latter feature has its roots rather in the late-medieval nominalist handling of *dominium* in the context of the sacrament of penance, penance that demands restitution as a condition of satisfaction.[5] Here, anything that can be taken away injuriously, that is, in a way liable to restitution, is a case of *dominium*, making right in things coincident with *dominium*. The heritage of this way of thinking is very clear in Vitoria's commentary on Aquinas's *Secunda secundae*, where he distinguishes between three different senses of the term *dominium*. The first and second of these are "lordship" and "property," and in these senses, he concedes, *dominium* is not the same as right. But "in a third sense *dominium* is taken more broadly inasmuch as it denotes a certain faculty for using a thing according to the laws.... And in this sense ... right and *dominium* will be the same.... in the matter of restitution and morals *dominium* can be taken in this third sense.... Because for me to be bound to restitution, it is enough that I do some injury to someone in a thing to which he had a faculty; i.e. whatever that faculty were, if I do him injury,

---

[3] Salas, *Tractatus de legibus*, tract. 13, disp. 2, sect. 2, fo. 35.
[4] Ibid.
[5] See my *Liberty, right and nature*, ch. 1, for the general outlines of this way of thinking.

I am bound to restitution."[6] This "negative" definition of right was restated in the Jesuit scholastic by Luis de Molina in his *De iustitia et iure*: "It is a faculty of doing something, or getting something, or keeping something, or relating to something in some other way, in which, if contravened without legitimate cause, injury is done to the one who has it. Hence it comes that right in this sense is as if the measure of injury."[7] Nevertheless, Molina did not accept the coincidence of *dominium* and *ius* in Vitoria's terms—as neither, indeed, had Soto before him. For Soto, a subjective right over or in something is a faculty in the sense of a "facility," something that an individual has over what he can use or otherwise handle without having to be licensed by someone else. But *dominium* "does not signify any right and power whatsoever, but only that which is in a thing that we can use at our own pleasure for our own profit."[8] Molina argued rather differently. Although his discussion of *dominium* reveals Soto's influence at certain points, he suggested that to posit *ius* as the genus of *dominium* was a mistake: the right to which Soto had referred was a consequence of *dominium*, not *dominium* itself. In Molina's handling, *dominium* emerges rather as a separate kind of legal relation, arising from just title, which necessarily generates a cluster of rights such as Soto had attempted to encapsulate in his definition.[9]

Despite their differences, however, *dominium* for both authors implicates right in its subjective sense as a faculty of the individual, whether it be my natural *dominium* over the animals, or my civil *dominium* over something that is mine by civil law, a book, for example. In this sense, natural liberty, or natural *dominium* over one's own actions, is a natural right, or at least has such rights consequent upon it; and this generated the problem of how the loss of liberty, the institution of servitude under the *ius gentium* (*ex hoc iure … servitutes*), could ever be licit. Aquinas had said that liberty belongs to natural law only in a negative sense, that is, in the sense that natural law does not positively command the contrary.[10] In his question on whether the natural law can be changed, Soto endorsed precisely that solution, without any discussion. But that solution does not seem so readily available to someone who thinks of liberty as a natural right; and indeed in his question on *dominium*, three books further on, Soto did not rely on that locus of Aquinas. Rather he answered that servitude is licit

---

[6] Vitoria, *Comentarios a la Secunda secundae de Santo Tomás*, on q. 62, a. 1, nn. 6–8.

[7] Molina, *De iustitia et iure*, tom. I, tract. 2, disp. 1, n. 1.

[8] Domingo de Soto, *De iustitia et iure*, lib. IV, q. 1, a. 1.

[9] Molina, *De iustitia et iure*, tom. I, tract. 2, disp. 3, nn. 1, 5 and 6; see M. Kaufmann, "Das Verhältnis von Recht und Gesetz bei Luis de Molina," in A. Fidora et al. eds., *Lex und ius. Lex and ius. Beiträge zur Begründung des Rechts in der Philosophie des Mittelalters und der frühen Neuzeit* (Stuttgart-Bad Cannstatt: Frommann Holzboog 2010), 369–91, at p. 375.

[10] Aquinas, *ST* 1a2ae, q. 94, a. 5 ad 3.

both as a consequence of war, to save captives from death—the usual justification—and also if the individual himself sells himself into servitude. This latter is licit because, like all *dominium*, liberty is alienable.[11] But only *at the limit*: Soto argues that it can only morally be alienated in exchange for life itself. To give it up is always morally problematic; we brutalise ourselves in a sense if we do so. As is well known, Molina had a far sunnier attitude: a human being "is the owner (*dominus*) of his own liberty, and therefore, even standing solely under natural law, he can alienate it and drive himself into slavery."[12] But Juan de Salas shared Soto's reluctance. In the state of natural law before the Fall,

> natural reason, and therefore the law of nature, would have obliged to liberty: for even though the deed would hold (*factum teneret*) if someone willed to become the slave of another, and the other accepted, because man is the owner of his own works and can sell or give them to another in perpetuity; nevertheless, both would sin mortally, and would *eo ipso* lose grace and original justice; because each out of charity for himself is bound not to lose his liberty except from grave cause, such as then there was not, and of charity for his neighbour existing in that state not to accept a gift of liberty made by him without cause and necessity.[13]

Self-enslavement is justified under natural law only after the Fall, when iniquity has caused the kind of pressure that would necessitate such a course of action.

It is not the case, then, that there is a sharp break between the Dominican and the Jesuit meditation on this controversial issue, which had not only a theoretical but a practical dimension. Both Soto and Salas adverted explicitly to the troubled question of the legitimacy of the Portuguese slave trade and the conditions under which the "voluntary" self-sale of black Africans was supposedly occurring.[14] However, with Salas and especially with Suárez we do find a new element in the construction of *dominium* as a right. As we saw in chapter 2, the Jesuits effectively reconfigured Aquinas's language of the human and the animal into a language

---

[11] Ibid., q. 2, a. 2.

[12] Molina, *De iustitia et iure*, tom. I, tract. 2, disp. 33, n. 3. See M. Kaufmann, "Luis de Molina über subjective Rechte, Herrschaft und Sklaverei," in Kaufmann and Schnepf eds., *Politische Metaphysik*, 205–26; R. Tuck, *Natural rights thories. Their origin and development* (Cambridge: Cambridge University Press 1979), p. 54.

[13] Juan de Salas, *Tractatus de legibus*, tract. 14, disp. 2, sect. 5, n. 31, fo. 44.

[14] See J. Eisenberg, "Cultural encounters, theoretical adventures: The Jesuit missions to the New World and the justification of voluntary slavery," in Kaufmann and Schnepf eds., *Politische Metaphysik*, 357–83.

of the free and the natural, coinciding with the moral and the physical. Apparently paradoxically, this led Salas to argue that man's intrinsic, that is, his natural *dominium* over his own actions is a physical *dominium*: man's actions being physically under his control. This is distinct from, although analogous to, the *dominium* that man has "politically, civilly or morally speaking."[15] It is in this same sense that, quite early on in his career, while he was lecturing at the Collegio Romano between 1580 and 1585, Francisco Suárez separated out two things: on the one hand the "*dominium*, as a physical thing" that I have over my own actions, which "consists in the intrinsic faculty of acting freely"; on the other, the "*dominium* [of those actions] in a moral sense, or right."[16] Such a separation is wholly alien to the Thomist tradition. For a Thomist like Soto, all *dominium* is moral, if you like—though he would never use that language—and all *dominium* is a right: the *dominium* that I have over my own actions, which frees me from natural necessity and distinguishes me from being an animal, is the same *dominium* that makes me not naturally the slave of any other human being. Slavery militates against the very essence of humanity. The right is innate. But for Suárez, rights—*moral* faculties—in whatever sense they might be natural, are not *physically* innate, with the crucial consequence that they can be given up without threatening the essence of human being as a free nature. The alienability of liberty in the early Suárez, then, depends upon his separation of a moral from a physical ontology; and when we come to read the language of the moral in his much later *De legibus* of 1612, we need to understand it as contradistinguished against the physical in this way.[17]

In the *De legibus*, Suárez distinguished between law, understood as a *moral* obligation in the sense we looked at in the previous chapter, and

---

[15] Juan de Salas, *In primam secundae*, tom. I, disp. 4, sect. 1, fo. 31.

[16] Francisco Suárez, *De iustitia et iure*, ca. 1580–85, ed. in J. Giers, *Die Gerechtigkeitslehre des jungen Suárez. Edition und Untersuchung seiner römischen Vorlesungen De iustitia et iure* (Freiburg: Herder 1958), q. 12, p. 34: "Although *dominium*, as a physical thing, consists in the intrinsic faculty of acting freely and cannot be transferred to another, nevertheless *dominium* in a moral sense, or right, in a free act of mine can certainly be transferred to another. As is clear in a servant, who is in justice bound to perform his actions at the will of his master, because the master has the right to those actions before they happen." Suárez's argument is in fact directed expressly against a passage of Soto, which, however, does not seem quite to the point.

[17] It is important to note that this view did not come to dominate the Jesuit understanding of rights. Juan de Lugo and Rodrigo de Arriaga offered a fundamental critique of this line of thought, based on their nominalist rejection of the entire notion of a separate sphere of "moral being" that is neither physical being nor the pure invention of the mind, *ens fictum*. In their view, moral being must in some way reduce to physical being if it is to exist at all.

right, understood specifically as a *moral* faculty that someone has either in something that is his own or something that is his due.[18] This allowed him to divide each domain of *ius*—natural *ius*, the *ius gentium*, civil *ius*—into two components. On the one hand we have law, the "*ius* that commands," *ius praeceptivum*; on the other hand we have right, the "*ius* of *dominium*," *ius dominativum*. Individual right is, then, a sphere of *dominium* taken broadly.[19] This contrast is what allowed Suárez his distinctive handling of the relationship between natural law and the natural right that is liberty. He began by disagreeing with Aquinas that liberty is only of natural law negatively, rather than positively. "Liberty," Suárez contradicted, "is of natural law positively, and not only negatively, because nature itself gave man true *dominium* of his own liberty." But this did not mean that the common liberty of all is immutable. "For first of all, by the very fact that man has *dominium* of his own liberty, he can sell it or alienate it." More generally, however, he argued that the difference between natural law and right is that "the former contains rules and principles of acting well which contain a necessary truth, and are therefore immutable. For they are founded in the intrinsic rightness or wrongness of their objects. But right in the form of *dominium* is only the material of the other, commanding right and consists (so to speak) in fact or in a certain condition or circumstance of things. But it is certain that all created things ... have from nature many conditions which are mutable and which can be taken away by different causes"—by which he means either the will of the individual, or, once a commonwealth has been established, the will of the commonwealth itself.[20] Thus although it seemed at first as if Suárez had made moral right and moral law equally positive components of the juridical universe, it turns out that this is not so. In comparison with law, right—including the natural right of liberty—recedes to a more passive role, as "fact," the circumstance or the "material" of law. As we shall see in the subsequent chapter, it is in this sense that natural human liberty is the site of the state.

I want to turn now to the juridical status of natural liberty within legal humanist and Aristotelian thinking. These intellectual traditions do not share (at least initially) either the sharp distinction between right and law, or the metaphysics of the moral that underlies Suárez's account. Nevertheless, both equally involve the idea of liberty as a natural faculty of

---

[18] Suárez, *De legibus*, lib. I, cap. 2, n. 5.

[19] He thus loses entirely the sense of individual right as a pure right of agency, which in Soto and Salas crosses the animal–human divide.

[20] Suárez, *De legibus*, lib. II, cap. 14 nn. 16, 18, 19. See Westerman, *Disintegration of natural law*, pp. 112–16, Tierney, *Idea of natural rights*, pp. 306–307.

some kind. It was axiomatic for the Roman lawyers that all men are born free, primarily from Ulpian's assertion in the opening title of the Digest that manumission belongs to the *ius gentium*, "since by natural law all men were born free and manumission was unknown, since no servitude was recognised; but when later servitude came in under the law of nations, then the benefit of manumission followed."[21] Liberty was defined by them, following the Roman law, as "the natural faculty of doing that which it pleases anyone [to do], except it be prohibited in something by force or law."[22] Commentary on this passage focused initially on the definition of liberty as a *faculty*, not a right. It then moved to a similarly intense discussion of the "except" clause, which raised multiple problems for them. The first issue was whether the exception should be read, as seems intuitively obvious, as a restriction of liberty, in which case it is not clear why it is included as part of the *definition* of liberty. The second problem concerned the dual nature of the "prohibition," either by force or by law. What single faculty can there be that can be impeded both physically, by force, and by law, which is not something physical? As we shall see, this led some commentators to posit a dual liberty, of body and soul. As a final problem, if freedom is something that we have unless we are prohibited by force or law, then what is the difference between a free man and a slave? Surely both equally can do what they like unless they are prohibited in either of these two ways, in which case the whole point of the definition, to define freemen against slaves, is entirely lost.

Within the broadly Aristotelian political literature there are two places where the question of a natural liberty surfaces. One comes in Book I of the *Politics*, where Aristotle argued for the existence of natural slaves. Now Aristotle did not here contrast natural slavery with natural liberty but with natural mastery or *dominium*. Nevertheless, commentators and philosophers moved to supply the definition of liberty as a natural faculty taken from the Roman law—a move that was not unproblematic since, as we have seen, it was axiomatic for the Roman legal tradition that all men are born free, and so there *are* no natural slaves. In some authors this raised the whole question of the relationship between legal and philosophical discourse. Secondly, Aristotle in Book V of the *Politics* defined the democratic understanding of liberty as "to live as one likes" and for "the fancy of the moment"—a misguided understanding, because "it ought

---

[21] D.1.1.4: *utpote cum iure naturali omnes liberi nascerentur nec esset nota manumissio, cum servitus esset incognita: sed posteaquam iure gentium servitus invasit, secutum est beneficium manumissionis.*
[22] *Libertas est naturalis facultas eius quod cuique facere libet, nisi si quid vi aut iure prohibetur:* D.1.5.4, Inst.1.3.1. I have translated *ius* by "law" since the commentaries we shall be looking at all take it in that sense.

not to be regarded as slavery to live according to the constitution, but rather as salvation."[23] But this democratic definition of liberty seemed fairly close both to the definition of liberty in the Roman law, and to Cicero's definition of liberty as "to live as you like," *sic vivere ut velis*.[24] This prompted intense discussion of how to understand the "except" clause of the legal definition so as to preserve Aristotle's critique of democratic freedom at the same time as the authority of Cicero and of the Roman law.

In this way, the discussion of liberty as a natural faculty was intimately connected with the question of the proper understanding of civil liberty. The situation was similar in the legal commentaries, since the definition of liberty comes in the discussion of the status or right of persons,[25] who divide into "slave" and "free." But this division, and this placing of liberty, necessarily already implicates the *ius gentium*, if not civil law, since by natural law no one is a slave.[26] In neither of these two literatures, then, do we find a notion of natural liberty in the sense with which we are concerned in this chapter, that is, as an essentially pre-civic condition from which the city is constructed (although it does have some of this sense, because all men, at least in Roman law, were free *before* the institutions of the *ius gentium*). Accordingly, I defer a discussion of these texts to chapter 6, once we have seen the city constituted. For the present, I want to concentrate mainly on that aspect of the definition which posits that liberty is a natural faculty, in which the important point is that it is not a *right*. A faculty is something that lies purely in the will or the mind (*animus*) of the person who has it, so that it is entirely up to him whether he exercises it or not. As such, it is a matter of fact rather than of right, with an implicit etymology connecting *facultas* with *factum*: *facultas est quid facti*, "a faculty is a thing of fact."[27] Antoine Favre in his *Iurisprudentiae Papinianeae scientia*, first published in 1607, gave a clear account of the difference in the context of the definition of liberty.

> [Liberty] is called a natural faculty, not a right: because it consists not in right but in the pure [*mera*] faculty of a person, so that he can

[23] Aristotle, *Politics*, bk. V, 1310a31–36.

[24] Cicero, *De officiis*, I. 20. 70.

[25] The title in the Institutes in which the definition appears is "On the right of persons" (*De iure personarum*), while in the Digest it is "On the status of men" (*De statu hominum*). Hugues Doneau commented that status and right are related as cause and effect: *Commentarii de iure civili* (Frankfurt 1589), lib. II, cap. ix, fo. 85.

[26] The distinguished humanist lawyer Antoine Favre argued that strictly speaking the division between slave and free *only* relates to the *ius gentium*, since natural law is a law of free men and civil law has for its subjects only those who have citizenship and are therefore, likewise, free. Antonius Faber, *Iurisprudentiae papinianeae scientia* (Geneva 1631), tit. III, princ. i, p. 81 [recte 83].

[27] For this sense of "faculty," see my *Liberty, right and nature*, ch. 5, pp. 192–95.

do whatever he likes as long as he is not prohibited from doing it by force or by law [*lex*]. For when someone says "a right of doing something," he signifies that it is something which could not take place if the right of doing so had not been granted. But by nature all men are born free, nor can any instant be pointed to in which man acquires the right of liberty, in the sense that before that instant he did not have full liberty. Therefore it is a natural faculty and not a right. And when we say "faculty," we understand a bare power [*nuda potestas*] which has its cause solely in the will to do something, as if to say "the will of doing" [*faciendi voluntas*], not a right. So that we say that it is in your faculty, not your right, to go through and walk in your estate: but rightfully to go through and walk in another's estate is not in your faculty unless you also do it by right.[28]

This notion of faculty, and of liberty as a natural faculty, is prominent in two of the most philosophically ambitious legal works of the mid-sixteenth century, which we encountered in the last chapter: the *Illustrious controversies* of Fernando Vázquez and the *Commentaries on the civil law* of François Connan. For Vázquez, liberty is the original natural condition of all things, human or otherwise.[29] It therefore belongs to the natural law that is common to human beings and to animals, Ulpian's *ius naturale*, that purely non-coercive, instinctual sphere of right action. It is guaranteed to all human beings under the *ius gentium primaevum*, the human law of natural reason. Under the *ius gentium secundarium*, which saw the introduction of wars, servitudes, divided domains—private property—and civil states, it is lost to most human beings as well as to many animals and things (though not the sea, as we have seen). Subjection to civil principate is a "servitude" contrary to natural liberty, as much as is the servitude of captivity that follows from war. Nevertheless, under civil principate, a remnant of that natural liberty remains: and it is found not only in our remaining faculty to act as we will, but also in our *dominium* over our own property, with which the prince may not interfere. Vázquez explicitly used the Roman legal definition of liberty to define this relationship to our own things. Both are *liberrima facultas*, the faculty of doing whatever you like. This paralleling of *libertas* and *dominium* would be highly influential on the early Grotius, as we shall see.

Less well known than Vázquez's treatment, but equally important, is the treatment of natural liberty at the hands of François Connan. We saw in the last chapter how Connan understood that natural *ius* has two aspects:

[28] Favre, *Iurisprudentiae papinianeae scientia*, tit. III (*De iure personarum*), princ. ii (*De libertatis definitione*), p. 89.
[29] I have discussed his conception of freedom at more length in *Liberty, right and nature*, ch. 5.

one, an immutable law commanding what is just and forbidding what is unjust; two, an aspect that regulates the considerations of utility that human life demands, and that is mutable according to circumstances. Now Connan posited in parallel with these two aspects of natural *ius* two capabilities of nature: justice and freedom. As he wrote, "nature made us just, and she made us free: from which, I mean justice and freedom, derive all the other things that belong to this natural law. For it is justice that makes us bring up our children ... return goods and money owed ... repel force." "These," he continued, "are those things that flow far and wide from the justice of nature as if from a pure spring and filter down into all parts of human society.... The other thing was liberty, which we derived from the same spring, but by another route. For liberty does not have the ability to coerce, since it does not contain any rationale of the just and the unjust, but only a licence of doing what you will so long as you hurt no one. Wherefore it does not properly have any part in natural *ius*, since it does not forbid or command anything, but exists only in those things that are permitted."[30] Liberty in relation to the precepts of natural law, then, is not itself a juridical quality or right: it is juridically passive, if you like, simply natural human liberty itself, so far as it does not contravene the demands of natural sociability. It is a facility in something like Soto's sense, an ease of doing something that does not run up against the rightful claims of somebody else.

This natural ease, however, was destroyed—even if necessarily so— under the *ius gentium*, from which, for Connan, the juridical institution of servitude was instituted as a consequence of war.[31] And once servitude is juridically instituted, liberty itself becomes a juridical institution, or a right. As he put it in his discussion of liberty in the Digest title *De statu hominum*, let us imagine the case of wearing your hair long, or wearing a beard. In this case, he argued, "anybody is allowed to have hair or a beard, not by any privilege accorded by other men, or by any institution of nature or by any law, but because each of us has that licence by nature. But if it should happen that plebeians, or any other class of men should be ordered by an edict to shave, then the rest, to whom the edict does not pertain, will commence to grow their beards or hair *by their own right*; and that which had been a matter of the natural faculty of all, will now be a civil right and belong only to a few." Similarly with natural liberty after the introduction of servitude by the *ius gentium*, what had once been a faculty that belonged to all is now a right that belongs to some and not

---

[30] Connan, *Commentariorum*, lib. I, cap. 6, nn. 7, 8.

[31] Ibid.: "to limit something of that facility [*facilitas*] and liberality [*liberalitas*] of nature not only was not iniquitous, but was actually necessary."

to others.[32] Connan was cited by Oswald Hilliger in his *Donellus enucleatus* of 1619 in defence of the genus "faculty" for liberty. "Correctly, *facultas*: because by the law of nature it [i.e., liberty] is a matter of fact rather than of right. But it began to be a matter of right after servitude was introduced, because what was previously licit by a natural faculty thereafter became licit by a special right."[33]

This solution of Connan's to the juridical status of liberty was also taken over, this time word for word, by the Aristotelian political philosopher Henning Arnisaeus in his *De republica* of 1615.[34] The broad context is the discussion of natural slavery, which Arnisaeus sought to defend against the insistence of the lawyers on the common natural liberty of all. However, he deployed the sharp separation between liberty as a faculty and as a right in a very different way. Connan had wanted to see the natural faculty of liberty as a kind of negative, and generous, juridical space of action. Arnisaeus took it out of any relationship to *ius* by conceiving it in terms of the Stoic freedom of the mind, whereby a human being can be free even if his actions are constrained by another.[35] He coupled his reference to the Stoic authority Seneca with Aquinas's question on obedience in the *Secunda secundae*, who had, indeed, also quoted the same passage of Seneca. As we shall see in chapter 6, this aspect of Aquinas's thought was taken up by Jesuit authors in considering the scope of the law, and their discussions may well have been the source for Arnisaeus's references here. Whatever the case, his familiarity with the Catholic scholastic tradition is attested by his reference to the metaphysical works of the fifteenth-century Thomist Paulus Soncinas and of Suárez himself. He used their terminology to characterise the Stoic freedom of the mind as "liberty of contradiction," that is, free will, which can never be taken away and thus does not enter the domain of law.[36] The opposite of this natural freedom is natural slavery, likewise a mental characteristic, but this time of those who have "an imperfect mind," being "not much different from animals."[37] These people are entirely lacking in *dominium* and consequently naturally subject; Aristotle and the Aristotelians are right, and the jurists are wrong, on the question of a universal natural human liberty.[38]

---

[32] Ibid., lib. II, cap. 1, n. 3, emphasis mine.

[33] Oswald Hilliger, *Donellus enucleatus* (Lyon 1619), *Notata* on lib. II, cap. 9, fo. 20.

[34] Arnisaeus, *De republica*, lib. I, cap. 3, sect. 2, n. 17.

[35] Ibid., sect. 1, n. 8 [recte 9] (referring to Seneca, *De beneficiis*, lib. III, 19 and 20); n. 10.

[36] Ibid., sect. 2, nn. 2–3. See above, ch. 2, n. 61, for the intellectual context of Arnisaeus's use of Jesuit metaphysics.

[37] Arnisaeus, *De republica*, lib. I, cap. 3 sect. 1, n. 10.

[38] Ibid., sect. 3, nn. 8–9, 15–25.

Far from being an empty philosophical category, Arnisaeus saw natural slaves everywhere in his contemporary world, beginning with the plebs and the peasants whose continual labour, without which they cannot survive, is their natural servitude.[39] On top of this, some early Christians "for love of religion" manumitted their slaves, thus releasing into the world hordes of impotent individuals, unable to look after themselves, who then had to be put up in hospitals of various kinds. Their action was misguided, "for truly," he explained,

> just as it is inhumane wrongly to oppress the best intelligences with perpetual servitude, so too it is disadvantageous to the commonwealth for every dimwit, whose invincible need has eaten up his virtue, to be thrust into a harmful liberty. For nothing can be expected from this except cohorts of beggars; and after they have wasted away through their own laziness the commonwealth is forced either to feed them at public expense, like drones, or leave them to the private alms of its citizens, when previously their masters would have given them food at private expense, and forced them to work.

Echoing the language of the Ypres legislation that we looked at in chapter 1, Arnisaeus compared such individuals to birds (*aviculi*, the diminutive form), who would prefer to die of cold or hunger as long as they are permitted to wheel around (*circumcursitare*) freely through the air.[40] The contrast with the Dominican attitude could hardly be clearer. Instead of interpreting natural *dominium* over one's own actions as a right, and extending it to every human being even if they are of dimmer intelligence, Arnisaeus not only denied that such command is a right—it is purely a natural faculty—but limited it to those who have the intelligence to live an independent life. The sphere of the city is a sphere of beings who are free in this sense; the presence of beggars within political space is an anomaly, and a burden, which would be better privatised.

In the second part of this chapter, I want to look at the ways in which liberty as a natural faculty came to be understood, within Protestant jurisprudence, as a natural *right*. The first step in this process was the instatement of the very notion of right in a subjective sense, that is, a power of acting that belongs to the individual as opposed to an objective juridical relationship or law. A key figure here was Hugues Doneau, who began his *Commentary on the civil law* of 1589 with a discussion of the various different senses of right that is very similar to what we find in contemporary

---

[39] Ibid., nn. 6–7.
[40] Ibid., nn. 12–13.

Jesuit authors.[41] The primary sense of *ius* is a command with coercive force: "*ius* means a constitution bidding, as a command, those things that are upright." However, various other significations of *ius* are derived from this, in one of which "*ius* does not mean generally that which belongs to anyone by law (*iure*), but specifically a power or faculty that is granted by the law.... Hence some are said to be of their own right, some subject to the right of another: 'of their own right,' that is, of their own power and judgement; 'subject to the right of another,' that is, to another's power, which the law grants."[42] Liberty, then, is a central case of a right in this subjective sense, which is confirmed when Doneau discusses the definition of liberty in the second book and distinguishes between liberty as a status and as a right: "Status is the condition of a person; right is the faculty of living and of doing what you will, which is granted to that condition."[43] Is liberty, however, in any sense for him a *natural* right? Doneau explicitly argued that liberty belongs to natural law—*ius naturale*—in its "first" sense, which Ulpian called common to all animals because of "the likeness and commonality of this law expressed in the nature of all animals." Servitude is contrary to nature, "as long as we understand nature as the first condition in which men were created, common even to brute animals."[44] From Doneau's remarks on "condition" in the context of the definition of liberty, the language here might suggest, if we pressed on it, that the liberty that belongs to the original natural condition is a natural right. But such pressure is not warranted by the text, since it would give a natural right to animals; and Doneau, while accepting the idea that there is a *likeness* of *ius* in animals, did not endorse the unqualified reading of Ulpian's text, which posits that animals and human beings *share* the same natural *ius*. It would seem something of a contradiction if this were not true for *ius* as law but true for *ius* as right, since, as we have seen, Doneau derived the latter from the former.

It was rather Hugo Grotius who took the key step in translating natural liberty into natural right, and he did so ultimately by importing the scholastic concept of rights into a legal framework that he derived, as we saw in the last chapter, from a different tradition of thought. There is a clear evolution here between his earlier work, the *De iure praedae*, and the later *De iure belli ac pacis*. The title of the former is normally translated as

---

[41] See H. Coing, "Zur Geschichte des Begriffs "subjektives Rechts,'" in idem ed., *Das subjektives Recht und der Rechtsschutz der Persönlichkeit* (Frankfurt: Metzner 1959), 7–23, at pp. 15–17.

[42] Donellus, *Commentarii*, lib. I, cap. iii, fo. 6.

[43] Ibid., lib. II, cap. ix, fo. 83.

[44] Ibid., lib. I, cap. vii, fo. 16.

On the law of prize, but in fact, in the *Prolegomena* to the work, which sets out the juridical framework of his argument, Grotius did not conceive *ius* either as law or as individual rights. *Ius* instead has a more objective sense of what is rightful, the object of the virtue of justice with which the work is centrally concerned.[45] It is determined in successive stages by an authoritative will, beginning with God's, and from *ius* in this sense there flow *leges* or laws of behaviour relative to that particular determination. Grotius placed human liberty within the second determination created by the consensus of all mankind, that is, the primary *ius gentium*. "God made man *autexousios*, that is, free and *sui iuris*, in such a way that each man's actions and the use of his goods should be subject to his own will and not to another's. And this is approved by the consensus of all the nations. For what else is that natural liberty, than the faculty of doing what it pleases anyone? And what liberty is with regard to actions, the same is *dominium* in things."[46] That parallelism between our faculty with regard to our actions and our faculty with regard to our things was straight out of Vázquez and is cited as such. The critical point for our present discussion is the relationship between freedom and right. Freedom as *autexousia* is, in the theological controversy that we examined in the second chapter, associated with having *dominium* over one's own actions—liberty of contradiction, the freedom to will one thing rather than another. But in Grotius it is juridicised in a way that it is not in Arnisaeus. It is part of *ius* in the sense of what is determined by the consensus of all mankind. It is because liberty is juridically sanctioned in this way that individual acts of will themselves acquire juridical force, and constitute the third determinant of right after the will of God and of all mankind: "What each has signified that he wills, that is *ius* with respect to him."[47] This in itself provides the possibility of pacts or mutual determinations of right *between* individuals.[48] And it is on this possibility that Grotius grounded the mutual *res publica*, the commonwealth, which is created by pact and whose will in turn provides the fourth determinant of right: "What the commonwealth has signified that it wills, that is *ius* with respect to the citizens taken universally."[49]

---

[45] This is not to say that Grotius does not use a subjective sense of "right" in this work at all: see B. Straumann, *Hugo Grotius und die Antike* (Baden-Baden: Nomos 2007), pp. 58–66.

[46] Grotius, *De iure praedae*, vol. 1, cap. 2 (*Prolegomena*), fo. 10; vol. II, p. 000.

[47] Ibid.

[48] Ibid., vol. I, fo. 10'. Compare Antoine Favre, who in his commentary on the definition of liberty equally moves directly from the consideration of man as having a free faculty to dispose of himself and his own goods to the origin of all contracts and commerce, which presuppose such a subject. Favre, *Iurisprudentia papinianea*, tit. III, princ. ii, fo. 89.

[49] Grotius, *De iure praedae*, cap. 2, fo. 11–11'; vol. I, p. 23.

From 1613, however, we find a new element in Grotius's philosophy of right, which is his adoption of the language of "moral faculty" to characterise a right as something that belongs to the individual. In 1612, as we have seen, Suárez's *De legibus* had appeared, with its juridical deployment of the fundamental contrast between the physical and the moral. It is, then, very striking that in 1613, in his reply to Welwod's critique of the *Mare liberum*, Grotius was already using the locution of right as a "moral faculty" and as a *dominium*, explicitly separated, in exactly the same way as in Suárez, from right in the sense of law.[50] The sea, he argued, is not only in common by the law of nations but by the right of nations, right in the sense of faculty or ownership. To attempt to appropriate the sea is therefore not merely an offence against an objective legal order, but an offence against the community of mankind which subjectively holds common property in it. Grotius was using the distinction opportunistically here, to strengthen a case essentially already made in the *Mare liberum*. However, in his *De iure belli ac pacis* of 1625, he made it into one of his central juridical concepts, defining right in a subjective sense as a "moral quality" of the person and explicitly understanding this as a kind of translation of the jurists' language of faculty.[51] However, this very association moved the meaning of a right away from Suárez's conception. Grotius defined the objective sense of right, from which the subjective is said to derive, deliberately negatively, as "that which is not unjust," the unjust being "that which conflicts the society of those who use reason"—an inflection quite alien to Suárez.[52] Grotius imported the Jesuit concept into a much more traditionally Protestant framework of sociability rather than individual agency, and subjective right, though a moral quality of the individual, still occupies the negative space that liberty as a natural faculty had for Connan.

Nevertheless, the difference with Connan is there, because Grotius does not conceive subjective right as a liberty of agency. Right is rather a relationship to or over things, and it has three species: power, which is either over ourselves or over others; *dominium*; and credit, the contrary of debt. The moral quality of power over oneself is, precisely, liberty, "which for this reason" (Grotius noted) "the Roman lawyers very well define with the name of 'faculty.'"[53] Thus liberty is a power relationship to one's own self (and its actions, as we shall see), analogous—as it was in the *De iure praedae*—to the relationship one has to property and (a new addition

---

[50] Hugo Grotius, "Defense of Chapter V of the *Mare liberum*," tr. in Hugo Grotius, *The free sea*, ed. D. Armitage (Indianapolis: Liberty Fund 2004), p. 107.

[51] Grotius, *De iure belli ac pacis*, lib. I, cap. 1, sect. 4.

[52] Ibid., sect. 3, n. 1.

[53] Ibid., sect. 5 and note.

in the *De iure belli*) to the debts that are owed to one. Much as for the later scholastics, these juridical relationships or rights are detachable from the individual and can be alienated or acquired by an act of will—indeed, we may speculate that it is precisely because of the advantages for analysis of contracts that Grotius imported the scholastic concept. Importantly, Grotius insisted that such contracts or pacts are possible between human beings outside any civil state—a possibility that is crucial, because, as in the *De iure praedae*, it is upon pact that the civil state itself rests.[54] The argument was directed against Connan, who had argued that under the law of nations, "promises and compacts [*conventiones*] made purely verbally [*verbotenus factae*]" do not oblige to their performance. Where no *sunallagma* or exchange has actually occurred, nobody's utility—and this is the field of the *ius gentium*, as we saw—is compromised by reneging on a promise, even if this is indeed something to be ashamed of in view of natural law, the principle of an honest life. On the contrary, to insist on fulfilment of a promise in such circumstances, possibly by threats, is illegitimately to privilege the utility of one party over that of the other.[55] In Book II of *De iure belli ac pacis*, Grotius rejected Connan's proposition to argue that a bargain in words alone can be made and can be binding even upon the seas or a desert island, regulated solely by the law of nature. Promising is a mode of natural self-obligation. By a promise of giving we alienate something of our own—our property—while by a promise of action we alienate "a particle of our liberty,"[56] "since we have as much power over our actions as we do over our own goods."[57] Either way, what we do, by an act of determination of our own will declared by word or other sign, is to transfer a right, a moral quality, incurring its obverse, an obligation, a moral necessity.[58]

Grotius's analysis of promising therefore posited, in a human being with the use of reason outside any civil state, a natural power of disposing of his or her own actions at will that is, by implication, liberty *as a natural right* and can be transferred or alienated by an act of that same will. Gro-

---

[54] Ibid., *Prolegomena*, nn. 16–17.

[55] Connan, *Commentariorum*, lib. I, cap. 16, n. 12, and especially n. 13, crudely summed up by Grotius at *De iure belli ac pacis*, lib. II, cap. 11, sect. 1. See M. Diesselhorst, *Die Lehre des Hugo Grotius vom Versprechen* (Köln: Böhlau 1959), pp. 31–34.

[56] Grotius, *De iure belli ac pacis*, lib. II, cap. 11, sect. 3.

[57] Ibid., sect. 1, n. 3.

[58] Ibid., n. 4. Talking here in the context of alienation of property, Grotius affirms that the one who is obliged to pay is the debtor of the person to which he is obliged; later on, he seems to extend the language of debt to all promises: a promise is a "natural debt," sect. 11, n. 10. But debt is not the obverse of subjective right in the sense of a power over persons, or even of *dominium*, but of credit. It seems, then, that Grotius does not always strictly hold apart his three kinds of "moral quality" or subjective right.

tius held, along with his scholastic contemporaries, that an individual can voluntarily alienate the entirety of his liberty, even if this is—in an individual context—a shameful act.[59] However, I stress "by implication" since, just as in Doneau, this sense of liberty as a natural *potestas suiipsius*, a power of determining oneself, the foundation of contracts, is discussed separately from *ius naturale* in the sense of natural law, and what Grotius had to say about liberty in that context is more ambivalent. So, considering unjust causes of war in chapter 22 of Book II, Grotius agreed with the jurists that there is no such thing as a natural slave in an Aristotelian sense.[60] Even so, "liberty, whether of individuals or commonwealths, i.e. autonomy, does not give a right to war, as if it belonged naturally and always to anyone. For when liberty is said to belong by nature to men or to peoples, this should be understood as of the law of nature preceding any human act, and of liberty 'privatively,' not as 'forbidding the contrary': that is, that by nature no one is a servant, not that he has the right not ever to serve. For in this sense no one is free."[61] It does not, therefore, belong to anyone "positively," as Suárez would say—for Grotius was clearly employing the scholastic categories here, even if he used Greek terminology—but only by juridical default, as it were.

The position is similar in Book I, where Grotius discussed the natural rights of individuals prior to the institution of the commonwealth. Analysing the contents of natural law in the first chapter of Book I, Grotius argued, consistently with the Prolegomena, that they comprise the demands of rational nature as social nature, and did not mention liberty at all.[62] However, "there are also," he added, "some things that are of natural law not absolutely, but for a certain condition (*status*): thus the common use of things was natural for as long as properties were not introduced; and the right of pursuing one's own by force before laws were laid down."[63] In this passage, the natural right of defensive resort to force takes the place of "the common liberty of all" with which common possession is habitually coupled both in other lawyers and in the scholastics. If we now ask what category of subjective right, or moral quality, this natural right belongs to in Grotius's own typology, it seems that it must be a species of power over oneself or liberty.[64] This natural right of self-defence is a right prior to the commonwealth: everyone "naturally has a right of resisting,

---

[59] Ibid., cap. 5, sect. 27: *ignobilissima*.

[60] Ibid., cap. 22, sect. 10.

[61] Ibid., sect. 11: *kata sterēsin, kat' enantiotēta* (explained in Grotius's notes).

[62] Ibid., lib. I, cap. 1, sect. 10.

[63] Ibid., n. 7.

[64] The eighteenth-century English version translates Grotius's word *ius* ("right") by the term "Liberty" at lib. I, cap. 1, sect. 7.

to ward off injury from themselves."[65] Grotius went on to argue that although there are some occasions within the civil state when an individual may still use what is now described as this "licence,"[66] the creation of the commonwealth necessarily takes it away, generally speaking; for if it still remains, there is no commonwealth, but only a dissociated multitude. Quoting Sallust, such a multitude is "without laws, without sovereign power, *free* and unfettered" (emphasis mine).[67] It seems, then, that we have *a* natural liberty as a natural right insofar as it is the right to resist, that is, to use force ourselves in defence of our "lives, limbs and liberties."[68] And insofar as civil society is instituted "to safeguard tranquillity,"[69] that is, to allow us to enjoy our own "with a *common* help and joint accord" (emphasis mine),[70] it has to be restricted almost entirely.

Taking the *De iure belli ac pacis* as a whole, therefore, it seems fair to say that it deploys, at least implicitly, a concept of natural liberty figured as a natural right. But it does not link up the natural right to determine oneself in a promise with the natural right to defend oneself with the use of force that is given up to form the commonwealth. Nor does it explicitly figure either juridical quality as "natural liberty," nor see it as the *only* right or liberty that we naturally possess.[71] It was Thomas Hobbes's masterstroke to knit these strands together into a complete account of natural liberty as natural right, an account that will at once both describe the juridical condition of men before the institution of the commonwealth and provide the means for them to leave it, by pact or (in Hobbes's English terminology) covenant. However, this account of natural liberty as natural right is only fully in place in *Leviathan*, where he can speak without qualification of "the Right of Nature, that is, the naturall Liberty of man."[72] It has a long gestation from the first version of the condition of nature presented in *The elements of law*, in which it is not so clear that natural liberty, understood as the absence of subjection, is a purely juridical condition, the absence of obligation.[73] The process is complicated from the outset by Hobbes's insistence that we can be subject to another

---

[65] Grotius, *De iure belli ac pacis*, lib. I, cap. 4, sect. 2, and see the discussion in Straumann, *Grotius und die Antike*, pp. 179–91.

[66] Grotius, *De iure belli ac pacis*, lib. I, cap. 3, sect. 2: *licentia*. Again the eighteenth-century translation uses "liberty."

[67] Ibid., cap. 4, sect. 2.

[68] Ibid, cap. 2, sect. 1, n. 3.

[69] Ibid., cap. 4, sect. 2.

[70] Ibid., cap. 2, sect. 1, n. 3: *communi ope ac conspiratione*, the latter almost untranslatable into English.

[71] Hence I broadly agree with Zagorin, *Hobbes and the law of nature*, p. 25, that "Grotius never achieved a well-defined and fully articulated conception of natural rights."

[72] Hobbes, *Leviathan*, Ch. 26, p. 185.

[73] As urged recently by Skinner, *Hobbes and republican liberty*, p. 44.

in one of two ways: either by being mastered by force, as a slave is, or by being obliged by the ties of covenant, as is a servant. It is further complicated, from *De cive* onwards, by Hobbes's introduction of the notion of "liberty in the proper signification," or the absence of impediments to motion. We shall address the first complication in this chapter, leaving the second, again, until chapter 6.

As we saw in chapter 2, Hobbes attributed to all animates the liberty to act or not to act according to their own appetite or aversion. This liberty is ended by the will as the last appetite in deliberation—etymologised in *Leviathan* as de-liberation—which deliberates or determines a creature upon one course of action rather than another, at which point it is no longer free to do that other thing.[74] This liberty is not characterised as a right. Indeed, in *Leviathan*, the transition to juridical language in chapter 14 comes very much out of the blue. However, *The elements of law* and *De cive*—and implicitly, *Leviathan* itself—supply the rationale behind that move.[75] Hobbes wrote in *The elements of law* that "that which is not against reason, men call *ius*, or right, or blameless liberty. It is therefore a right of nature, that every man may pursue his conservation with all the power he hath."[76] Similarly in *De cive*, Hobbes argued that "by the term 'right' nothing else is signified than the liberty that each man has of using his natural faculties in accordance with right reason."[77] In *Leviathan*, the explicit reference to reason is missing. Nonetheless it is clear that here, too, right is not simply the liberty to act at will but the liberty to use one's power *for the preservation of one's own nature*, which is a demand of reason.[78] Hobbes, then, delineated a juridical world without importing, as Suárez and Grotius had done, a moral ontology on top of a natural or physical ontology. A right is not something ontologically different from natural liberty, which is a physical or corporeal ability to use one's own (physical) power at one's own (physical, and naturally determined) will, and which stones, for example, don't have. Rather, it is that same liberty, but understood in relation to the dictates of right reason and signified accordingly.

Hobbes's elegant solution avoids not merely a moral ontology but also Grotius's tripartite typology of right. A right is not a relationship to a thing, not even to one's own self and its actions. It is the liberty of action itself. For the same reason, Hobbes was able to do without Grotius's

---

[74] Hobbes, *Leviathan*, p. 44. See the discussion in my *Liberty, right and nature*, ch. 6; P. Pettit, "Liberty and Leviathan," *Politics, philosophy and economics* 4/1 (2005), 131–51.
[75] See D. Gauthier, *The logic of Leviathan* (Oxford: Oxford University Press 1969), pp. 29–32.
[76] Hobbes, *The elements of law*, part I, ch. 14, p. 71.
[77] Id., *De cive*, cap. I, p. 94.
[78] Id., *Leviathan*, ch. 14, p. 91.

distinction within promises between promises of doing and promises of giving. According to Hobbes, any promise is an act of will, or last appetite in deliberation, which ends the liberty to do otherwise.[79] It is always, therefore, an alienation of "a particle of our liberty," in Grotius's terms; a promise of "giving" is not the alienation of one of our things, or our property, but the renunciation of our latitude or liberty of action in respect of that particular thing.[80] Exclusive or secure relationships to things do not precede but are a function of deliberation through promises or covenants, which are relationships between persons and not between persons and things. However, it is important to stress that, differently from the act of deliberation involved in every doing on the part of every creature, what is ended in a promise is not simply liberty, but right; and it is ended not simply by the natural act of deliberation, but by the mutually understood signification of that will to another, to whom the promiser is then obliged or bound.[81] Without involving a moral ontology, therefore, Hobbes's analysis of promising does depend on a second kind of being, this time the artificial world of signs. A covenant is both a natural and an artificial act; it is, as we shall explore more fully in chapter 6, a crossing point between nature and artifice.

The reductive elegance of Hobbes's construction is complicated, however, by his continued attachment to some sense of right as a relationship to things. In *The elements of law*, *De cive* and *Leviathan*, Hobbes held that the natural right of all men equates to a natural "right to all things," a *ius in omnia*.[82] In itself this is not vicious, so long as it is understood merely as a translation into a more rhetorically effective language of the central

---

[79] Ibid., p. 97.

[80] Clearest ibid., p. 92; implicit in *The elements of law*, part I, ch. 15, pp. 75–76 and *De cive*, cap. II, p. 100.

[81] No covenants are possible, therefore, with animals, which cannot make signs: "it is impossible to make covenant with those living creatures, of whose wills we have no sufficient sign, for want of common language." Hobbes, *The elements of law*, part I, ch. 15, p. 79. See most recently P. Pettit, *Made with words. Hobbes on language, mind and politics* (Princeton: Princeton University Press 2008), for the critical role of language in all dimensions of Hobbes's politics; B. Ludwig, *Die Wiederentdeckung des Epikureischen Naturrechts. Zu Thomas Hobbes' philosophischer Entwicklung von De cive zum Leviathan im Pariser Exil 1640–1651* (Frankfurt: Klostermann 1998), pp. 257–60, also emphasises the importance of speech for Hobbes's theory of contract and obligation. I am sceptical, however, of the further claim that in *Leviathan* (as opposed to *De cive*) the obligation of covenant is grounded *solely* in Hobbes's theory of signs (*Sprachtheorie*), divorced from the third law of nature dictating the performance of covenants, thus marking a shift from a Stoic-Christian to an Epicurean natural law theory. While I agree that there is a development on the question of obligation between *De cive* and *Leviathan*, on the issue of the third law of nature Hobbes expressly says the contrary in chapter 30 of *Leviathan*: see below, chapter 6, p. 160.

[82] Hobbes, *The elements of law*, part I, ch. 14, p. 72; *De cive*, cap. II, p. 95; *Leviathan*, ch. 14, p. 91.

point about liberty: prior to any covenants, and therefore to any obligation, all individuals have an unrestricted and "blameless" liberty of action in respect of all things necessary to their self-preservation. But one problem is that Hobbes never adds this critical qualification to the phrase;[83] another is that Hobbes does not consistently hold "right ... to" apart from "right ... over," that is, dominion (*dominium* in *De cive*). Both are *ius in ...* in the Latin of *De cive*. And dominion is directly—as it is indeed for all the authors we have been looking at—a relationship to another thing or another person that has in some sense been secured. Not only that, but Hobbes throughout the three works continued to posit that this relationship could be natural, that is, not a function of any act of covenant but of strength and force. Indeed, in *The elements of law* and *De cive* he went so far as to suggest that it could obtain between human beings and animals, creatures that are *incapable* of covenant because they cannot use signs.[84] It therefore apparently runs counter to the revolution in the language of right that he had effected through his focus on liberty and his appeal to speech.

Nevertheless, there is an important evolution in Hobbes's thought on natural dominion between the three works, an index of which is the absence of a corresponding passage on dominion over animals in *Leviathan*. In the two earlier works, Hobbes devoted two chapters each to showing how dominion can be acquired, the first concerning masters and slaves and the second parents and children, with the passage concerning animals occurring in the first.[85] Dominion in these chapters is a "right ... over," a *ius ... in*.[86] In these works, the dominion that we acquire over animals, by force, is the same as the dominion we acquire over other men, by force. In either case, such force gives the (successful) invader a right over the conquered, and he has "absolute dominion" over such a person; indeed, Hobbes's concern is more to point out that the same goes for one who has covenanted with him and whose body he therefore "leaveth at liberty."[87] In *The elements*, the right of parents over children is said to have as its title the power of the parent not to generate but to preserve the child. Hobbes adds to this a "presumed" promise of obedience on the

---

[83] See Malcolm, "Hobbes's theory of international relations," pp. 445–46.

[84] Hobbes, *The elements of law*, part II, ch. 3, pp. 130–31; *De cive*, cap.VIII, p. 163; cf. above, n. 81. He even implied that animals could have the same natural dominion, or right, over human beings.

[85] Hobbes, *The elements of law*, part II, chs. 3 and 4; *De cive*, caps.VIII and IX.

[86] Hobbes, *The elements of law*, part II, ch. 3, p. 127: "upon what title man may acquire right, that is to say, property or dominion, over the person of another"; *De cive*, cap.VIII, p. 160: "*quibus modis ius Dominij acquiri potest in* personas *hominum*."

[87] Hobbes, *The elements of law*, part II, ch. 3, pp. 126–27, cf. *De cive*, cap.VIII, p. 161: the master has no less right, *non minus iuris*, in the one than in the other.

part of the child, but this is given explicitly as a second reason ("also"), not as the primary rationale; and in *De cive*, that addition is lacking.[88] Dominion is therefore not necessarily correlate with any obligation on the part of the object of that dominion.[89] Slaves (and animals) are equally as much under the dominion of their master as the servant who has obliged himself by promise, and thus both equally lack their natural liberty in the sense of freedom from subjection. In these two works, then, natural liberty does not always equate to the absence of obligation, although it does always involve the absence of a "right over," a *ius in*, held by another.

In *Leviathan*, the two chapters have been run together to create a single chapter, "*Of Dominion* paternall, *and* despoticall." Hobbes began by including them both under what he calls commonwealths "by Acquisition."[90] This understanding of master-slave and parent-child relationships as little commonwealths or bodies politic is there in the earlier works as well; indeed, in *De cive*, Hobbes was prepared to call them a natural *civitas*.[91] However, by the time of *Leviathan* Hobbes was clear that conquest—successful invasion—does not by itself yield any dominion over the vanquished. With regard to a captive who has not yet consented, the master has no *right over*, but only the natural right *by which* he may act toward that captive in any way consistent with self-preservation. Equally, the conquered has that right in respect of the master. Such a captive is a slave. By contrast, "right ... over," dominion, is only acquired by covenant or other sufficient sign of the will, which transforms the captive from a slave to a servant. "It is not therefore the Victory, that giveth the right of Dominion over the Vanquished, but his own Covenant." Similarly, the right of parent over child is now based solely on consent.[92] Although animals receive no consideration here, we may compare the passage from *The questions concerning liberty, necessity and chance* of 1656 that we looked at in chapter 2, in which Hobbes disallowed any more "natural" dominion of a man over a lion than of a lion over a man.[93] Crucially, Hobbes added a qualification here that is absent in *The elements* and *De cive*: "if that of man over Lions, or over Sheep, or Oxen, may be called dominion *which properly it cannot*" (emphasis mine).

---

[88] Hobbes, *The elements of law*, part II, ch. 4, p. 132; *De cive*, cap. IX, p. 164.

[89] This point is made in the context of dominion over animals in K. Hoekstra, "The *de facto* turn in Hobbes's political philosophy," in T. Sorell and L. Foisneau eds., *Leviathan after 350 years* (Oxford: Clarendon 2005), 33–73, at pp. 64–65.

[90] Hobbes, *Leviathan*, ch. 20, p. 138.

[91] Id., *De cive*, cap. V, p. 135.

[92] Id., *Leviathan*, ch. 20, pp. 141, 139. For a similar understanding of the change between *De cive* and *Leviathan*, see Ludwig, *Wiederentdeckung*, pp. 328–31.

[93] Above, ch. 2, p. 81.

Dominion in these later works, then, *is* (properly speaking) correlate with an obligation arising from consent, which explains why there is silence about dominion over animals—there can be none, for they can give no sign of their will. A human being forcibly restrained by another is not, properly speaking, a subject; natural liberty as the absence of subjection has therefore been pushed into being a purely juridical phenomenon, the absence of obligation. But there remains a problem, which is that, even in *Leviathan*, Hobbes does not always hold "the right of Dominion" apart from the right of nature, that is, the liberty by which we preserve ourselves; and the slippage depends precisely on the idea of a natural *ius in omnia*, the right *to* all things, that Hobbes was not prepared to give up. The slide remains and is glaring in chapter 31 of that work, entitled "*Of the* kingdome of god by nature." Here Hobbes started out with what we might expect from the chapter on dominion: "he onely is properly said to Raigne, that governs his Subjects, by his Word"; consequently, inanimate bodies, irrational creatures (which appears here to include plants as well as animals), atheists, and those who think of the deity as not caring about human actions are not God's subjects, "because they acknowledge no Word for his." His kingdom, strictly speaking, does not extend to them, although his power does. But Hobbes went on to assert that "the Right of Nature, whereby God reigneth over men," is derived purely from his "*Irresistible Power.*" And this is argued by direct analogy with the unqualified *ius in omnia* that individual human beings are said to have in the condition of nature. "Seeing all men by Nature had Right to all things, they had the Right every one to reigne over all the rest." Since none of them were individually powerful enough to have "obtained" this right by force, they laid aside this right to set up a commonwealth. But God's power being irresistible, "the dominion of all men adhaereth naturally" to him, and kingdom over men belongs naturally to God.[94]

This is a notorious problem, and it goes to the heart of the questions whether Hobbes was a de facto theorist of government as opposed to a consent theorist, whether he moved from the one to the other in *Leviathan*, and what is the relation between human power and the power of God. These issues run very deep.[95] For the present I shall only remark that even if God (unlike any man) can by his power vindicate or secure his right to all things, this is still not the same as the dominion that is

---

[94] Hobbes, *Leviathan*, ch. 31, pp. 245–47.
[95] In addition to Hoekstra, "*De facto* turn," see Q. Skinner, "Hobbes on the proper signification of liberty" in id., *Visions of politics*, vol. III (Cambridge: Cambridge University Press 2002), 209–37; L. Foisneau, "Omnipotence, necessity and sovereignty," in P. Springborg ed., *The Cambridge companion to Hobbes's* Leviathan (Cambridge: Cambridge University Press 2007), 271–90.

described in chapter 20, which cannot be "obtained" by force at all. A conqueror with his sword at the throat of a captive has secured by force complete access to that captive, he has every right *to* him, but no dominion. The thrust of that discussion is to isolate dominion as a peculiar kind of right, one that is created by consent. It is explicitly political as opposed to natural, the surface polarity that governs the argument of *Leviathan*. However, as suggested in the introduction, that polarity is not the whole of the Hobbesian story about the relationship between nature and the city. It is not a simple either/or: the natural is implicated in the political, and vice versa; there is a passage from one to the other.[96] We shall explore a further dimension of this when we come to consider obligation more fully in chapter 6. But such an interpretative strategy cannot wholly dissolve the tension in *Leviathan*. The unmodulated argument over from the "Right to all things" to a "Right ... to reigne" remains problematic in the context of that work. As we saw in chapter 2, Bishop Bramhall's thesis of a natural dominion of humans over animals gave Hobbes no reason to expect "any very shrewd answer from him, to my *Leviathan*."

To sum up, however, Hobbes had created—even if not entirely clearly—a sense of natural liberty as natural right that can be alienated, and can only be alienated, by an act of will on the part of the individual who is the subject of that right. He thus joined hands both with Grotius and with the later scholastics in constructing a sense of liberty that does not resist the commonwealth but is in fact the very basis upon which it can be erected. As an interpersonal juridical structure, the commonwealth depends upon the alienation of liberty through the medium of pacts or covenants that bind individuals together. The precise nature of that structure is what we turn to next.

---

[96] Hoekstra, "*De facto* turn," pp. 64–73, suggests that we replace the opposition between "consent" and "de facto" with a view of Hobbes as a "political naturalist." His argument concentrates on Hobbes's naturalisation of the will, which entails that there are things we cannot naturally not will—most prominently to avoid death—and thus our consent is both natural and to be presumed (as Hobbes does) in a wide latitude of cases when we are confronted with an overwhelmingly superior force.

CHAPTER FIVE

KINGDOMS FOUNDED

One of the key markers of the early modern natural law tradition is the pervasive understanding of the unsustainability of a condition of equal natural liberty governed only by natural law. The writers with whom we are concerned use various words to indicate the pressure on that pristine juridical situation: "convenience," "commodity," "necessity," and—perhaps most prominently of all—"utility." Of themselves, these words are not part of a juridical vocabulary: they refer to the concrete goods of life. As such, they draw in considerations not of rights but of psychological attitudes, which all our authors explore to a greater or lesser extent. But since those concrete goods are part of a life that must be lived alongside other people, they have to be put in relation to the legal framework that governs interpersonal relations; and the key insight of this tradition is that they force changes in that framework, the critical change being the establishment of the commonwealth or state. The story of that genesis is accordingly a mix of juridical possibility and what I am tempted to call the pathology of the *ius gentium*, be that understood purely as natural law or as a kind of second stage of juridical organisation. *Ex hoc iure gentium*, "of this law of nations," Hermogenianus said, "wars were brought in, peoples separated, kingdoms founded, properties distinguished, boundaries put on fields, buildings set in place, trade, buyings and sellings, lettings and hirings, and obligations instituted: except for some that were brought in by civil law." The drive of early-modern natural law is to pick out and to privilege "kingdoms founded," no longer one among many institutions of the *ius gentium* but the one that critically alters juridical relations both inside and outside the state.

The deepest exploration of the psychopathology of the "condition of nature" was put forward by Hobbes to explain his crucial thesis that man's natural condition is a state of war. In *De cive*, where Hobbes started the story *in medias res*, as it were, he introduced this thesis by way of a contrast between himself and the majority of other writers on "matters public," who have begun with Aristotle's idea that man is *zōon politikon*, "an animal born fit for society." Hobbes understands this to mean that man has a natural love of other men, a notion that he thinks is purely false. Men by nature love themselves, not other men, and their pursuit of society is a function of two pursuits that spring from self-love, that of honour and that of advantage (*commodum*).[1] Here, then, and equally in *The elements of law* and *Leviathan*, Hobbes made it clear that the pressure exerted on the condition of nature is not simply the strain created by human beings looking out for their own utility. Human self-love is a complex passion that is satisfied not simply by getting what one wants, but by the regard of other men; indeed, the account in *The elements* suggests that conflict is purely a function of the destabilisation caused by the excessive desire for reputation and esteem.[2] However, in *De cive* and *Leviathan* it is clear that the pursuit of esteem is not the only reason for the state of war in which men naturally find themselves, and that the pursuit of advantage will cause conflict in itself. *De cive* separates the mutual desire for the same thing from the argument from reputation,[3] and equally in *Leviathan* there is no suggestion here that those who "invade for Gain" are *always* the vainglorious, though they may be so.[4]

In all these works, the idea that mutual appetite for the same thing will cause war is put forward as an implicit negation of any idea of a secondary *ius gentium* or *ius naturale*, under which the original community of property cedes to "divided domains" without involving the civil order. Thus, Hobbes wrote in *The elements*, "considering that many men's ap-

---

[1] Hobbes, *De cive*, cap. I, p. 90.

[2] Id., *The elements of law*, part I, ch. 14, p. 71: "And thus the greatest part of men, upon no assurance of odds, do nevertheless, through vanity, or comparison, or appetite, provoke the rest, that otherwise would be contented with equality." Here, appetite is connected with the desire for superiority and forms part of the same psychological complex.

[3] Id., *De cive*, cap. I, p. 94; Hobbes drops the sentence quoted in the previous note, which ends the parallel passage in *The elements of law*, thus disconnecting mutual appetite for the same thing from the pathological superiority complex.

[4] Id., *Leviathan*, ch. 13, pp. 87–88.

petites carry them to one and the same end; which end sometimes *can neither be enjoyed in common, nor divided*, it followeth, that the stronger must enjoy it alone, and that it be decided by battle who is the stronger."[5] In this state, Hobbes said, "*jus* and *utile*, right and profit is the same thing."[6] Similarly in *Leviathan*, in the condition of nature there is "no Propriety, no Dominion, no *Mine* and *Thine* distinct."[7] In consequence, the situation that for the jurists applies only to those things that have not been divided up under the secondary *ius gentium*—namely, that they fall to the first occupier—applies universally to everything. Thus, the tacit engagement with the broader natural law tradition helps fill out the sense and the attraction for Hobbes of the problematic *ius in omnia* that we explored in the previous chapter: "every man has a Right to every thing, even unto anothers body."[8] This ontological reduction of even our bodies to things that belong to no one—*res nullius*, if you like—that lie about promiscuously for the use of others if they can get them is the true horror of the condition of nature. The best defence is what *The elements* calls "preoccupation," *Leviathan* "anticipation," but it is the same thing: occupy something before the other party does. It is a stratagem of war.

The contrary of this position, that human beings are naturally sociable, and that therefore the city is not motivated by utility or need in a situation of war, Hobbes by his use of the phrase "*zōon politikon*" implicitly attributed to Aristotle and the Aristotelians. But if we look at contemporary Aristotelian interpretations, both scholastic and humanist, we find that they do not see the picture in such simple terms. It is true that they all follow Aristotle in saying that men find a natural pleasure in one another's company, that they have a natural instinct for society and would seek it even without the pressure of necessity. Nonetheless, they all pay very close attention to the first half of Aristotle's famous saying in Book I of the *Politics*, that "the city comes into being for the sake of living, but exists for the sake of living well."[9] The first end that men seek, then, is simply to live. In Book I of Aristotle's *Politics*, this is seen as the need to secure self-sufficiency, and it is apparently figured in purely economic terms. But early-modern Aristotelians saw the pre-civic state not merely as one of need, but of danger. This is true even in the Catholic scholastic that Hobbes so despises. So, for example, Francisco Suárez posited as part of the motivation for the formation of the civil community the insecurity of justice outside the state. Thus he explained that the primitive

---

[5] Id., *The elements of law*, part I, ch. 14, p. 71, emphasis mine.
[6] Ibid., p. 72.
[7] Id., *Leviathan*, ch. 13, p. 90.
[8] Ibid., ch. 14, p. 91.
[9] Aristotle, *Politics*, I. 2, 1252b29–30.

condition of human society, composed of separate households, would not only be insufficient to the needs of human life—Aristotle's explanation; it would also "scarcely be possible to keep peace among men, nor repulse or revenge violations of right in any ordered fashion."[10] Juan de Salas, while holding that man is naturally in need of social and political life because he cannot live alone, also argued that civil law is necessary because most people are incapable of recognising and following the demands of natural law. He offered an extensive list of classical citations in support of his contention, which tell a story of danger and injustice outside the civil state. These include Plato, *Laws*, Book IX: "it is necessary to impose laws on men, for if they lived without them, they would in no way differ from the most savage wild beasts,"[11] and Aristotle, *Politics* Book I: "Just as man, if he is endowed with the virtues, is the best of animals, so, removed from justice, he is the worst of all"—to which Salas added in Hobbesian tones that "without law man is a wolf to man, or a lion; but with law, man is a God to man."[12] He referred to Machiavelli on the need for laws given the general iniquity of human nature, and juxtaposed this with a quotation from Horace, *Satires* I, 3, which was, as we shall see, a ubiquitous point of reference around the turn of the seventeenth century: "It must be admitted that laws were invented from fear of injustice ... nor can nature distinguish between the just and the iniquitous."[13]

This emphasis on inadequacy, fear, and defence is still more pronounced if we look at contemporary humanist Aristotelians. After all, Cicero himself had said in the second book of his *De Officiis* that "even if men gathered together at the guidance of nature, nevertheless it was in the hope of safeguarding their own things that they sought the protection of walled cities (*urbes*)."[14] The Ferrarese humanist, Antonio Montecatini, transferred this remark from *urbes* to the *polis* or *civitas* itself; thus he wrote in his 1587 commentary on Book I of the *Politics* that "we cannot live, simply speaking, unless we defend both ourselves and our own." In consequence, the original political communities, societies for the sake of living, were "like societies of war, that is, *summachiai*, against

---

[10] Francisco Suárez, *De legibus*, lib. III, cap. 1, n. 3.

[11] Salas, *Tractatus de legibus*, disp. 6, sect. 1, n. 4, fo. 98, col. 1.

[12] Ibid., col. 2. *Homo homini Deus, & Homo homini Lupus*, is of course the classical quotation on which Hobbes in the preface offers *De cive* as a kind of extended commentary (*De cive*, p. 73). I am not sure where Salas's *vel leo* comes from. For source of the twin formulae in Erasmus's *Adagia*, see F. Tricaud, "'Homo homini Deus,' 'Homo homini Lupus': Recherche des sources des deux formules de Hobbes," in R. Koselleck and R. Schnur eds., *Hobbes-Forschungen* (Berlin: Duncker and Humblot 1969), 61–70.

[13] Salas, *Tractatus de legibus*, disp. 6, sect. 1, n. 4, fo. 98, col. 2.

[14] Cicero, *De officiis*, II. 20, 73.

wild beasts and against unjust and monstrous men, who would want to violate and to seize us and our own."[15] Living well is a second end that supervenes upon the end of simply living once that end has been achieved. In this dual understanding of the motivation of the city, Montecatini was (among others) a source for Henning Arnisaeus. Arnisaeus insisted that man is by nature an animal *sociale*, and that "men came together in the beginning not for the sake of living, but for the sake of living well."[16] Nevertheless, "it happens from time to time that men enter society, not at the guidance of nature, but compelled by necessity or indigence." The intention of nature is that men should enter it for the sake of the good and from natural instinct, but "secondarily and of the intention of the men who come together it often happens, that someone proposes for himself a different end."[17] So Cain founded a city from fear, and Nimrod from the desire of domination. Arnisaeus both endorsed and denied Horace's dictum in *Satires* I, 3: endorsed, because fear and defence *are* a motivation;[18] denied, because they are not the only driving force.[19]

Arnisaeus held, true to Aristotle in Book I of the *Politics*, that entry into political society goes through the lesser society of the family. Here again he was concerned to stress that the origins of the family are not purely in need or indigence, but in the impulse of nature. That impulse is at base the desire for self-preservation, something that is suggested directly by Aristotle's text. However, Arnisaeus fused material from Cicero's *De finibus* and from Aristotle in the *Nicomachean Ethics* to extend self-preservation into a global force that governs all nature, a natural love of self or *philautia* in all things, "by which they are driven to their own self-preservation, and to the removal of anything that could get in the way of this." Why, he asked, does the Roman law derive self-defence from natural law, unless it is "that we wish our own things to be safe before those of others, and this from the innate love with which we pursue our own, even if we not infrequently abuse it."[20] This coupling of Aristotle and Cicero is exactly the same pairing that the early Grotius used in *De iure praedae* to argue

---

[15] Antonio Montecatini, *In politica, hoc est, in civiles libros Aristotelis progymnasmata* (Ferrara 1587), fo. 49.
[16] Henning Arnisaeus, *De republica*, lib. I, cap. 1, titles to sects. 1 and 2.
[17] Ibid., sect. 2, nn. 1, 6.
[18] Ibid., n. 8.
[19] Ibid., sect. 3, n. 2.
[20] Ibid., sect. 7. nn. 4–5. The Stoic reference is to Book III of Cicero's *De finibus*, where Cicero discusses the universal self-love of all creatures. Again, unlike Aristotle (although partially suggested by the text), Arnisaeus distinguished between a universal nature, which intends the preservation of the species, and a particular nature, which looks out for the preservation of that individual.

for a natural *philautia* and a natural *ius* of all things to pursue their self-preservation.[21] Differently from Arnisaeus, however, Grotius connected this directly with the language of "utility," agreeing with Horace in *Satires* I, 3 that utility is the mother of the just and the unjust.[22] As we saw in chapter 3, in the later *De iure belli* Grotius changed his position on the primacy of utility. In this work, human beings are naturally sociable independent of the pressure of utility; and it is no longer true, as Horace said, that "nature cannot discern the just from the unequal."[23] However, when Grotius came to explain the genesis of the specifically civil community he located it squarely in the pursuit of utility, positing a disjunction in motivation between natural and civil society.[24]

We have seen, then, that Hobbes and the Aristotelians, despite Hobbes's caricature, did share some common ground on the question of the motivation for the city. I want now to turn to the question of its formation, where the parallel passages in *The elements of law*, *De cive*, and *Leviathan* are equally directed against the Aristotelian thesis of natural sociability. Here, Hobbes charged the Aristotelians with the idea that because human beings are naturally sociable, *zōon politikon*, all that is needed is a few pacts and everything will go swimmingly.[25] In the question of formation, then, as distinct from motivation, his criticism of the natural sociability thesis is directed against its role in underpinning pact. This is key to his argument, because if pacts can hold of themselves, there is no need for a Leviathan and we can be satisfied with the classical account of the city as a mutual *res publica*: a civic body that may transfer its power to a governor, but need not, and any such governor will be a magistrate rather than a sovereign. Accordingly, Hobbes began his critique in chapter 17 of *Leviathan* by telling us that "it is true, that certain living creatures, as Bees, and Ants, live sociably one with another, (which are therefore by Aristotle numbred amongst Politicall creatures;) and therefore some man may perhaps desire to know, why Man-kind cannot do the same."[26] He gave a number of reasons why human nature differs from animal nature so as to make this impossible, one of which is the human capacity for speech, which instead of being an instrument of sociability is rather, as he puts it in *De cive*, "a trumpet of war," *tuba belli*. (We might remark in passing that this is a little disingenuous: speech may lead to faction and sedition, but in being the

---

[21] See above, ch. 3, p. 70.

[22] Grotius, *De iure praedae*, cap. 2, fo. 5'a.

[23] Id., *De iure belli ac pacis*, Prolegomena, n. 6. Compare Denys Lambin's commentary on the satire, in which he rejected Horace's argument from utility: Dionysius Lambinus, *In Q. Horatium Flaccum commentarii* (Frankfurt 1577), *Satyrarum* lib. I, *Satyra* 3, fo. 39.

[24] Grotius, *De iure belli ac pacis*, Prolegomena, n. 16.

[25] Hobbes, *De cive*, cap. I. 2, p. 90.

[26] Id., *Leviathan*, ch. 17, p. 119.

means of covenant, it is also the crucial instrument of peace.) "Lastly," Hobbes concluded, "the agreement of these creatures is Naturall; that of men is by Covenant only, which is Artificiall; and therefore it is no wonder if there be somewhat else required (besides Covenant) to make their Agreement constant and lasting"[27]—and this is the institution of a common power to hold men to their covenants, the heart of *Leviathan*.

Now, the introduction to this passage is not really to the point. Pace Hobbes, contemporary Aristotelians were not sitting around wondering why human beings cannot behave like bees and ants. Human beings are distinguished from such natural creatures, which act by natural necessity and are "determined to one," as we have seen, by the possession of will: they are capable not merely of the natural, but of the voluntary. Every early modern commentary on the *Politics* that I have read incorporates the voluntary and elective aspect of human agency into its account of the formation of the city and distinguishes it from the natural. This voluntary aspect does not necessarily make the city *un*natural, but it demands a complex explanation that involves both natural communicative instinct and an act of the will. Thus the Oxford Aristotelian John Case, in his *Sphaera civitatis* of 1588, allowed his "objector" to put the proposition that the city is unnatural: "the voluntary and the natural are opposed: but to be a political animal is voluntary: therefore not natural. The major premise is proved, because the will acts from freedom, nature from necessity. The minor, because those who live a solitary life choose solitude over the city." Case's response was to argue that "the will and nature do not conflict always and in all things, for we choose many things which are by nature, such as life and health."[28] In the same vein, Suárez asserted that "man is a social animal and naturally or properly desires to live in a community"; the political community is "consonant with reason and with natural law." But "the natural law cannot by itself create political subjection without the intervention of the human will."[29]

Nevertheless, Hobbes was absolutely right in his essential perception that the voluntary aspect of the city is, for these theorists, underpinned by its naturalness in the sense of natural inclination. Even those commentators who have the most acute appreciation of the double natural inclination of mankind—both to sociability and to love of self—nevertheless used sociability to ground the city along with the voluntary act of the utility-pursuing individual. Thus, Hubert van Giffen argued both that "what holds the city together is utility ... which is why Horace elegantly calls utility the mother of the just and the unjust," and that "the city belongs

[27] Ibid., p. 120.
[28] John Case, *Sphaera civitatis* (Oxford 1588), lib. I, cap. 2, p. 26.
[29] Suárez, *De legibus*, lib. III, cap. 1, n. 11.

to that group of societies which hold together by nature, and not just by utility or institution or compact."[30] But for Hobbes, the Aristotelian account, even at its most sophisticated, gets human nature wrong: it provides no such underpinning to pact. So it is not that we need both nature and covenant; rather, we cannot rely on nature, so we must have covenant plus something else: "a Common Power, to keep them in awe."[31]

The question of the formation of the commonwealth implicates precisely the question of its *form*, the metaphysics of which pervades even the most anti-Aristotelian of our theorists, Hobbes, whose *Leviathan* is subtitled "the Matter, Forme and Power of a Common-wealth." Form gives to the commonwealth both its essence—its being as a distinct entity that is not given in nature—and its identity as a particular structure of government. The writers with whom we are concerned used two key words to elucidate the form of the commonwealth, "unity" (or "union") and "order." The central issue around which the debate turned is the separability or otherwise of these two aspects of its being: that is, whether the commonwealth can exist as a unity independently of the particular order of command and obedience that informs it, or whether that order just *is* the commonwealth. As I hope to show, the story of concept of the state in this period is given by the clash of these two competing narratives, narratives that are not purely philosophical but carry with them the most fundamental political implications.

Both medieval and early modern legal and scholastic discourse is saturated with the idea that the city is a unity. *Civitas* was even defined, in a pseudo-etymology, as *civium unitas*, a unity of citizens; a definition that was repeated in early modern legal lexicons like that of Johannes Calvinus,[32] or again by Althusius.[33] The dominant interpretation of this unity is the unity of *one body*. It relies on two ideas that, although originally distinct, tended to fuse together. One is the "organic metaphor" of the political body as analogous to a natural body. The other is so-called corporation theory, the legal conception whereby distinct individuals can act as one at law if they are incorporated into one legal body. These two ideas together make the "body politic"—a corporate unity at a different ontological level from the unity of individual natural bodies. They operate in tandem because the point of the corporate conception is to make

---

[30] Hubert van Giffen (Obertus Giphanius), *Commentarii in politicorum opus Aristotelis* (Frankfurt 1608), p. 32–33, 28.

[31] Hobbes, *Leviathan*, ch. 17, p. 120.

[32] Johannes Calvinus, *Lexicon iuridicum iuris romani* (Frankfurt 1600), col. 412.

[33] Althusius, *Politica*, p. 44. A caveat needs to be entered here, which is that Althusius does not think that the *civitas* coincides with the *res publica*; see below, p. 133.

the body politic capable of *agency* in the same way as a natural body. Hence the analogy between the two kinds of bodies remains central to this way of thinking, and it issues in a pervasive language of "head and members." The members of the body are united, and are able to act in concert, through the direction of a head that in some sense both represents and creates the body as a single agent, a "one." The "head" analogy for the rector, or ruler, is associated with this necessary directive function.

There was a distinct Aristotelian prompt for the idea of the city as a body. In Book I of the *Politics*, Aristotle described how the political community is formed as a development from smaller communities, the household and the village, and he also described how the city is logically prior to the individual, just as the body is prior to its constituent parts. It was easy to read the genesis of the city in *Politics* I, then, as the forming of a body politic—*one body*—and we find this sort of reading in the first chapter of Aquinas's *De regno* (also known as *De regimine principum*), which sketched how individuals come together for need of society, but also how that company requires to be ruled as one if it is not to disintegrate again —just as the natural body requires a *vis regitiva communis*, a common ruling and directive force.[34] However, this "body" interpretation did not sit so easily with Aristotle's continuing analysis, in Books II and III of the *Politics*, of what makes the city a distinct entity. In Book II of the *Politics*, Aristotle criticised Plato's idea of unity as the characteristic of a city. Platonic oneness, he said, is more the principle of a household, or even of one man. For Aristotle, the unity of the city is *disanalogous* with the kind of unity that characterises one individual human being. The city is not a unity in this sense, but a sharing or a communication: it demands, not one, but a multitude, a *plēthos*; not sameness, but difference. Multitude and difference are structured by an order (*taxis*), which is the "constitution" of the city, the *politeia*, the standard early-modern translation of which is *respublica* or "commonwealth." In chapter 6 of Book III, Aristotle characterised the *politeia* as the order of ruling offices, and particularly of the most sovereign. Moreover, in chapter 3 of that book he suggested, in an important passage for our theorists, that the criterion for the continued identity of the city is precisely its constitution: if the constitution changes, we no longer have the same city.[35] Thus it is *order*, not the unity of a body, that was in fact the key concept for Aristotle in thinking about the formal nature of the city.

The Catholic scholastic was heir to the late medieval corporate conception of the political community through the debate over the location

---

[34]Thomas Aquinas, *De regno*, tr. (under the title *De regimine principum*) in R. Dyson ed., *Aquinas. Political writings* (Cambridge: Cambridge University Press 2002), ch. 1.
[35]Aristotle, *Politics* III. 3, 1276b11.

of power in the church between Jacques Almain and Tommaso de Vio, Cardinal Cajetan, at the beginning of the sixteenth century. Cajetan marshalled the Dominican heritage, going back to Aquinas but transformed into a thesis about *power* in the furious polemics of the early fourteenth century, to allow Almain much of what he wanted to say about the nature of the political community and consequently the location of its power, but to deny that the same arguments extended to the church. For both Cajetan and Almain (who indeed also appealed to Aquinas), the city is a body analogous to a natural body, and analogously with that body it has a power of self-preservation and self-defence that Almain glossed as a natural right under natural law. The power that the political ruler exercises is the power of this body to preserve itself. In other words, the power of the head is the people's power. Thus Cajetan said forcefully that

> a king, whether appointed by the people or given by God, represents the people and its power. For, although they differ among themselves in their appointment, because one is raised up by the people, the other by God, they do not differ in the nature of [their] office and power. For, just as a natural organ, like a hand, if it exists miraculously by the power of God, is the same as if it existed naturally, so a political organ, like a king, when he is appointed by God, is the same as if he were appointed by the people; and, therefore, in whichever way he was appointed, he represents and exercises their power.[36]

The conclusions concerning political power generated by this debate permeate Vitoria's relection *On civil power*, where he reproduced Almain's analogy between the individual and the political community, which both equally by natural law have the natural right of self-preservation and self-defence.[37] Unlike both Almain and Cajetan, however, he sought to defuse the potentially revolutionary implications of the people's power by insisting that in the specific constitution that is a monarchy, the power comes from God, and only the authority to exercise it from the people.[38]

In a crucial move, Domingo de Soto transformed the juridical analogy between the natural human being and the civic community into a juridical dynamic, running up from the individual to the community and on to a governing part, the head. So, in a famous passage defending the naturalness of political power, he began by saying that "God through nature

---

[36] Cajetan, *Apology* (1512), tr. in J. Burns and T. Izbicki eds., *Conciliarism and papalism* (Cambridge: Cambridge University Press 1997), 201–84, at p. 232.
[37] Vitoria, *On civil power*, 1. 4, tr. Pagden and Lawrance, p. 11.
[38] Ibid., 1. 5, p. 16, and see the Introduction, pp. xix–xx.

gave to individual things the faculty of preserving themselves, not only with regard to the safekeeping of their temporal well-being, but also through his grace with regard to the prosperity of their spiritual well-being. But since in their scattered state they were not able to exercise this faculty conveniently, he added to them the instinct of living together, so that united they might be sufficient each to each other."[39] Now it is true that Soto does not here explicitly characterise this "faculty" as a right. But the passage occurs in Book IV of his *On justice and right*, at the opening of which he had defined "faculty" as right in a subjective sense;[40] and Soto spoke elsewhere in the work of the "desire and right" of self-preservation innate in all things.[41] We are justified, then, in understanding by "faculty" in the present context a juridical faculty, or natural right. "However," Soto went on, "the commonwealth thus congregated could in no way govern itself, drive off enemies and check the temerity of malefactors unless it selected magistrates, to whom it granted its faculty: for otherwise the community, without order or head, would not represent one body, nor could it provide for those things that were expedient."[42] Here, the faculty of the congregated commonwealth—the body—is implied but instantly transferred to a head. The body cannot act, it cannot even *be* a body, without a head, and it is the head that exercises the faculty of preserving it. This account, then, centred as it is on the idea of body, incorporates the idea of order in the sense of ordination to a head. But the relationship between body and head is reciprocal, because the power that the head exercises is only the body's power of preserving itself.

Soto's elliptical account glided over the moment of creation of the body and its power. By contrast, Francisco Suárez offered in his *De legibus* a precise analysis of this moment, developing and refining Soto's juridico-genetic perspective by using the Jesuit metaphysical distinction between the physical and the moral to characterise the city as a *moral* union. So, he wrote,

> we must be aware that a multitude of men is considered in two ways. Firstly just as it is an aggregate of some kind without any order or union, physical or moral, in which way they do not make up a "one" either physically or morally; and therefore they are not properly one political body, and therefore they do not need one head or prince. But the human multitude is to be considered in a second way, insofar as with a specific will or common consensus they congregate

[39] Soto, *De iustitia et iure*, lib. IV, q. 4, a. 1.
[40] See above, chapter 4, p. 93.
[41] See my *Liberty, right and nature*, p. 152, for instances of such passages.
[42] Soto, *De iustitia et iure*, lib. IV, q. 4, a. 1.

into one political body with one bond of society and in order that they might mutually help each other in order to one political end; in which way they make up one mystical body, which morally speaking can be said to be of itself 'one': and that body consequently needs a head."[43]

Suárez's account implicitly posits the individual as a subject of rights, that is, naturally equipped with a range of "dominative" faculties including the natural right of liberty, which (as we saw in the last chapter) can be ceded at the will of the individual. It is not clear that the act of will involved has the specific form of a contract; it is a more general intention for an end, the moral effect of which is not simply obligation, but union.[44] Nevertheless, it is still very clear that the creation of the body politic is a function of individual acts of will, and that the creation of that body is at one and the same time the creation of its power. "Therefore, in such a community, as such, there is this power of the nature of the thing, so that it is not in the power of men to congregate in this way and to obstruct this power."[45] This power, political power, is characterised at the outset as a power "of governing" or "of ruling" the community for the common good.[46] It is held by "the civil magistrate," which (as we shall see) can be one man or a multitude of men. It necessarily includes the power to make civil laws, one of the acts most necessary for its function. But this is to the extent that "this power of making human laws is convertible with the human magistrate" in this sense: it is impossible to hold apart legislative and political power.[47] Hence, what the individuals create is at one and the same time the community's power to govern itself for the common good, primarily through law, and a power, a "peculiar dominion," over the individual members themselves.[48] Just as in Soto, unity and subjection go hand in hand: "without political government or ordination towards it the notion of one political body is unintelligible ... because

[43] Suárez, *De legibus*, lib. III, cap. 2, n. 4.
[44] Gemmeke, *Metaphysik des sittlich Guten*, p. 128, argues strenuously against any contractual reading: it is not a contract, the terms of which are up to the parties involved, but the creation of a new entity with properties that cannot be stipulated as part of a deal.
[45] Suárez, *De legibus*, lib. III, cap. 2, n. 4.
[46] Ibid., cap. 1, n. 4: *potestas gubernandi*; n. 5: *potestas regendi*. Here the "a priori reason" for the existence of such a power is taken from Aquinas's work *De regimine principum* (or *De regno*), lib. I, cap. 1, which is that if there are a multitude of men consulting their own good, there must be something or someone to look to the common good, or the society will disintegrate. See above, n. 34.
[47] Suárez, *De legibus*, lib. III, cap. 1, nn. 5–7.
[48] Ibid., cap. 3, n. 6: *corpus politicum hominum, eo ipso quod suo modo producitur, habet potestatem et regimen suiipsius et consequenter habet etiam potestatem supra membra sua et peculiare dominium in illa.*

this unity in great part arises from subjection to the same regime and to some common and superior power."[49]

Suárez was clear that the original location of power is in the community itself. Moreover, his dual conception of the community's power, both as a power over itself and a power over individual members, allowed him (differently from Soto) to conceive of the ordination of subjects to a head without transfer of that power. In the *Defensio fidei* of 1613, Suárez held that the state of un-transferred power is pure democracy, the original constitution of all commonwealths.[50] In the *De legibus*, this is ambiguous, because in this work he suggested that democracy is one among three basic types of regime (the others being monarchy and aristocracy) that the community may choose for itself, and is thus something different from power being exercised "immediately through the whole community itself."[51] Even here, however, he did not assert the absolute necessity of a transfer of power. Nevertheless, he made it clear that the community can, and in fact almost always will (because of the extreme difficulty of making laws "with the votes of everyone"), transfer that power to a determinate person or persons, precisely to further that political end for which this new moral body is formed. The terms of that transfer are up to the community itself, and it is here that the contractual language of "pact" clearly comes into play.[52] The community may choose to reserve to itself some of the power, or it may alienate it completely by analogy with a voluntary slave. As we saw in the last chapter, an individual can

---

[49] Ibid., cap. 2, n. 4

[50] Francisco Suárez, *Defensio fidei III*, ed. E. Elorduy and L. Peña (Madrid: CSIC 1965), cap. 2, n. 8. See M. Walther, "*Potestas multitudinis* und *potentia multitudinis*. Zur Transformation der Demokratietheorie zu Beginn der Neuzeit," in Grunert and Seelmann eds., *Ordnung der Praxis*, 281–97, at pp. 283–86.

[51] Suárez, *De legibus*, lib. III, cap. 4, n. 1.

[52] Höpfl, *Jesuit political thought*, p. 251, argues that Suárez systematically runs together the *pactum* that creates a regime with the original agreement to form the body politic. Kremer, *Den Frieden verantworten*, pp. 109–12, argues by contrast (following the analyses of Soder and Wilenius) for a sharp distinction between the two, the former being a contract and the latter an act of consent, with the former being responsible for creating a commonwealth as opposed simply to a political community. It seems to me undeniable that *De legibus*, at least, appeals to two different moments. However, I agree with Höpfl to the extent that the original act of will creates not simply a community, a potential but not actual subject of political government, but a full commonwealth in which political power over itself and over its members necessarily and actually inheres. Suárez has no name for the primary form of government in *De legibus*, but that does not mean it is not a form of government at all; as we have seen, power would have been exercised "immediately through the whole community itself." Suárez presumably has in mind the difference between an absolutely direct democracy (which he clearly thinks is unsustainable) and an "institutional" democracy with a formal assembly, even if that assembly is open to every member of the community.

alienate his moral faculty of liberty entirely without threatening his underlying essence as such. Here in Book III Suárez made exactly the same distinction between physical and moral properties in the context of the individual body politic.[53] The consequence is that the city can alienate its moral property of liberty without ceasing to be the body that it is, and this is critically important. The body does not disappear into the head, but remains in being throughout; as in Soto, it is the good or preservation of the body that regulates both the concept and the exercise of the power. Thus, although all members of the second scholastic were strongly monarchist in outlook (hence the slightly exasperated tone of Suárez's address to James VI and I in the *Defensio fidei*), the body of the people continues to play a regulatory role in the commonwealth even if it has totally alienated its power.[54] This is its continuity with the more revolutionary, so-called monarchomach or "king-killing" versions of the theory deployed *against* kings in the civil wars of France and the Netherlands, which insist that power always remains in some sense with the people and may be recovered by them if the monarch goes against the good of the people: for which, and only for which, the power exists in the first place. It is this that so disturbed defenders of monarchy like Robert Filmer, whose caricature of Suárez and his fellow Jesuit, Robert Bellarmine, in the first chapter of his *Patriarcha* foisted upon them a revolutionary attitude that both of them strenuously resisted.[55]

One writer often associated with "monarchomach" thought in its French and Dutch Calvinist handling is Johannes Althusius, whose situation in East Friesland placed him in close proximity to events in the Netherlands.[56] Nevertheless, his political theory was far from a simple defence of popular sovereignty. Like other writers in the *politica* genre, one of his central concerns was with the "functional necessity" of "magistrates in command over obedient subjects,"[57] and his analysis of the structures of political life, life alongside other human beings, is an analysis of the order that must necessarily govern them. Althusius took as his fundamental category the *consociatio*, which he made a term of art to denote

[53] Suárez, *De legibus*, lib. III, cap. 3, n. 8.
[54] See Höpfl, *Jesuit political thought*, pp. 256–57.
[55] Robert Filmer, *Patriarcha*, in J. P. Sommerville ed., *Patriarcha and other writings* (Cambridge: Cambridge University Press 1991), pp. 2–3.
[56] See H. Lloyd, "Constitutionalism," in J. Burns ed., *The Cambridge history of political thought 1450–1700* (Cambridge: Cambridge University Press 1991), 254–97, at pp. 287–92; M. van Gelderen, "Aristotelians, monarchomachs and republicans," in M. van Gelderen and Q. Skinner eds., *Republicanism*, vol. I (Cambridge: Cambridge University Press 2002), 195–217, at pp. 204–207; R. von Friedeburg, *Self-defence and religious strife in early modern Europe* (Aldershot: Ashgate 2002), pp. 106–10.
[57] Von Friedeburg, *Self-defence*, p. 105.

the primary subject of politics. In the opening chapter of the third edition of the *Politica* of 1614, he declared that "the object of political science is the consociation (*consociatio*), by which those who have their life together (*symbiotici*) oblige themselves to each other, in an express or tacit pact, to the mutual communication of those things that are useful and necessary to the use and interchange of social life."[58] "Consociation" is therefore a juridical phenomenon that necessarily involves a *jus symbioticum*, that is, a juridical principle or norm of life-sharing. In parallel, a consociation is always *one body*, as distinct from a simple congregation or gathering.[59] For Althusius it was a category that covers all types of association, from the natural associations of marriage, family, and kinship to the voluntary associations of colleges and guilds; from these private forms to the public forms of village, town, city, metropolis, province, and ultimately the "universal" consociation that is the *regnum*, the "realm," or the *respublica*, the "commonwealth." The "one body" argument is thus decoupled from the argument for the location of *sovereign* power, which occurs a great deal further on in Althusius's account when he came to discuss the ultimate, "universal" consociation, which alone is in possession of *maiestas* or supreme and absolute power.[60] Instead, the argument for an order of subjection in consociation in general is an argument about the need for some kind of ruler-ruled relationship in any composite body. Althusius posits this as the "common and perpetual law" of every consociation, separate from the more specific laws by which it is governed.[61] To elucidate the point, he turned to the Catholic legal and political theorist at the university of Pont-à-Mousson in Lorraine, Pierre Grégoire—a move that of itself shows how problematic is the unqualified designation of "monarchomach" for Althusius's thought.[62]

Grégoire had begun his *De republica* of 1596 by declaring that "the commonwealth is a kind of community of life and goods in one society, which makes one civil body, composed of many different individuals, as

---

[58] Johannes Althusius, *Politica methodice digesta*, repr. from the third edition of 1614 with an Introduction by C. J. Friedrich (Cambridge, Mass.: Harvard University Press 1932), cap. I, n. 2, p. 15.

[59] For example, ibid., cap. V, n. 4, p. 39, on the specific consociation that is the *universitas* or public corporation: "men congregated without symbiotic right are a crowd, a gathering, a multitude, a congregation, a people, a nation." But the specific consociation that is the household also involves a *jus symbioticum*, and its members are equally "the members of one body": ibid., cap. II, n. 5, p. 21.

[60] Ibid., cap. IX, nn. 18–27, pp. 92–94.

[61] Ibid., cap. I, n. 11, p. 16.

[62] Grégoire is described as a "moderate absolutist" by J. Salmon: "Catholic resistance theory," in Burns ed., *Cambridge history*, 219–53, at p. 235; more strongly, Strohm characterises his *De republica* as a programmatic rebuttal of monarchomach ideas (*Calvinismus und Recht*, p. 212).

if they were its members, under one supreme power, as if it were one head and one spirit, to live well and conveniently in this mortal life, so as to come more easily to the eternal life."[63] But as Grégoire developed the argument, he dropped the language of "head," and what he instead described was how the members of a political body, just like those of a natural body, must be bound together by one "spirit," or "soul," which is the necessarily single "supreme power" and whose function it is to command (*imperare*) the members.[64] The notion of spirit and soul as having a *uniting* function, not just a *commanding* function, is a debt not to Aristotelian but to Stoic physics, in which the *pneuma*—in Latin, *spiritus*—holds the body together in a kind of "tenor" (*hexis*), soul being the *pneuma* of a specifically animate body.[65] It is spirit, then, that makes the body the specific body that it is, playing the role of form in Aristotelian physics; and accordingly "the form of the society," Grégoire went on, "is the union of the body with the concord of the members under one spirit."[66] Althusius adopted this conception directly from Grégoire, to make the role of the ruler in the consociation analogous to what he called the *animus*—the "mind"—in the human body.[67]

This language marks a departure from the scholastic Aristotelian analysis, in which the power of the community is always a power for an act—the act of preserving the body—and is thus intimately knitted in to the agent-centred perspective that dominates Aquinas's *Prima secundae* and all the commentaries upon it that we have been studying so far. It is centrally a teleological conception in which ruling is an art of directing to an end.[68] Certainly, after the Fall, achieving the political end always requires in addition a *vis coactiva*, a coercive force; but coercive force does not exist independently of the directive force that constitutes its sole rationale.[69] It is this concept of direction that underlies the metaphor of the ruler as the "head" of the body. By contrast, in Althusius and Grégoire the

[63] Pierre Grégoire, *De republica libri sex et viginti* (Pont-à-Mousson 1596), cap. I, n. 6, p. 3.

[64] Ibid., n. 8: *utque in uno corpore physico, membrorum concordia et colligatione, actiones suas mens exerit et perficit, et unico spiritu eadem membra colligat: ita unum imperium, cum potestate unius vel plurium in republica regit, imperat;* and n. 9: *Et quot sunt respublicae tot debent esse supremae potestates, in unaquaque una, sicut in uno corpore physico, una anima quae imperat, non duo.*

[65] See A. Long and D. Sedley, *The Hellenistic philosophers*, vol. 1 (Cambridge: Cambridge University Press 1987), pp. 280–89.

[66] Grégoire, *De republica*, cap. I, n. 10, p. 3.

[67] Althusius, *Politica*, cap. I, n. 13, p. 17, referring to Grégoire, *De republica*, lib. I cap. 1, n. 18, where he sums up: "Therefore in a commonwealth that is to be well-established, this will be fundamental, that there be some who rule ... and some who obey."

[68] See M. Senellart, *Les arts de gouverner. Du* regimen *médiéval au concept de gouvernement* (Paris: Seuil 1995), p. 19; on the transformation from an individual to a political concept of *regimen* in Aquinas, ibid., pp. 158–79.

[69] For "directive" and "coercive" authority, see Höpfl, *Jesuit political thought*, pp. 208–11.

power of the ruler is not the specifically directive function of the head. It is, in the first instance, a unifying force, a force that works through its command of the members. It is a superior *imperium* rather than the *potestas* of the scholastics. Nevertheless, the two conceptions are not couched in completely different languages. Soto and Suárez insist, as we have seen, on the notion of order, of subordination and subjection; and equally Althusius and Grégoire also appeal to the notion of a "head." Thus, Althusius asserts that if there were no command and subjection, this would be monstrous, "no otherwise than to see a body without a head, and a head without members legitimately and appropriately ordered,"[70] and echoes Grégoire directly in the phrase "under one head and spirit," *sub uno capite et spiritu*.[71] Crucially, both also share the language of "one body," *unum corpus*, and both appeal to the juridical language of the corporation, the *universitas*, in their characterisation of public communities. And it is thus that Althusius saw no tension, when he came to the question of sovereign power or *maiestas*, in using a fundamentally scholastic thesis of the location of *potestas* in the body to join hands with the "monarchomach" literature in combating the absolutism of the French *politique* Jean Bodin.[72] Althusius kept the consequence of the scholastic juridico-genetic story—in its radical, inalienable version—without the underlying narrative.

The infiltration of the "body" conception into the Aristotelian political literature on the commonwealth, *de republica*, was attacked as a fundamental confusion by Henning Arnisaeus, who took himself to be returning to a more authentically Aristotelian conception of the *respublica* or commonwealth as order—the ordering of the *plēthos* or multitude that is described in *Politics* Book II and Book III. It is a terrible mistake, according to Arnisaeus, to confuse the *polis*, the *civitas*, of Book I, with the *politeia*, the *respublica*, of Book III, and thus to offer a "body"-type account of

---

[70] Althusius, *Politica*, cap. I, n. 34, p. 19; the quotation can be found in Grégoire, *De republica*, lib.VI, cap. 1, n 1.

[71] Grégoire, *De republica*, as for n. 72; Althusius, *Politica*, cap. II, n. 4, p. 20 (on the domestic consociation).

[72] Opinions differ as to Althusius's relation to Bodin. One view is that Althusius kept a Bodinian concept of indivisible and absolute sovereignty, but located it permanently in the associated body: Lloyd, "Constitutionalism," pp. 290–91; cf. von Friedeburg, *Self-defence*, p. 116. By contrast, van Gelderen ("Aristotelians, monarchomachs and republicans," p. 204) argues for Althusius's rejection of Bodin's theory of sovereignty. Merio Scattola suggests that the successive editions of the *Politica* show Althusius's increasing independence from Bodin, from the acceptance of his conception in the 1603 edition to its displacement and ultimate rejection in the 1614 edition: M. Scattola, "Von der *maiestas* zur *symbiosis*," in E. Bonfatti, G. Duso, and M. Scattola eds., *Politische Begriffe und historisches Umfeld in der Politica methodice digesta des Johannes Althusius* (Wiesbaden: Harrassowitz 2002), 211–49. I offer my own interpretation of the changes between the 1603 and the 1614 editions below, ch. 8, pp. 215–19.

the latter. The definition Arnisaeus explicitly attacked was that of Pierre Grégoire. According to him, as we have seen, "the *respublica* is a kind of community of life and goods in one society, which makes one civil body, composed of many different individuals, as if they were its members, under one supreme power, as if it were one head and one spirit, to live well and conveniently in this mortal life, so as to come more easily to the eternal life." Arnisaeus's response was that this "one body" definition confuses two things that are separate: the community of men, which is the city, and the structure of rule, which is the commonwealth of his title, *De republica*. For Arnisaeus, the "community of life and goods" for living well, the city, does not create the distinctive new entity that is the commonwealth. The assembly—*coetus*—of human beings into a city is still only a "multitude" in this respect. The multitude becomes a commonwealth not by coming together as a body but by *taxis*, the order of command and subjection. This "is imposed upon such a multitude ... and circumscribes it with laws, limiting it for the sake of the public well-being."[73] Law, then, belongs to the commonwealth and not to the city. In parallel with making this distinction between city and *respublica*, Arnisaeus also distinguished between citizen and subject. An individual is a *citizen* insofar as he is a member of the political community that is the city. But he is a *subject* of the *respublica*, understood as an order of command and subjection, which "with all different kinds of limits contracts and circumscribes the indeterminate liberty of citizens."[74]

Arnisaeus's critique was sweeping and not entirely fair. Arnisaeus included in the confused both Bodin and Althusius, neither of whom had in fact identified the city and the commonwealth. Bodin had explicitly criticised Aristotle for *not* distinguishing between a city and a *respublica* or commonwealth.[75] For Bodin in the sixth chapter of the first book of *Les six livres de la République*—although it is important that Arnisaeus was reading Bodin's later Latin translation, the *De republica* of 1586—a city is a legal construction, *un mot de droit*, and it is governed by laws and magistrates; but it is not a commonwealth, which is defined by common subjection to a sovereign power. Thus, you could have a city that is not a commonwealth, such as the cities of the Veneto which are subject to the commonwealth that is Venice.[76] However, despite distinguishing between city and commonwealth, Bodin had also criticised Aristotle's definition of the citizen, substituting his own, which is "a free subject of the sovereign power of

[73] Arnisaeus, *De republica*, lib. II, cap. 1, sect. 1, n. 5.

[74] Ibid., lib. I, cap. 5, sect. 5, n. 4.

[75] Jean Bodin, *Les six livres de la république* (Paris: Fayard 1986), livre I, ch. 6, p. 118; *De republica libri sex* (Paris 1586), lib. I, cap. 6, fo. 49.

[76] *Les six livres*, pp. 119–120; my thanks to Anna Becker on this point.

another."[77] This, in Arnisaeus's view, pointed to fundamental confusion: how can the city be distinguished from the commonwealth if the citizen is not distinguished from the subject?[78] Moreover, Bodin had included law in his definition of the city, a mistake on Arnisaeus's terms; and in his definition of the *respublica* he had included families and property, which for Arnisaeus belong in the city as distinct from the commonwealth.[79] Althusius, for his part, had also overtly distinguished between city and commonwealth. The city is a public consociation, but it is a lesser consociation than the commonwealth which is made up of many cities and provinces. Nevertheless, Althusius had done the same as Bodin by including law in the definition of the city and "works" and "property" in the definition of the commonwealth, thus equally falling foul of Arnisaeus's critique.[80]

For Arnisaeus, therefore, the confusion still stands, and it is related to the more fundamental mistake of both of them—and of practically everyone else—which is to define the *respublica*, the commonwealth, as he put it, "through the men themselves,"[81] as congregated into one body, or assembly, or society, or consociation, or whatever you choose to call it; and thus, if not to identify city and commonwealth, to use the same genus for both.[82] For Arnisaeus, by contrast, the political community, the city, stands to the *respublica* as the material to the form.[83] This form he described, following Aristotle, as the "life" of the city, or, following Isocrates, as the

---

[77] *Les six livres*, p. 113: "le franc subject, tenant de la souveraineté d'autruy"; *De republica*, fo. 47: *liberum hominem, qui summae potestatis imperio teneatur.*

[78] Arnisaeus, *De republica*, lib. I, cap. 5, sect. 5, nn. 5–6. Hubert van Giffen had already offered this critique of Bodin: van Giffen, *Commentarii*, cap. 1, lib. III, p. 298.

[79] On the question of law and the city, Bodin had indeed asserted, in the first book of the *Six livres*, chapter 6, that there can be no city where there are no laws. In chapter 8 of the same book, however, he had clearly linked the power to make laws with sovereignty. Still, this had necessitated the injection of a "strict sense" of law, since magistrates too can make law over persons within their jurisdiction so long as they are not in conflict with those of the sovereign. Thus "law" in a more general sense is not exclusively tied to sovereignty, and to that extent Bodin's text supports Arnisaeus's interpretation. On the question of families and property it gave him much clearer ammunition: *Les six livres*, livre I, ch. 1, p. 27: "République est un droit gouvernement de plusieurs mesnages, et de ce qui leur est commun, avec puissance souveraine"; *De republica*, lib. I, cap. 1, fo. 1: *Respublica est familiarum rerumque inter ipsas communium summa potestate ac ratione moderata multitudo.*

[80] Arnisaeus, *De republica*, lib. II, cap. 1, sect. 1, n. 1.

[81] Ibid., lib. I, *Ratio ordinis*, n. 5. The critique of Bodin here really only applies to the Latin version, in which he had defined the commonwealth as a "multitude" governed by supreme power and reason. The French version stresses that the commonwealth is the *gouvernement* itself.

[82] Ibid., lib. II, cap. 1, sect. 1, n. 1.

[83] Ibid., n. 2. See Dreitzel, *Protestantischer Aristotelismus*, p. 119; on Arnisaeus's debt to the broader Aristotelian commentary literature on this point, and especially the work of Pier Vettori, see ibid., pp. 344–45. See also van Gelderen, "Aristotelians, monarchomachs and republicans," p. 209.

"soul" of the city.[84] And with the introduction of the notions of "life" and "soul," Arnisaeus could use Aristotle's categories not simply of matter and form, but of matter and form in the context of a living body, from Book II of Aristotle's work *On the soul*. The soul should not be defined as the body itself but as the formal actuality of the body, as Aristotle says—what actually makes it a living body, without which the body is not a body at all, but just matter. In the same sense, Arnisaeus wrote, the city can no more survive without the *respublica* than an organic body without its soul.[85] And this, the commonwealth, is synonymous with the state: "For," he said, "the word *status*, drawn from the Italian language, in the signification in which it is used here denotes the *respublica* itself, and when it is translated into the Latin tongue, is given as *respublica*."[86]

Let us turn back now to the natural law tradition and consider the later work of Hugo Grotius, which lies interestingly between these two stories —juridical and political—about what the city is. In the *De iure praedae*, Grotius had unequivocally envisaged a process of congregation and of individual self-incorporation into a civil body, a new "one" or unity that is distinct from the individual human unities who create it. This assembly, *coetus*, is the *civitas* that is also the *respublica*.[87] In the *Prolegomena* and Book I of the *De iure belli ac pacis*, describing the genesis and the form of the city as the source of civil law—as in Suárez—we have essentially this same familiar story about forming into a body. Grotius defined the *civitas* in broadly Aristotelian terms as "a perfect assembly [*coetus*] of free men, associated [*sociatus*] for the sake of enjoying right and the common utility."[88] By perfect he meant being what he calls the "common" subject of civil power, capable of making its own laws, autonomous.[89] I say that it is *essentially* the same story as in the earlier work because, in the very brief account of the formation of the *civitas* in the *Prolegomena*, the commonwealth is described as "an association [*consociatio*] or subjection" (emphasis mine): men either congregate into an assembly, or subject themselves to some person or persons.[90] Nevertheless, putting together the

---

[84] Arnisaeus, *De republica*, lib. II, cap. 1, sect. 1, n. 1; cf. lib. I, *Ratio ordinis*, n. 5; lib. I, cap. 5, sect. 3, nn. 4–5. The references are: Aristotle, *Politics*, IV. 11, 1295a40–b41: "the *politeia* is in a sense the life of the city" (*res publica est vita civitatis* in the Latin, "the Commonweale is the life of the City," in the 1598 English translation); Isocrates, *Areopagiticus*, "the soul of the city is nothing other than the *politeia*," *nec enim alia civitatis anima est, quam forma Reipublicae: Isocrates Graeco-Latinus*, tr. H. Wolfius (Basel 1567), vol. I, p. 420.

[85] Arnisaeus, *De republica* lib. I, cap. 5, sect. 5, nn. 3, 4.

[86] Ibid., lib. II, cap. 1, sect. 1, n. 4.

[87] Grotius, *De iure praedae*, cap. 2, fo. 11; vol. I, p. 20.

[88] Id., *De iure belli*, lib. I, cap. 1, sect. 14, n. 2.

[89] Ibid., cap. 3, sect. 6, n. 1, and sect. 7, nn. 1–3.

[90] Ibid., *Prolegomena*, nn. 15–16.

very brief words in the *Prolegomena* with the more extended analysis in Book I, it does not seem that Grotius is here offering us two fundamentally different genetic accounts. Even in the *Prolegomena*, it is implicit that subjection to a person or persons still involves a body, because Grotius spoke of this person or persons as "those to whom the power has been transferred." We need to connect this phrase rather with his famous insistence in Book I, chapter 3 that it is not necessary that civil power be always in the people.[91] Like Suárez, Grotius in this later work held that the power can be entirely alienated and the commonwealth still be legitimate, with the same slave analogy. The *proper* subject of civil power can be one absolute ruler alone, even while the *common* subject remains the *civitas*.[92] The *civitas*, then, is fundamentally a united body of individuals, which explains Grotius's tendency to move easily between the term *civitas* and the term "people," *populus*. Not every people is a city—there can be a subject people, which, because it is not autonomous, is not a *civitas*, juridically self-sufficient, or "perfect."[93] But a *populus* in the sense of being the common subject of civil power is equivalent to a *civitas* even if, as we have seen, it has alienated its power to a ruler as the proper subject. In line with Grotius's adoption of the Suarezian metaphysics of right as a moral faculty, this people or *civitas*, created by pact or the transfer of right, is characterised as a *moral* body, and civil or sovereign power, the power to make civil law, as a *moral faculty* of governing the city.[94]

However, the picture changes if we move on to look not at the genesis of the city in Book I, but at Grotius's account of the loss of *imperium* or sovereign power in Book II, chapter 9.[95] To undertake his analysis, he changes from a language of moral bodies to one of *artificial* bodies that belongs to the Roman law tradition rather than to the Aristotelian, but that nevertheless brings him much closer to the matter-form distinction that Arnisaeus had deployed. I say much closer, because Grotius's terms are not the same: he speaks rather of body (*corpus*) and what I shall call specific form (*species*).[96] However, Grotius's arguments are in part a commentary on the key chapter of Aristotle mentioned at the outset of this discussion, Book III, chapter 3, which is about the continued identity of the city, and they are deliberately brought into relation with the language of political Aristotelianism. Thus, he began:

---

[91] Ibid., lib. I, cap. 3, sect. 8, n. 1. See Tuck, *Natural rights theories*, pp. 77–78.

[92] Grotius, *De iure belli*, lib. I, cap. 3, sect. 7, n. 3; sect. 8, nn. 1–2.

[93] Ibid., sect. 7, n. 2.

[94] Ibid., and sect. 6, n. 1.

[95] It should be noted that here too Grotius slips between "city" and "people."

[96] The eighteenth-century translation does not hesitate to use the simple term "Form" to translate the latter but, as we shall see, Grotius's debts are to Stoic rather than to Aristotelian physics.

Isocrates said … that cities are immortal, that is, they can be; because a people belongs to that genus of bodies, which is made up from separate parts, but bears one name insofar as it has one disposition … or one spirit. That spirit, or disposition in the people is the full and perfect association of civil life, the primary product of which is sovereign power, the bond through which the commonwealth co-heres, the vital breath which so many thousands draw, as Seneca says. But clearly these artificial bodies are in the likeness of a natural body. A natural body does not cease to be the same, if its parts are gradually changed, so long as its specific form remains the same.[97]

We have already met "spirit" in the Stoic sense of a *hexis*, here translated as "disposition." The term *species* Grotius imported from the Roman jurist Alfenus, in a celebrated passage arguing for the continued identity of a composite body, like a ship, even as its parts are gradually replaced.[98] Another passage from the Digest distinguished composite bodies into those that are made up from pieces joined together (*sunnēmena*), like a ship or a building, and those that are made up of things that are separated from one another (*diestōta*), "but are subject to one name, like a people, a legion, a flock."[99] Althusius in his *Dicaeologica* posited both of these as subtypes of "artificial bodies," *corpora technica*,[100] while Arnisaeus, discussing the ideal size of the city in his *De republica*, referred to quantity as a perfection "that embraces not only all bodily things that are natural [*physicae*] … but all artificial collections [*congregationes artificiales*], which imitate nature," and of which the city is one.[101] Hubert van Giffen had already imported this legal language of bodies into his commentary on Aristotle's *Politics*, both in Book I and in the critical chapter 3 of Book III.[102] Grotius was using a familiar language, therefore, one that was originally Stoic and legal but had been assimilated into political Aristotelianism. And Grotius made the Aristotelian connection clear when in his notes he added the same quotation from Aristotle that Arnisaeus had relied upon to separate the city from the commonwealth. "This spirit or disposition in the people is 'the constitution (*politeia*), the life of the city.'"[103]

[97] Grotius, *De iure belli*, lib. II, cap. 9, sect. 3, n. 1.

[98] D. 5.1.76.

[99] D. 41.3.30.

[100] Althusius, *Dicaeologica*, lib. I, cap. 4, n. 4, p. 9.

[101] Arnisaeus, *De republica*, lib. I, cap. 5, sect. 6, n. 12.

[102] Van Giffen, *Commentarii*, lib. I, cap. 1, p. 54; lib. III, cap. 2 (modern editions ch. 3), pp. 305–306. See further Brett, "Natural right and civil community," p. 49.

[103] Grotius, *De iure belli*, lib. II, cap. 9, sect. 3, n. 1. The eighteenth-century translation has here: "The government is the life of the state," indicating the huge gulf separating their political terminology from the debates of the early seventeenth century. It should be noted that in Book II, chapter 6, concerning alienation of *imperium*, Grotius had already spoken

According to Grotius, a people dies when either the body or "the spirit or *species*" dies. The body dies if its particles disappear or are forcibly dispersed. The *species* dies when either all the individuals are reduced to personal slavery, or they are left in personal liberty but deprived of sovereignty. This leaves them a mere "multitude," not a commonwealth.[104] The case is different, however, if the sovereignty changes hands. Thus he insists that a people remains the same people whatever its form of government: the Roman people is the same "under kings, under consuls, and under emperors." Whether the people is *sui juris* or has alienated its right over itself entirely, "the people will be the same as it was before," since "the king is superior to it as the head of that people, not as the head of another people." To give the reason for this, Grotius went back to the language he had developed in Book I of his work. "For the sovereign power that is in the king as in the head, remains in the people as in the whole, of which the head is a part."[105] The people, then, continues to be the underlying or common subject of *imperium*; and it is here that Grotius made his difference with the political Aristotelian tradition plain. On an Aristotelian form-matter analysis, if the form changes—and the *respublica*, the *politeia*, the "constitution" *is* the form—we no longer have the same thing, because a thing is identified by its form rather than its matter. Likewise, in Roman law, a thing is the same if its *species* is the same.[106] Accordingly, contemporary commentators on *Politics* Book III, chapter 3 agreed with Aristotle that if the form of government changes, so too does the city itself. But Grotius disagreed: "do not let anyone object to me that passage of Aristotle, who says that if the form of the commonwealth"—*forma rei publicae*—"changes, it is no longer the same city." "For," he went on, "you should know that of one artificial thing, there can be several specific forms.... In this sense, one specific form of the city is an association of right and sovereign power; another, the mutual relationship of the parts that rule and the parts that are ruled. The political scientist [*politicus*] looks at the latter; the jurist looks at the former."[107]

Grotius here deliberately juxtaposes the two stories we have been looking at, the juridical and the political. Both of them offer themselves as complete analyses of the *respublica* or commonwealth: either as moral body, or as form of government, a *state*. Grotius puts the latter in its place as an incomplete understanding of the commonwealth. But he does so at

---

of it as pervading the whole body like the soul, without, however, filling out his meaning properly or making this any more than a simile: ibid., lib. II, cap. 6, sect. 6, n. 6.

[104] Ibid., cap. 9, sect. 6. Grotius gives the example of Capua, which the Romans decided that *tanquam urbs habitaretur*: see below, ch. 8, p. 211.

[105] Ibid., cap. 9, sect. 8, n. 1.

[106] D. 5.1.76.

[107] Grotius, *De iure belli*, cap. 9, sect. 8, nn. 1, 2.

some cost to the "moral body" analysis with which he himself had started out. It seems clear, although Grotius does not say so, that the *species* of the *civitas* at which the jurist looks—the association of right and sovereign power, the full and perfect association of civil life—is the moral body of Book I. But that just *is* the *civitas*, not a *species* of the *civitas*. Here in Book II, by contrast, the moral body is only a *species*—albeit apparently the more consequential *species*—of the artificial body that is the *civitas*. The two analyses simply do not join up.

I want to turn finally to look at Hobbes's account of the state in the light of these alternative models. Hobbes was deeply opposed to the "moral body" account of the scholastic natural law tradition. As we have seen with Grotius and Suárez, it was, even at its most "absolutist," dangerous in positing the body of the people as the underlying subject of *potestas* or *imperium*, a subject that cannot be destroyed without destroying the very notion of sovereign power. It was also open to the charge of dividing the sovereignty. At its most popular, it was the tenet of revolutionaries.[108] As such, the alternative model of Arnisaeus must have looked much more appealing: either *imperium* or disunited multitude. But Hobbes appreciated the power of the juridical account of the *creation* of sovereign power—something the political Aristotelian tradition could not offer—as well as its huge parallel strength in involving the people in their own subjection. The task was, then, to create the power without creating the body; and Hobbes accomplished this with his startling new account of the original covenant. Individuals covenant, each with each, to give up their natural liberty by submitting their will to the will of one man or body of men, and in so doing they create in one and the same instant both the sovereign power itself, *summum imperium*, and the holder or subject of sovereign power, the sovereign.[109] They themselves are never the subject of sovereign power. This strategy elides both the "moral body" of Suárez's account and the *civitas* that persists, albeit unformed, in the thought of Arnisaeus, and exists as an identifiable juridical structure in Bodin and Althusius. For Hobbes, the *civitas* slides into the state, and the citizen, the *civis*, has no identity other than as subject or *subditus*.

From the outset, in *The elements of law*, Hobbes insisted that what is being created thereby is a "union," one thing out of many.[110] As we have seen, the stress on unity marks not only the legal and Stoic-inspired ac-

---

[108] See Q. Skinner, "Hobbes on representation," *European Journal of Philosophy* 13 (2005), 155–84, for Hobbes's opposition to parliamentarian notions of the body of the people and their claims to represent it.

[109] Hobbes, *Leviathan*, ch. 17, p. 120.

[110] Hobbes, *The elements of law*, Part I, ch. 19, p. 103; *De cive*, cap. V, sect. IX, p. 134; *Leviathan*, ch. 17, p. 120.

counts but also Suárez's understanding of the "moral body." It was in *De cive*, however, that Hobbes first used the language of "soul" to describe the sovereign, in explicit opposition to the "head" conception that dominates the scholastic accounts.

> Those who have the habit of comparing the city and the citizens with a man and his members almost all of them say that he who has the sovereignty in the city is, in relation to the whole city, what the head is in relation to the whole man. But it is plain from what we have said before that he who is furnished with this sovereignty (be this a man or a council) has in respect of the city the nature of a soul, not a head. For it is the soul by which a man has a will, that is, can will and not-will; and thus it is by him who has the sovereignty, and [not] otherwise, that the city has a will, and can will and not-will. It is rather the assembly of counsellors that should be compared with the head ... for it is the function of the head to advise, as it is of the soul to command.[111]

Hobbes here clearly rejected the "directive" understanding of *potestas* that we have seen govern the scholastic accounts from their ultimate debt to Aquinas and the medieval concept of *regimen*. The directive capacity is relegated to counsel, not command.

Hobbes in *Leviathan* developed the language of soul further, by involving it in the contrast between nature and artifice that pervades the work. In the Introduction to *Leviathan*, he wrote that "by Art is made that great leviathan called a common-wealth, or state, (in latine civitas) which is but an Artificiall Man ... in which, the *Soveraignty* is an Artificiall *Soul*, as giving life and motion to the whole body."[112] In chapter 21, he asserted that the "Soveraignty is the Soule of the Common-wealth; which once departed from the Body, the members doe no more receive their motion from it." In these passages, differently from *De cive*, it is the sovereignty, the *summum imperium*, that is the soul, rather than its holder. But in the chapter on the dissolution of the commonwealth, chapter 29, the soul is once again the sovereign: "the Sovereign is the publique Soule, giving Life and Motion to the Common-wealth; which expiring, the Members are governed by it no more, than the Carcasse of a man, by his own departed (though Immortall) Soule."[113] The chapter that is new in *Leviathan*, chapter 16 on persons and personation, makes clear on a close reading the difference between the sovereign and the state: the sovereign is an artificial person, that is, one whose words and actions represent those

---

[111] Hobbes, *De cive*, cap. VI, sect. XIX, p. 148.
[112] Id., *Leviathan*, p. 9.
[113] Ibid., p. 230.

Figure 3 Thomas Hobbes, *Leviathan* (London, 1651). Reproduced by kind permission of the Syndics of Cambridge University Library.

of another, and the person that he bears is the person of the state. It is as if the sovereign were an actor on stage wearing the mask of *civitas*. But, unlike any natural person, the state that he personates, the *civitas*, only exists as a person through his personation—that is, it is a person purely by fiction—and hence tends to slip into the artificial person of the sovereign, or simply to disappear entirely.[114]

For the very same reason (and this is really just another way of putting the same point) sovereign power does not exist except as it is held by some man or men, which means that the state does not exist except in the specific form of being a monarchy, an aristocracy or a democracy. In *De cive*, these are explicitly described as *species* of *civitas*, although the sense seems closer to our own usage of the term than to the technical meaning it has in Book II, chapter 9 of Grotius's *De iure belli*.[115] The major difference is, of course, that Hobbes has entirely lost the other *species* of the *civitas*, the moral body, that Grotius had borrowed from the scholastic analysis to keep the continued identity of the state even under change of regime. In Grotius's terms in that chapter, Hobbes provides an account that is solely that of a *politicus*, a political scientist, not of a jurist. And yet that is not quite right. If we compare Hobbes's account with that of Arnisaeus, we see that he is making a serious Arnisaean mistake in equating the state with the *civitas*, the city. But it is not a Hobbesian mistake. Hobbes deliberately combined both what Arnisaeus criticised and what he proposed instead. He usurped the juridico-genetic account of the natural law tradition, the product of which is the moral body, to produce the artificial body that belongs to a very different mode of analysis. But, in a tense negotiation, he combined that artificial body with the organic analogy to produce the artificial *man*, Leviathan.[116] As a pure structure of *imperium*, what Hobbesian individuals create is something that looks very much like Arnisaeus's state. But, unlike in Arnisaeus, and precisely because they created it, the state *is* defined "through the men themselves," as a multitude of men united in one person. The city *is* the state. This is the revolutionary strength of Hobbes's conception, and what he tried so hard to make his contemporaries see in the extraordinary frontispiece to *Leviathan*.[117]

---

[114] See the analysis in D. Runciman, *Pluralism and the personality of the state* (Cambridge: Cambridge University Press 1997), pp. 8–13, 19.

[115] Hobbes, *De cive*, cap. VII, sect. I, p. 150; the corresponding chapter in *Leviathan* has "kinds" for *species*: ch. 19, p. 129.

[116] See Runciman, *Pluralism,* pp. 21–23, for a discussion of the problems involved.

[117] See fig. 5. As Skinner notes, however (*Hobbes and republican liberty*, p. 190), Hobbes was unable satisfactorily to render in visual terms the idea of the soul, and hence resorted to the more familiar imagery of the head.

CHAPTER SIX

the lives of subjects

In the last chapter we saw how the commonwealth or state is constructed as a union of human beings in a moral, juridical, or artificial body, the being of which is by definition different from that of the individual human beings by whom it is made or who constitute its matter. In one way or another, the civic balloon has gone up. But where does that leave the natural bodies of its members? In this chapter we turn to look at the relationship of the state to its subjects as necessarily physically embodied beings.

The primary way in which the commonwealth commands its subjects is through the medium of its law. As we saw in the previous chapter, Suárez holds that legislative power is convertible with supreme political power; and as we shall explore in more detail below, all the Jesuits with whom we are concerned think that for men to establish a human power to legislate irreducible to either God or nature is the same as for them to establish a commonwealth. The law is for the common good and obliges the community as a whole, and thus the ontological status of the law, as distinct from any particular command of a superior to an individual, is intimately tied to that of the body politic. As Salas put it, "union in positive laws is necessary to the unity of the commonwealth and the body politic, for they belong to the same body politic because they are governed by the same laws; nor would it be enough to have a living law, that is, a superior governing with temporary commands that are not perpetual and do not have the rationale of law: for it is necessary for the good of the community, which is perpetual, that there should be commands that are of themselves perpetual, and obligatory without any limitation of time."[1] Hobbes, having refused the existence of the moral body, could not accept the distinction between law and command in these terms; rather, he held that a law is a law whether it be passed on all the subjects, or only on particular provinces or professions, or just on certain individuals.[2] Nevertheless, he too, in chapter 21 of *Leviathan*, allowed the civil laws to mirror the ontological status of the commonwealth as an artificial man by describing them as artificial chains.[3] Arnisaeus, as we have seen, tied the existence of civil law to the *respublica* as the form of the city; and, while other Aristotelians may have disagreed with his analysis, they still saw civil law as the law not just of a throng or crowd of persons—by definition, a crowd has no law—but of a civil body of some kind. The metaphysics of the city and of its law are inseparably linked.

Our question, then, concerning the relationship of the state to the natural body of the individual can be framed in terms of the extent of the obligation, the "take," of the civil law. Now it is common to all our authors that by definition, the natural body is not civilly obliged. Incorporation into the state creates a moral, juridical, or artificial union, not a physical or natural union of bodies. In parallel, its members are bound not by physical chains but by law. Indeed, subjection to the state is precisely contrasted with the bodily subjection of enslavement. In one sense, therefore, the body is purely and simply excluded from the civic sphere. And yet the matter is infinitely more complex. Bodies are not purely natural, like an animal that accompanies the person: they are subject to the mind and will of individuals, the same mind and will by which those

---

[1] Juan de Salas, *Tractatus de legibus*, disp. 6, sect. 1, n. 4, fo. 98, col. 1. Cf. Gabriel Vázquez's distinction between a law and a command: law is a "common precept," in making which the superior acts "in the name of the commonwealth" whereas in giving a command to an individual or individuals, he acts "in his own name," as holding a special position of responsibility. Vázquez, *Commentarii in primam secundae*, disp. 151, cap. 3, n. 16, fo. 8, col. 2. In the former case, "the commonwealth speaks through [the prince] as if through its head": ibid., disp. 152, cap. 3, n. 33, fo. 32, col. 1. These conditions of universality and perpetuity and the consequent distinction between law and command were, however, denied by Rodrigo de Arriaga, on the basis of his nominalist metaphysics: "it is certain, that all men are nothing other than Peter, Paul and John; and if the commonwealth gave the prince jurisdiction to govern Peter when at the same time he governs John, it also gave it to govern Peter even if he did not govern Paul." Arriaga, *Disputationes theologicae in primam secundae*, tom. II, disp. 3, sect. 1, n. 5, fo. 24, col. 2.

[2] Hobbes, *Leviathan*, ch. 26, p. 183.

[3] Ibid., ch. 21, p. 147.

individuals are subject to the state. And while the state is not in any way
a natural body, it exercises its command through the medium of its offi-
cers who are bodily individuals and whose enforcement of its laws can
only have for its scope what is visible to them—that is, the physical acts
and traces of its subjects. It is axiomatic for our theorists that the mind
and will are largely hidden from the law and transparent only to God.
Individuals are subject, then, not *as* bodies but nevertheless *through* their
bodies. And while the law does not command bodies, but minds and wills,
the law enforces its commands by sanctions directed ultimately against
the body: corporal punishment or death, in the extreme case. Thus the
law systematically exploits its subjects' attachment to their own body; but
precisely in so doing, it recognises a lien that is far stronger than any tie
of its own. That link between body and soul is simply human life itself,
for the furtherance of which the state was instituted in the first place. Thus
the relationship of the state to the natural bodies of its subjects turns out
to be a much deeper question of its relation to their natural *lives*.

Let us begin with the conversation among the Jesuits with whom we
are by now familiar—Vázquez, Salas, Suárez, and Arriaga—and their common insistence that the obligation of the law covers only what they call
the "external acts" of the human being. There was support for this position in the rationale that Aquinas had offered, in his treatment of laws in
the *Prima secundae*, for the necessity of divine law: human judgement can
only concern exterior motions, and thus a divine law and a divine judge
are necessary to regulate their interior acts.[4] However, while Vázquez
handled the question in relation to the text of the *Prima secundae*, Suárez,
Salas, and Arriaga preferred to focus instead on something that Aquinas
had said when discussing the virtue of obedience in Question 104 of the
Secundae secundae. Here he had asked whether subjects are bound to obey
their superiors in all things, and had replied that "... an inferior is not
bound to obey his superior, if he commands something in a matter in
which the inferior is not subject. For Seneca says, *De beneficiis* Book III:
'A person is in error, if he thinks that servitude covers the whole man; for
the better part is excepted. Their bodies are liable, and given over to their
masters; but the mind is independent, *sui juris.*' And therefore," Aquinas
went on, "in matters that pertain to the interior motion of the will, a man
is not bound to obey man, but God alone; but a man is bound to obey
man in those things that are enacted externally by means of the body."[5]
That Aquinas had in mind not just the servitude of personal slavery but
the servitude involved in subjection to law is clear from his next question,

---

[4] Aquinas, *ST* 1a2ae, q. 91, a. 4.
[5] Aquinas, *ST* 2a2ae, q. 104, a. 5; Seneca, *De beneficiis*, III. 20. We have already encountered
this quotation in Arnisaeus's discussion of liberty: above, ch. 4, p. 101.

"whether Christians are bound to obey the secular powers." Here he repeated his previous assertion: "the servitude, by which man is subject to man, pertains to the body, not to the soul, which remains free."[6]

Now one might find this quite a surprising thing for Aquinas to say. The Stoic overtones of this split between the internal and the external seem at odds with his treatment of human law in the *Prima secundae*. It is true that, even here, Aquinas did not reduce political government to moral government: men are governed to the common good, not their individual good, and in parallel the human law can only prescribe those acts of the virtues that can be ordained to the common good (and must even allow some vices, granted the frail nature of the multitude).[7] But this is not to suggest that subjection to the human law is a purely bodily affair. In Question 92 he argued, along with Aristotle, that the law of the human city, provided it is good absolutely speaking, will function to make men good absolutely, by habituating them to the moral virtues and disposing them to the theological virtues of faith, hope, and charity.[8] Aquinas's appropriation here of the Aristotelian thesis of moral habituation means that the city is not just a realm of purely external government; the law of the city may in the first instance have a coercive function in this respect, but ultimately it goes further. So he argued in Question 95 that it is certainly necessary for the law to coerce through force, and fear, so that at least malefactors might be prevented from disturbing the peace; but also so that "they themselves, through this kind of habituation, might be brought to the point where they do willingly, what they had formerly done through fear, and should in this way become virtuous."[9]

In the Dominican commentaries of Soto and Vitoria, we find a marked emphasis on this Aristotelian aspect of Aquinas's argument. Vitoria deliberately rejected the perspective of some who say that the laws are "like artificers, who do not aim at moral goodness, but at an artificial goodness"; on the contrary, he insisted, "the intention of the king is without doubt to make men good absolutely speaking and to direct them to virtue."[10] Soto equally argued that "all civil laws ... are to be instituted for the good of the soul, in which our felicity is in question.... For by the reason that man is born to felicity, by that same reason he is a civil animal."[11] However, Vitoria had also been very careful to argue that the end of the political community and its power is not the same as that of the church,

---

[6] Aquinas, *ST* 2a2ae, q. 104, a. 6.

[7] Ibid., 1a2ae, q. 96, a.2 and a.3.

[8] Ibid., q. 92, a. 1.

[9] Ibid., q. 95, a. 1.

[10] Vitoria, *Comentario al tratado de la ley*, q. 92, a.1, pp. 20–21.

[11] Soto, *De iustitia et iure*, lib. I, q. 2, a. 1.

and he had gone on from there to craft a delicate relationship between temporal and spiritual power. The former does not depend completely on the latter, because "even if there existed no spiritual power, nor any supernatural felicity, there would still be some kind of order in the temporal commonwealth, and some kind of power." Nevertheless, the temporal community is not fully independent vis-à-vis the spiritual, as it would be vis-à-vis another sovereign state; it is, instead, "a matter of dependency and hierarchy."[12] In the handling of Jesuit theologians, and especially the leading controversialist of the Society, Cardinal Robert Bellarmine (1542–1621), this became the contested doctrine of the "indirect power" of the pope in temporals.[13] Its corollary was a conception of political community as a sphere stripped of spiritual function and ordained solely towards "external peace."[14]

Francisco Suárez developed this position by drawing expressly on the theology of "pure nature" that he had earlier deployed in the context of the ultimate end of human life. Challenging the Thomist understanding of the continuity between natural and supernatural, Suárez held that there is no natural appetite in man for his supernatural end because there is no natural potential for that end. "Purely naturally," man is ordered only towards the end of natural felicity; his being ordered towards supernatural felicity is something *added* to that nature.[15] Suárez used this theological stance to argue that political power is "simply natural," *mere naturalis*, and therefore does not and cannot have for its end the supernatural felicity of the future life, except by some extrinsic relation. Neither does it have for its end the spiritual felicity of this life, because that felicity is a disposition intrinsically ordered to future, supernatural felicity and therefore equally falls outside the scope of civil power. Finally, "the civil legislative power, even considered purely naturally, does not have for its intrinsic and *per se* intended end the natural felicity of the future life, and not even the proper felicity of the present life insofar as it pertains to individual men in their aspects as particular persons. Its end is rather the natural felicity of the perfect human community of which it is charged

---

[12] Vitoria, *Relection I On the power of the church* (1532), q. 5, a. 4, tr. Pagden and Lawrance pp. 89, 91.

[13] See Höpfl, *Jesuit political thought*, ch. 14.

[14] Robert Bellarmine, *Disputationum de controversiis Christianae fidei, adversus huius temporis haereticos*, tom. II (Ingolstadt 1611), lib. III (*De laicis*), cap. 11, col. 651.

[15] Suárez, *De ultimo fine hominis*, esp. disp. 16, sect. 2. The classic studies of *pura natura* are by Henri de Lubac: *Surnaturel: études historiques* (Paris: Aubier 1946) and *Augustinisme et théologie moderne* (Paris: Aubier 1965). De Lubac's thought is discussed in G. Chantraine, "Le surnaturel: Discernement de la pensée catholique selon Henri de Lubac," *Revue Thomiste* 101 (2002), 31–51; the political ramifications are studied in Courtine, *Nature et empire de la loi*, ch. 2.

with the care, and of individual men in their aspect as members of such a city, that they might live in it in peace and justice, with a sufficiency of those goods that relate to the preservation and comfort of bodily life."[16] The city figures in this sense as a necessary condition of individual human felicity rather than the intrinsic locus of it, a position that was repeated by Arriaga with direct reference to Suárez.[17] Arriaga in particular deployed the externality of the civic function as a structuring principle to determine the limits of obligation.[18]

Suárez, then, used a theology that isolated the natural from the supernatural through the concept of "pure nature" to block the continuity between natural and spiritual felicity that had characterised the Dominican understanding of the end of the city. It was in this context that Suárez held that the civil power "does not care very much about internal acts."[19] This, he said, was the intention of Aquinas in his questions on human law in the *Prima secundae*. Civil law is there to govern the community, not individuals or even families; and men "communicate" with one another politically, that is, they are harmful or useful to one another, only in their external acts.[20] It is in this context, of the essential focus of the civil law on external rather than internal acts, that Suárez, Salas, and Arriaga all cited the passage from Aquinas on obedience in the *Secunda secundae*.[21] As Salas said in his development of the theme, "civil power is external, and is ordained for the sake of ruling an external community";[22] and he quoted Vázquez to the effect that "the law is the command of a superior, to which subjects are bound to conform according to their own mode; and therefore since it is peculiar to man among rational creatures to be corporeal, it is in corporeal, and external matters that he must conform to his superiors ... not in internal, in which he shares with the angels."[23] All of these authors, however, added a qualification on "external" and "corporeal" acts. By their own arguments, as we saw in chapter 3, law can only fall on moral acts, that is, acts that are the result of free will. As Suárez said, an external *human* act "cannot take place without an internal,

---

[16] Suárez, *De legibus*, lib. III, cap. 11, nn. 4–7.

[17] Arriaga, *Disputationes in primam secundae,* tom. II, disp. 13, sect. 9, fo. 148, cols. 1–2.

[18] Ibid., disp. 14, sects. 2 and 3.

[19] Suárez, *De legibus*, lib. III, cap. 11, n. 8.

[20] Ibid., nn. 7–8; cap. 13, n. 3.

[21] Ibid.; Salas, *Tractatus de legibus*, disp. 9, sect. 1, fo. 193–96; Arriaga, *Disputationes in primam secundae,* tom. II, disp. 14, sect. 3, subsect. 1, fo. 152, col. 1. For obedience as a leitmotif of all Jesuit thinking on government, see Höpfl, *Jesuit political thought*, esp. pp. 26–34, although I do not think that it has quite the explanatory force that he attributes to it.

[22] Salas, *Tractatus de legibus*, disp. 9, sect. 1, n. 5, fo. 195, col. 2.

[23] Vázquez, *Commentarii in primam secundae*, disp. 160, cap. 2, n. 3, fo. 71, col. 1.

for the external act has its quality as human and moral from the internal act, as providing its moral form ... just as a human being is made up of body and soul."[24] How then to save the principal thesis of the externality of the city and its law? It was Gabriel Vázquez—otherwise anathema to Suárez—who supplied the answer, which is that *indirectly* the human law must, and does, command those acts of will that are involved in external acts. However, it has no need to, and cannot, command purely internal acts.[25]

Rodrigo de Arriaga offered an interesting coda to this discussion, considering the question of external acts that are hidden or "occult." The common opinion, put forward by Suárez among others, was that while purely internal acts are *per se* occult, external acts are only *per accidens* occult in certain circumstances. They are of their nature cognisable, and thus they remain appropriate subject matter for the human law and the human judge (should they come to light). Hence it is a crime to act externally against the law in secret. Arriaga objected, however, that there is no difference between these two kinds of occult act as regards the "external and common administration of the commonwealth." The law governs Peter not as a private person but as a public person, a member of the commonwealth, and "making a moral one with the others" as Suárez himself tells us. "But in that action which is totally occult, Peter conducts himself as if he were, as I said, a solitary man, and in no way a member of the community.... therefore his action does not fall under the law."[26] Arriaga took care to specify that he did not mean acts that are in some way harmful, like selling something at higher than the set price on the quiet, because these involve third parties and therefore the community and its law. But supposing there is a law forbidding drinking from golden cups. A man has such a cup in his bedroom, and unobserved by anyone—and in the dark, if you like—pours water into it and drinks. Such an act, according to Arriaga, is "very probably" not the subject of civil law: not in the sense that the civil law cannot possibly cognise it (but it would be a crime if it could), but in the sense that it is *not a crime at all*.[27]

These related arguments of Salas, Suárez, and Arriaga turn on the conception of the commonwealth as a particular kind of community, a sharing or communication of our corporeal lives with those of others for the sake of an external security without which they cannot be lived at all.

[24] Suárez, *De legibus*, lib. III, cap. 13, n. 1.
[25] Vázquez, *Commentarii in primam secundae*, disp. 160, cap. 3; cf. Salas, disp. 9, sect. 1, n. 7, fo. 196, col. 2; Suárez, *De legibus*, lib. III, cap. 13, n.9 (who, however, does not cite Vázquez directly). For Vázquez's position in more detail, see L. Vereecke, *Conscience morale et loi humaine selon Gabriel Vazquez S.J.* (Tournai: Desclée 1957), esp. ch. 5.
[26] Arriaga, *Disputationes in primam secundae,* tom. II, disp. 14, sect. 3, subsect. 1, n. 15, fo. 152.
[27] Ibid., subsect. 1, n. 18, and 2, n. 19, fo. 153.

But as their own reasoning demonstrates, the obligations involved in membership of this community cannot be handled simply by shaving off the body from the soul. A human being is a complex of both, and to that extent subject both externally and internally. Living within the city is one aspect of a life that is both physical and moral. It demands a particular form of *regimen* or government, one that is not the same as the domestic government of a family or the moral government of an individual.[28] Nevertheless, political life cannot be entirely hived off from moral life on the grounds of its externality; the one is intrinsically connected to the other. Thus, asking whether the law has any moral effect on the individual, Arriaga considered the case of a law prohibiting someone from going down one street and obliging him to go down another. Certainly, this does not make him any morally better, "if we consider purely the physical motion." But if we consider the danger to his body or soul that the legislator is trying to prevent, then he is certainly rendered better thereby.[29] Equally, but from the opposite direction, Suárez rejected the view that civil law can only command in matters of justice and not of the other virtues, a view that, as he himself admitted, had some plausibility given what he himself had said about the specific and limited end of the city. The plausibility is specious, however: securing the external end of the city demands all the virtues, and "the civil laws intend to make good men, because they cannot otherwise make good citizens."[30]

By the same token, the fact that the city is a community or communication in external matters does not mean that the law obliges only to external punishments and not in conscience. As Cardinal Bellarmine put it in his treatise *De laicis*, part of his massive controversial work "against the heretics of this time," "from the fact that political power is temporal, and its end is external peace … it is a correct inference to argue that that power cannot oblige except to acts that are temporal and external; but *not* that it cannot oblige in conscience." Civil law is called "temporal" by reason of its object, but is nonetheless in itself a "spiritual" thing.[31] This obligation in conscience was, however, not an easy thing to establish on philosophical grounds. Detaching the city both from an individual's supernatural end and even from his moral end threatened correspondingly to detach its law from both divine and natural law, making it a crime to break it but in no way a sin. There was, moreover, a distinct Catholic

---

[28] Suárez, *De legibus*, lib. III, cap. 11, n. 8, demonstrating the continuing importance of the inherited medieval conception of *regimen* even while the specifically theological argument is radically new. See above, ch. 5, p. 130.

[29] Arriaga, *Disputationes in primam secundae,* tom. II, disp. 5, sect. 1, subsect. 1, n. 4, fo. 40.

[30] Suárez, *De legibus*, lib. III, cap. 12, nn. 3, 8.

[31] Bellarmine, *Disputationum de controversiis Christianae fidei*, tom. II, lib. III, cap. 11, col. 651, emphasis mine.

tradition of arguing that the civil law does not, of itself, have the power
to oblige in conscience. The fifteenth-century chancellor of the University of Paris, Jean Gerson, had argued in his *De vita spirituali animae* of
1402 that only God has the power to legislate under penalty of eternal
death, and that therefore any obligation in conscience to obey a civil law
is in fact an obligation to obey divine law, under which he subsumed
natural law. No transgression of a human law, as such, could ever be a
mortal sin.[32]

With varying degrees of severity, however, all the Jesuits attacked Gerson's position, as indeed had their Dominican predecessors. They regarded
it as undermining not just the civil law but the civil power itself, in a way
that was dangerously close to the anarchism with which they tarred Protestant understandings of "Christian liberty." Domingo de Soto had argued
that *all* human laws bind in conscience, and that the penalty attached to
them is no more than a function of this, there being no legitimate power
to impose a penalty on an act that is not a sin in conscience. Suárez did
not agree: he thought that some human laws do bind only to a civil penalty.[33] But even here, there is some obligation in conscience, that is, to pay
the penalty; and other human laws directly oblige to their performance
in conscience. If we look at Suárez's arguments for this, however, we find
an uncomfortable heap of separate reasons. The first is the thesis of Romans 13, that the civil legislator acts as the minister of God. To the objection that on the contrary, he has his power from the human community,
which could have restricted him to legislating without any obligation in
conscience, Suárez replied that at least the community itself will have the
power to oblige in conscience (and moreover that such a legislator would
not be a "full prince"). The second is the divine and natural law precept
to obey the just laws of legitimate superiors. Does this not reduce the
obligation of civil law to divine or natural law, ceding Gerson's position?
Suárez argued not, because the civil law is the proximate cause of the
obligation, which would not exist without it and which can therefore be
said to be simply speaking an obligation of civil law. His third argument
was, precisely, an argument from government or regime. So he said: "government without the power to coerce is ineffective and easily contemned.
But coercion without the power to oblige in conscience is either morally
impossible, because just coercion presupposes guilt ... or certainly is wholly
insufficient, because in many cases of necessity it would not be possible
to defend the commonwealth sufficiently."[34]

[32] See Vereecke, *Conscience morale*, ch. 1, "Une querelle autour de Gerson."
[33] Suárez, *De legibus*, lib. III, cap. 22, n. 6.
[34] Ibid., cap. 21, nn. 5, 6, 7, and 8.

The shakiness of Suárez's reasoning did not go unnoticed. Rodrigo de Arriaga agreed with him that civil law has the power to bind in conscience, but disagreed with his grounds, which he summarised as follows: "this power seems necessary to the good government of the human commonwealth ... for [otherwise] no one would bother about [the laws]." This is not very persuasive, however, because "civil laws lead men to observe them more by the coercive force that the commonwealth exercises, than by any other means, as Father Suárez himself often insinuates. But that coercive force exists solely in punishment in the external forum, coercing the subject by force, if he is in no other wise willing, to perform what is commanded."[35] Thus eliminating Suárez's third reason, Arriaga concentrated on the second, that natural law obliges subjects to obey legitimate superiors without the obligation of civil law simply reducing to that of natural law.[36] But he offered a refinement focusing on the precise nature of the act of will involved in subjection, developing a far more individualistic line of thought than we find in the other Jesuits we have studied. He suggested that the act of will involved in our subjection is either similar to a vow of obedience, which does bind in conscience to its performance, or to a contract. Pursuing the second analogy, he argued that the alienation of our liberty in subjecting ourselves to the civil power is similar to the alienation of anything else. Once I have given you my cloak, for example, it is morally wrong for me to use it without your permission. Likewise when once I have given the sovereign my liberty, it is morally wrong for me to use it at my own pleasure.[37] Arriaga then faced the objection that the obligation in conscience not to use the cloak is directly and purely a natural law obligation, defeating his argument about the irreducible obligation of civil law. He agreed that metaphysically there is no difference between the two cases, but still insisted that morally there is, because the alienation of liberty is about jurisdiction and obedience whereas the alienation of a cloak is not.[38] Arriaga's unwillingness to concede that subjection to authority is *morally* comparable to any contractual obligation demonstrates the continuing gulf between Jesuit political thought and any purely contractarian theories of political obligation.

If we turn now to the Protestant Aristotelian literature, we find that the body figures in a very different way in the context of the obligation of

---

[35] Arriaga, *Disputationes theologicae in primam secundae*, tom. II, disp. 16, sect. 1, nn. 7–8, fo. 178, col. 1–2.
[36] Ibid., and sect. 2; cf. disp. 4, sect. 4.
[37] Ibid., disp. 16, sect. 1, n. 9, fo. 178, col. 2.
[38] Ibid., sect. 2, n. 12, fo. 179, col. 1.

the law. Here we take up the discussion of liberty that was deferred from chapter 4 on the grounds that it is not a discourse of natural liberty in the sense that we were discussing in that chapter, that is, as an essential constituent of the juridico-genetic account of the commonwealth that characterises the natural lawyers. It is, however, an essential part of their defence of the power of the commonwealth and its law against a specifically political, democratic notion of liberty as a licence to act at one's pleasure, a liberty that is constrained by the law in what is, implicitly, a kind of slavery. In developing their position, political writers of the early seventeenth century drew heavily on the complex and fraught discussion of the legal definition of liberty that involved some of the best legal minds of the late sixteenth century.

Let us begin with Pierre Grégoire, the French Catholic lawyer whose political treatise, the *De republica* of 1596, we examined in the last chapter. Much less well known is his juridical treatise, the *Syntagma iuris* of 1582, which dates from some years previously but is equally innovative. Nowhere is it more so than in its consideration of the legal definition of liberty, which, to repeat, is "a natural faculty of doing that which pleases anyone [to do], except it be prohibited in something by force or law." As we saw in chapter 4, it was common to all the lawyers to understand this passage as defining liberty as a faculty *compatible with*, rather than *compromised by*, the restraints imposed by these "prohibitions" (presumably precisely because they are part of the definition, although this is not made clear). The challenge, then, was to understand what these prohibitions restrain if it is not liberty itself. Pierre Grégoire handled the problem by distinguishing between the faculty, as a power or possibility of action, and the act of doing that issues from it. Liberty as a natural faculty is an "innate power" of doing, or living, as you will, but it does not necessarily issue in an act. This consideration allows us to understand the exceptions of which the Roman law speaks. "And therefore although liberty is a natural faculty of doing what you will, nevertheless the act can be impeded (*impediri*) either externally (*extrinsecus*) or internally (*intrinsecus*)." An act is impeded externally by force, "by which the liberty of doing something is impeded even while the faculty still exists in the man: for it is not taken away, nor does it cease to be, just because it cannot operate. Thus, a man is no less an enemy for being conquered and subjected by his enemy by force: for force is the impact of a greater thing, which cannot be resisted and against which defence is little use." But we can equally think of force as impeding internally, in the form of our passions: "Aristotle says that those things that happen through cupidity happen through force intrinsically." And it is in both these ways, Grégoire went on, that "the faculty of liberty is prohibited from acting freely: just as, too, when law obstructs an evil act, so that it does not issue from the faculty, and conquers it so that it does not happen." For the law "is stronger, in having coercive force, and in striking fear by the terror of punishment."[39] Law, then, obstructs the act of liberty on the part of those who wish to act wrongly. Here in this passage, it does so in a dual way, both externally through force and internally through fear. Earlier on, however, Grégoire had suggested that force falls "on the body in external things; but the prohibition of law compels chiefly the soul."[40]

On the basis of this distinction between the two types of impediment, Grégoire posited a dual servitude and equally a dual liberty, of body and of soul, which can be either conjoined or separated in a man. We can see the attraction of this for one of Grégoire's philosophical leanings, because it allowed him to introduce philosophical considerations of the natural difference between human beings, considerations that the Roman law excludes. So, he said, the good, who command their own cupidity, are not impeded internally and are thus free in their souls even if they serve in their bodies. But there can be a natural slave, whose reason, as Aristotle says, does not fit him to command himself; and this man is a slave in his soul even if he is not subject to the power of a master. A man is also unfree in his soul if he is a slave to money or good fortune, or to fear: "he who contains himself only for fear of the punishment of the laws, he too merits being called a slave";[41] "those who do what is right through fear of the law, these indeed are under the servitude of the law."[42] Thus Grégoire saved liberty under the law by appropriating the Stoic paradox that the wise man is free; that is, as Cicero says, it is only the good man who in fact lives as he wills.[43] The laws do not limit this "true liberty"; indeed they conserve and foster it. For this reason, their coercive force is not, in fact, properly force, but a kind of medicine by which the evil are rescued from their own "voluntary servitude" and restored to "healthy liberty."[44]

An entirely different solution to the problem of the legal definition of liberty was offered by Alberico Gentili in a work published the next year, 1583, entitled *Lectiones et epistolae quae ad ius civile pertinent*, devoted to problem passages of Roman law. Here Gentili *opposed* the legal definition to the philosophical authority of Cicero, who says that liberty is the power

[39] Pierre Grégoire, *Syntagma iuris* (Lyon 1582), pars. II, lib. XIV, cap. 1, fo. 224.

[40] Ibid., lib. XI, cap. 1, fo. 148.

[41] Ibid., lib. XIV, cap. 1, fo. 224.

[42] Ibid., lib. XI, cap. 1, fo. 151.

[43] Ibid., lib. XIV, cap. 1, fo. 224: "Cicero says that 'liberty is the power of living as you will. Who therefore lives as [reading *ut* for *et*] he wills, except he who follows what is right? ... who does not obey the laws for fear, but follows and cultivates them because he judges it to be in the highest degree salutary.'" Likewise lib. XI, cap. 1, fo. 150: "Cicero, following the philosophy of the Stoics."

[44] Ibid., lib. XI, cap. 1, fo. 150.

of living as you will.[45] The Roman law is better than a thousand philosophers, if only we read it aright.[46] So, then, he said, some interpreters have suggested that the two exceptions (force and *ius*) refer to two different things: force to the servitude of the *ius gentium* (by which is commonly meant, although Gentili does not spell it out, captivity, originally in war); *ius* to the servitude of the civil law (*ius civile*). This interpretation is faulty for two reasons. Firstly, servitude that is legal under the *ius gentium* is precisely *ius*, not force. And as regards the second element, this interpretation does not separate out liberty from "unbridled licence" (*licentia effraenis*), which "we cannot call liberty without the confusion not only of words but of things."[47] The solution Gentili offered is that we are to understand the two exceptions as specific *differentiae* that qualify the genus of "natural faculty" so as to isolate "liberty" from any other species of it. So, the first exception—"except it be prohibited by force"—constitutes by a negative procedure the first specific difference of liberty. On the Roman law definition, liberty is something that is compatible with being prohibited or "impeded" by force. It cannot, therefore, be the specific faculty that Gentili with some hesitation ("so to speak") called *libertas facti*, the simple liberty of acting.[48] For this kind of faculty is *incompatible with the use of force, which takes it away. By inference, then, liberty is not a *facultas facti* but a *facultas iuris*, a juridical status, which cannot be destroyed except by a deed that itself has juridical sanction. We proceed likewise with the second exception, "except it be prohibited by *ius*." Liberty is by definition something compatible with being prohibited by *ius*, and this separates it off from the specific faculty that is *licentia* or licence, which cannot be limited by *ius*—and Gentili made plain that by this he meant laws—without ceasing, by definition, to be licence.[49]

Liberty, then, is "a faculty of doing what you will even if impeded by force or law." But if liberty is a *facultas impedita*, a faculty subject to impediment, then what—and this was a common objection, as we saw in chapter 4—is the difference between liberty and servitude, which is equally a *potestas impedita*? The difference is that servitude is a faculty that is al-

---

[45] Alberico Gentili, *Lectionum et epistolarum quae ad ius civile pertinent libri IV* (London 1583), lib. III, cap. V, p. 175.

[46] Diego Panizza, in his study *Alberico Gentili, giurista ideologico nell'Inghilterra elisabettiana* (Padua: La Garangola 1981), p. 43, places this work largely within Gentili's project of combating the philological methods of humanist jurisprudence. However, this passage points to the broader conception of the autonomy and superiority of law to other disciplines that he would develop more fully later on vis-à-vis theology. See below, ch. 7, p. 191.

[47] Gentili, *Lectiones*, lib. III, cap. V, p. 175.

[48] Ibid., p. 176. Gentili does not want to call it any kind of "liberty" because of course it is not liberty on his reading. He would prefer simply "faculty."

[49] Ibid., p. 177.

ways impeded. We can see this if we pay attention, as even the most recent commentators have not, to the crucial little word *quid* in the definition: "except if it be prohibited in something [*quid*] by force or law." For "it is not the case that in a slave 'something' is prohibited; but the very slave himself is prohibited."[50] He simply does not have any faculty left at all; this is, precisely, servitude. This solution was also put forward (without reference to Gentili) by Hugues Doneau, writing in 1589. Like Gentili, Doneau avoided importing a distinction between different senses of liberty in order to salvage liberty under the law. The law, he said, does not just prohibit immoral actions, but lots of things that are perfectly acceptable in themselves; and still we are free under the law. How so? Here he underlined the importance of *quid*.

> And clearly this definition would be vicious, if it were said without limitation, "unless prohibited by force or law": so that someone could be called free who was prohibited by law from acting in any way, even if all things were prohibited him. But in fact the words are "unless he be prohibited in something by force or law": so that we should understand that someone is free even if he is prohibited from doing something by law. And this correctly distinguishes a freeman from a slave. For freemen are those who are prohibited from doing many things, not all; but slaves by the law of nations are prohibited from doing everything, so that nothing is left them, since they are clearly in the *dominium* of their masters."[51]

These discussions were picked up and transformed into a specifically political understanding of liberty by Henning Arnisaeus in his *De republica* of 1615. We saw in chapter 4 how Arnisaeus had used the language of "natural faculty" to distinguish a natural master from a natural slave by the possession or otherwise of free will, liberty of contradiction. But this sense of liberty, on which the Stoics depend for their paradox that the wise man is free, has no place in politics: "here, where we are talking about political liberty, we should not attend to this, because it remains equally free in slave and freeman, subject and king, as Seneca admits."[52] Political liberty must rather be measured not from the pure freedom of the will, but from the freedom to carry out those acts that are commanded by the will. Putting the matter in the terms of the Roman law definition, liberty cannot simply be measured from the faculty, "which is always free,

---

[50] Ibid.

[51] Doneau, *Commentarii de iure civili*, lib. II, cap. 9, fo. 84. Doneau distinguished "slaves by the law of nations" from other conditions of servitude that are not absolute, and argued that these are not properly slaves in the sense in question here.

[52] Arnisaeus, *De republica*, lib. I, cap. 3, n. 5.

and liable (*obnoxius*) to no power," but from the "impediment that is in-
terjected between the faculty and the act."[53] But this means that liberty,
contrary to the interpretations of all the lawyers, is *not* compatible with
being prohibited by force, which Florentinus was therefore wrong to
include in his definition. Force is always an impediment to liberty, as we
can see from the very origins of servitude in the forcible and violent
subjection of those who are captured in war. Unlike the lawyers Gentili
and Doneau, then, who take the slavery of the *ius gentium* to be a legal
impediment, for Arnisaeus it is always an impediment of force, something
that gets between the human will and what it actually wants to do. And
everything that operates in this way necessarily diminishes liberty. However, Arnisaeus insisted, "not every diminution of liberty induces slavery,
as Aristotle says the common people in a democracy persuade themselves.... For if liberty is to be measured from any kind of impediment to
action, and limitation of licence, then no one on earth will be free. For
we are all compelled to be subject to majesty, and majesty to God and to
nature."[54] Human laws do coerce, then, in the sense that they are impediments to action and a function of being subject to a superior power. But
Arnisaeus held, and here he reverted to the sort of position we find in
Grégoire, that what they limit is not true liberty, but licence. We are prevented from doing everything we might have a whim to, but we are not
prevented from doing everything that a human being *naturally* wills to
do. The command of good laws furnishes us with a liberty that is distinct
from licence, a liberty that is only for good actions. Law is therefore not
forcible—contrary to the natural freedom of the mind—in the way that
slavery is forcible.[55] This is the difference between subjects and slaves.

In the light of this discussion, I want to turn now to Hobbes's discussion of liberty under *imperium* in chapter 9 of *De cive*. In this chapter
Hobbes, having founded the commonwealth on the surrender of natural
liberty, considered the liberty that individuals possess within the commonwealth, and he did so in implicit opposition to rival, "democratic"
understandings of freedom. "Commonly, to do everything at our whim,
and that, with impunity, is thought to be liberty; not to be able to do so,
slavery: which cannot happen in the city, and consistently with the peace
of the human race: because a city without sovereign power and right of
coercion, is none."[56] To get out of this impasse, Hobbes offered a definition of liberty as nothing other than the absence of impediments to motion. As we have seen, the terminology of "impeded" and "impediment"

[53] Ibid., n. 15.
[54] Ibid., n. 7.
[55] Ibid., nn. 11–13.
[56] Hobbes, *De cive*, cap. IX, sect. IX, p. 167.

is common to the legal and Aristotelian discussion. If Hobbes offered his definition as a political-scientific replacement of the legal definition, as, given the context, it is highly likely he did, then what strikes us is the absence of any reference to a "faculty."[57] Arnisaeus had removed the faculty from political consideration, because it always remains intact, and insisted that political liberty must be measured from the absence of any impediment coming between the faculty and the act. Hobbes went further in doing away with the faculty altogether. Liberty just is being unimpeded in act. Impediments, he pursued, fall into two types, and these distinguish the slave who is purely captive from every other kind of servitude, of servant, child or subject. The first type consists in "absolute and external" impediments that physically bar a man from a particular action just like any other body; Hobbes's example is water. In this sense, everyone is equally free who is not chained or incarcerated. Hobbes called the kind of slave who is kept in chains or imprisoned an *ergastulus*; not every slave is one.[58] It seems clearly equivalent to the *vis*, the force, of the legal definition. As to the other kind of impediment, which holds the place of *ius* in the legal definition, Hobbes made a move very similar to Grégoire's in seeing it as located in our own internal passions, which for Hobbes (as we saw in chapter 2) are nothing other than the will. This second type of impediment Hobbes called "arbitrary," that is, a matter of our own choice in the sense of what we are capable of willing. The penalties attached by superiors to various actions function as arbitrary impediments, implicitly, though Hobbes does not say so, by exciting the passion of fear.

At this point, as we saw, Grégoire had translated the two types of impediment into two types of liberty, of the body and of the soul, and had argued that fear of the law works only on those who are enslaved in their souls in a kind of servitude of the will. This is a move that Hobbes did not make. Liberty is one thing, not being impeded in motion, and both types of impediment restrict liberty to a greater or lesser degree—the fewer there are, the more liberty you have. In the matter of freedom from arbitrary impediments, then, Hobbes went further than Doneau and Gentili to posit a kind of sliding-scale of liberty whereby a slave (so long as he is not in chains or incarcerated) is precisely *not* distinguished from a freeman in kind; the distinction is only in degree, in that the free citizen serves only the city, the servant a citizen as well.[59] In this consists "civil liberty."[60] However, Hobbes did not mean to encourage the thought that

---

[57] This is also suggested by Skinner, *Hobbes and republican liberty*, p. 108, to whose account of liberty in *De cive* I am much indebted here.
[58] Hobbes, *De cive*, cap. VIII, sect. II, p. 161.
[59] Ibid., cap. IX, sect. IX, p. 168.
[60] Ibid., p. 167.

the less afraid of the laws you are, the more civil liberty you will have.[61] Rather, in a passage that is far more akin to the sort of argument we found in Grégoire and Arnisaeus, Hobbes moved directly to argue for the beneficial character of being subject to the threat of punishments that operate in some way to save us from ourselves. He argued that one who is impeded in this way "is not oppressed with slavery, but governed and sustained," because he has all the liberty he needs to pursue life and health and is prevented from destroying himself.[62] This goes for a servant subject to the commands of a master; but it equally goes for a citizen subject to the commands of the civil law. Hobbes insisted in chapter 13 that laws are not there to take away the actions of human beings, but to direct them in a healthy way, just like water that is neither stagnant nor dissipated but flows vigorously.[63] Thus Hobbes, too, saved liberty under the law.

To function in this directive way, civil laws must necessarily have penalties attached to them, which, Hobbes argued, are not there to force but to form the will of the man.[64] But this does not mean that he thought of the civil laws as what the scholastics would call "purely penal"—that is, simply as a system of penalties. At the end of his chapter on laws in *De cive*, chapter 14, Hobbes took issue with those who interpret them this way.

> There are those who think that acts contrary to civil law—when the penalty is laid down in the law itself—are expiated if they undergo the punishment willingly, and that those who have paid the penalty that the law demanded are not guilty before God of a violation of the law of nature (although in violating civil law, we also violate natural laws, which command that civil laws be observed). As if the act were not prohibited by the law, but the penalty was laid down as the price by which the licence of doing what the law prohibits is put up for sale. By the same reasoning they could infer, that no transgression of the law is any sin, but that a man has by right the liberty that he has bought at his own peril.[65]

That is, if you are such a person that the fear of penalty does not function as an arbitrary impediment, then you are entirely at liberty in the sense of not juridically subject—you have that liberty *by right*. But this is not true. Like Suárez, Hobbes thought there could be a law that did not oblige to a deed, but simply laid down a penalty for doing otherwise. But not every civil law is like this; and if you presume that a law is purely

---

[61] This reading is proposed in Ludwig, *Wiederentdeckung*, p. 325.

[62] Hobbes, *De cive*, cap. IX, sect. IX, pp. 168, 167.

[63] Ibid., cap. XIII, sect. XV, pp. 202–203.

[64] Ibid., sect. XVI, pp. 203–204.

[65] Ibid., cap. XIV, sect. XXIII, pp. 217–18.

penal where it is not clear that it is, this is contempt of the law and a violation of natural law. Where there is doubt, violation of the civil law is to be presumed to be sin. Thus, as for the scholastics, civil law obliges to sin, an obligation that, as for them, always involves—even if it does not always *reduce to*—the obligation of natural law to obey the command of a legitimate superior.

This passage highlights the difference between the liberty that is restricted (or not) by arbitrary impediments to motion and the juridical liberty that is restricted by the obligation of civil law, which is a function of the obligation arising from covenant even if it ultimately rests on the obligation of natural law.[66] But civil liberty and what we might, anticipating *Leviathan*, call "the liberty of subjects," are held together by Hobbes's positive view of arbitrary impediments as governing and sustaining the individual. The two types of restriction—the former termed at one point in *De cive* a "natural obligation," the latter a purely juridical form of obligation[67]—dovetail in keeping him in security and beneficial agency. In *Leviathan*, however, the link is broken, due to Hobbes's further reworking of the notion of liberty. In chapter 21 of that work, "Of the liberty of Subjects," Hobbes again confronts a rival understanding of political liberty, although this time less overtly the Aristotelian, "democratic," view (in which it is slavery to live according to the laws rather than as one likes), and more the "republican" understanding of a "free" city like Lucca (in which it is slavery to be commanded by the arbitrary will of another).[68] But by this time, Hobbes had changed his mind. It is liberty from external impediments to motion, he says here, that just is liberty, "in the proper, and generally received meaning of the word." For liberty from arbitrary impediments, he has now substituted "the Liberty of Subjects," which is not measured in relation to physical chains, but in relation to the "Artificiall Chains" of civil law, "which they themselves, by mutuall covenants, have fastned at one end, to the lips of that Man, or Assembly, to whom they have given the Soveraigne Power; and at the other end to their own Ears." Fear is not now itself any impediment to liberty, or "natural obligation," but something that shores up the artificial

[66] Ibid., sect II, p. 206: "Covenant (*pactum*) obliges of itself; law (*lex*) holds a man obliged, in virtue of the universal covenant to render obedience."

[67] The restriction of liberty through "hope and fear" is categorised as a species of "natural obligation" ibid., cap. XV, sect. VII, p. 223 (the context is our natural subjection to God's almighty power, linking Hobbes's developing thought on liberty with the continuing issue of the legitimacy of de facto government). By contrast, Hobbes calls the obligations arising from covenant *vincula pactitia*, ibid., cap. VIII, sect. III, p. 161.

[68] For this latter sense of freedom, see Q. Skinner, *Liberty before liberalism* (Cambridge: Cambridge University Press 1998), as well as *Hobbes and republican liberty*. Clearly, the two conceptions, "democratic" and "republican," are not entirely distinct.

chains, which may be "made to hold, by the danger, though not by the difficulty of breaking them."[69]

The question of liberty, then, has been subordinated to the polarity between nature and artifice that governs this later work. The result is to elide *De cive*'s "civil liberty" completely, and to present instead an absolute contrast between "the liberty of subjects," an artificial latitude presented as a function of a purely verbal or artificial act, and what Hobbes in this chapter, and in this chapter alone, calls "natural liberty"—a physical, not a juridical condition (as it is elsewhere in the work). This allows Hobbes to counter the rival understanding of political liberty on a different basis: subjection to the sovereign does not affect your liberty, in the proper signification, at all. However, while this may be rhetorically more effective, it does not obviously represent a theoretical gain on the account in *De cive*. It creates a kind of two-world theory, a natural world of bodies in motion and the artificial world of the state; in parallel, it splits the subject, an artificial being, from the man, a natural being, who remains untouched by the state like an animal at large.[70] It makes the state apparently purely dependent on words, with legal penalties pushed into the uglier position of threats to back them up. But it is not clear that this is what Hobbes really wants in the context of the work as a whole. In chapter 30, on the office of the sovereign representative, he kept *De cive*'s understanding of the directive function of the law, though changing the simile: "the use of laws ... is not to bind the people from all Voluntary actions; but to direct and keep them in such a motion, as not to hurt themselves by their own impetuous desires, rashnesse, or indiscretion; as Hedges are set, not to stop Travellers, but to keep them in the way."[71] The "traveller" here is neither an artificial being nor a natural body in any kind of motion, but a human agent in pursuit of his good: the same individual, in the same pursuit, who originally deliberated upon the original covenant in an act of will that was both natural and artificial. And he is kept to that deliberation not simply by "terrour of legall punishment," but by coming to know (with the help of a little state education) his "natural obligation," under the laws of nature, to do so.[72] Thus, Hobbes does not lose all notion of natural obligation in *Leviathan*: the obligation to preserve ourselves, dictated by natural reason, continues to underpin our subjection. In consequence, it is not simply the subject who is obliged;

---

[69] Hobbes, *Leviathan*, ch. 21, pp. 146–47; for the disappearance of *De cive*'s concept of "natural obligation," see Ludwig, *Wiederentdeckung*, pp. 326–27, although (as will be clear from what I say below) my analysis does not entirely coincide with his.

[70] See Skinner, "Proper signification of liberty," p. 225; *Hobbes and republican liberty*, p. 171.

[71] Hobbes, *Leviathan*, ch. 30, pp. 239–40.

[72] Ibid., p. 232.

it is the man himself, who is bound into the commonwealth both by nature and by artifice.

We have so far been exploring how the obligation of civil law falls on
subjects who are necessarily physically embodied entities. I now want to
turn to consider how far the body, or, more precisely, bodily life, functions as a limit to that obligation. Let us begin with Johannes Althusius,
whose analysis belongs in some respects within the political consideration of liberty that we examined in the previous section of this chapter.
The first book of his *Dicaeologica* of 1617 devotes chapter 25 to an extensive discussion of the definition of liberty, in an interesting contrast with his
first legal work, the *Iuris romani libri duo* of 1586. As we saw in chapter 3,
Althusius in this work characterised *ius* in traditional legal terms as what
is *aequum* or equitable, the object of *ius* in the sense of the *ars boni et aequi*,
"the science of the good and the equitable." The work moves through a
series of Ramist dichotomies to *dominium*, then to power (*potestas*), and
then to "the private power of a master." This chapter discusses slaves who
have lost their liberty, but there is no discussion of what liberty is at all.[73]
The later *Dicaeologica* equally proceeds by successive differentiation through
to *potestas*, which is defined as "a domination with the right of command
and the necessity of obedience."[74] However, Althusius now proceeded to
specify that this power can be either over oneself or over another. Power
over oneself is liberty, and it is "the right and licit authority of acting at
one's own judgement; that is, of commanding and obeying oneself; or a
free power of doing or omitting something."[75]

Like Pierre Grégoire in his *Syntagma iuris*, Althusius split liberty into a
liberty of the body (*libertas corporis*) and a liberty of the mind (*libertas
animi*).[76] Unlike Grégoire, however, Althusius defined both of these as a
right.[77] The liberty of the body "is that, by which under civil law the free
use of the members of the body is conceded, so that everyone is allowed
to do, handle and enact whatever things are conceded by natural law, unless something [*quid*] is specifically excepted."[78] Here, Althusius has substituted "whatever things are conceded by natural law" for the "whatever
it pleases anyone" of the legal definition. He has thus removed at a stroke
both the spectre of licence and the existence of a purely physical liberty;

[73] Althusius, *Iuris romani libri duo*, lib. I, cap. xi, pp. 25–26.

[74] Id., *Dicaeologica*, lib. I, cap. xxv, n. 1, fo. 96.

[75] Ibid., n. 5, fo. 96.

[76] Ibid., n. 6.

[77] Christoph Strohm argues that the *Dicaeologica* is a kind of deliberate anti-*Syntagma*: *Calvinismus und Recht*, pp. 211–12.

[78] Althusius, *Dicaeologica*, lib. I, cap. xxv, n. 7; see the discussion of the corporal dimension
of freedom in Witte, *Reformation of rights*, pp. 167–70.

but he has also made *ius* in the sense of the liberty of using the body something that is primarily governed by the *ius* of natural law. His treatment of the demands of natural law comes earlier in the work, in chapter 13 of Book I under the heading *De jure communi*. "Right" here is defined objectively rather than subjectively as something that is laid down between persons, a rule, a norm;[79] "common *ius*" is "that which is written immediately on the minds of men by nature or by God," and which is called by various names, among them *ius naturale*.[80] Natural law in this sense divides into *officia*—duties—towards the self and *officia* towards the other, and the duties towards the self explicitly concern the individual's conduct and care of his bodily life. They are listed as self-defence against force and injury; self-conservation "through necessary means;" and self-propagation in the joining of male and female and the education of children.[81] Althusius thus protected the individual's relationship not merely with his body, but with his personal life insofar as it involves his body, by natural law, and created the conceptual space for this protection to regulate the specific exceptions of civil law; but he did not offer any detailed discussion of when and in what circumstances it might do so.

By contrast, the Jesuit literature developed an extensive casuistry on the question. The issue is principally handled in the question whether the civil law can oblige with the danger of death. Again, the crucial locus in Aquinas was the article on obedience in the *Secunda secundae* with which we began this entire discussion. Aquinas, having laid down that the law only binds those external acts that are carried out through the body, now lays down a further limitation: even "within this class of acts, man is not bound to obey man, but only God, in those things that pertain to the nature of the body; because all men are by nature equal; that is, in those things that belong to the sustenance of the body, and the begetting of children."[82] The influential Ingolstadt professor Gregory de Valentia glossed this in terms of the power of one human being over another in matters that concern bodily *necessity*: "a man is not obliged to obey another man in those things that are necessary for the nature of the body, either in respect of the species, like having children, or in respect of the individual, like eating or drinking."[83] Salas set Valentia alongside Aquinas and Soto as authorities for the opinion that human law can never oblige citizens to obey it if there is a danger of death, because "to preserve one's life is of

---

[79] Althusius, *Dicaeologica*, lib. I, cap. 13, nn. 1–2, fo. 35.

[80] Ibid., n. 13, fo. 36–37.

[81] Ibid., n. 15, fo. 37.

[82] Aquinas, *ST* 2a2ae, q. 104, a. 5.

[83] Gregory de Valentia, *Commentariorum theologicorum tomi quattuor*, tom. III (Ingolstadt 1595), disp. 7, q. 3, pt. 3, col. 2101.

the law of nature, and human law cannot prejudice natural law."[84] As we shall see, the reference to Soto is misleading and probably depends on Valentia, who had interpreted Soto as saying that "no purely human laws can of themselves oblige in a case where they cannot be obeyed without endangering life." If there is any such obligation in any particular case, it derives from a concurrent obligation of natural or divine law.[85]

Aquinas himself had not moved directly to connect the question of obedience with that of the danger of death, either in the *Secunda secundae* or in the *Prima secundae* on the question of obligation in conscience. The terms of the Jesuit discussion were instead originally set by Cardinal Cajetan in his commentary on the *Prima secundae*. Here, in the helpful paraphrase offered by Gabriel Vázquez, Cajetan presented two arguments as to why human law can oblige with the danger of death. The first is that the human being is a member of the commonwealth and therefore subordinate to the community as the part to the whole. Therefore, where the safety of the whole is in question, the life of the part can be endangered. This argument parallels (as we shall see further below) Aquinas's arguments for why capital punishment is licit, and therefore remains squarely in the terms of Thomist thought. His second argument, however, was more radical: if the human law can oblige in conscience, that is, to mortal sin—and it most certainly can—then it must be able to oblige to the death of the body, because the death of the body should always be accepted as a condition of avoiding mortal sin, that is, preserving the life of the soul. As Vázquez summed up in his usual logical way, the first argument posits that the human law *can* oblige with the danger of death; the second that it *always does*.[86] Domingo de Soto, however, and most of the Jesuits who followed him (the Louvain professor Leonard Lessius in his *De iustitia* of 1605, Vázquez, Salas, Suárez) took a much more cautious attitude. There are cases where the survival of the commonwealth requires that its commands oblige with the danger of death—cases for example of external attack, where the city requires people to fight, or of plague, where the commonwealth can oblige citizens to stay where they are. But where the survival of the commonwealth is not in question, human law cannot oblige in this way.[87] Vázquez was careful to make clear, however, that it is not the case that the obligation stands but that you are somehow given a licence to disobey. This would be to allow sin on the grounds of

[84] Salas, *Tractatus de legibus*, disp. 11, sect. 1, fo. 255; Salas ultimately steers "a middle course."

[85] Valentia, *Commentariorum theologicorum*, tom. II (Ingolstadt 1592), disp. 7, q. 5, pt. 6, cols. 965–66.

[86] Vázquez, *Commentarii in primam secundae*, disp. 161, cap. 1, n. 2, fo. 74, col. 2.

[87] Soto, *De iustitia et iure*, lib. I, q. 6, a. 4; Lessius, as for n. 95 below; Salas, as for n. 84 above; Suárez, *De legibus*, lib. III, cap. 30, nn. 4–5.

danger, which cannot be right. Rather, we are to understand that the obligation simply ceases to exist, on a presumption of equity. No human legislator can be interpreted as wanting to oblige a citizen to die except in the case of danger to the commonwealth, because such a law would be unreasonable and not possible, thus negating some of the essential conditions of law.[88]

The parallel discussion in our sources is whether the civil law can oblige *criminals* to the danger of death. Now all of them followed Aquinas in holding that the commonwealth can both kill and mutilate citizens who break its laws.[89] The argument here again is the whole/part analogy: for the safety of the whole, the "corrupt member" of the body can be simply excised, or a bit of him excised. But this is a different question from whether a criminal, once condemned to death, can be obliged to go to his death. Aquinas had handled this question explicitly in the *Secunda secundae*, stipulating that the criminal cannot be obliged to cooperate in his death, but he *is* obliged not actively to resist the magistrate.[90] This demand is put in terms of just war: if a criminal actively resisted the magistrate, the magistrate would have a just war against the criminal; therefore the criminal cannot have a just war against the magistrate, since it is impossible for there to be a war that is just on both sides. Soto broadly followed Aquinas here, but put it in his own language of natural rights. If a person is condemned to a corporal punishment, "he is only obliged to suffer, but not to do anything himself.... For the right of nature granted us to defend our own lives, excuses us from any obedience forcing us to lay hands upon ourselves"; therefore, "although in this case no one can resist by force, he cannot be constrained not to evade death by flight or by any other means."[91]

---

[88] Vázquez, *Commentarii in primam secundae*, disp. 161, cap. 2, n. 11, fo. 75. The condition of "possibility," originally from Isidore of Seville's *Etymologies* (V. 21), is discussed by Vázquez ibid., disp. 55, cap. 1, to the effect that the law cannot impose anything too difficult for normal human nature. Compare the analysis of moral possibility in Knebel, *Wille, Würfel und Wahrscheinlichkeit*, esp. pp. 143–56 and pp. 197–218. Knebel identifies two different senses: the first appeals to the idea of frequency, so that something is morally possible if it can happen often and without great difficulty, morally impossible if it can occur only very seldom and with great difficulty (ibid., p. 147); the second is connected rather with motivation, so that something is morally impossible if it directly contravenes an "extremely strong" (*vehementissima*) human inclination (ibid., p. 197, and see the example from the Peruvian Jesuit Leonardo de Peñafiel, ibid., p. 210: it is morally impossible for a human being of sound mind to throw himself down a well or otherwise kill himself). The Jesuits with whom we are concerned in this section operate rather with the second conception: the law cannot justly command acts contrary to basic and urgent human inclinations unless the security of the commonwealth demands it.

[89] Aquinas, *ST* 2a2ae, q. 64, a. 2.

[90] Ibid., q. 69, a. 4.

[91] Soto, *De iustitia et iure*, lib. I, q. 6, a. 6, conc. 5.

Soto's discussion was thus handled explicitly in terms of the natural right of self-preservation that protects the body. Accordingly he argued that the criminal is obliged to cooperate in any punishments that do not inflict hurt on the body, including life imprisonment. But Salas set the question much more broadly in terms of the condition on human law that it cannot command the impossible—not physically impossible, evidently, but not morally impossible either, taking "morally impossible" as something that involves great difficulty for the human beings involved. Concerning this latter impossibility, he said, "I judge that, at least where there is not the weightiest and most pressing cause, human commands can have no place ... because human beings are not subjected to their princes in a servile manner, as slaves, but politically, as citizens."[92] That is, subjection is for the governance of their common lives, not the usurpation of their own individual lives. This principle of political subjection governs criminals as well as law-abiding citizens: for, Salas went on, "from the same principle many infer that no one is bound to stay in prison, if there is danger of death.... And although Cajetan, Soto and Covarruvias ... say that someone condemned to perpetual and severe imprisonment cannot escape, nevertheless others say, and better ... that he can." The same was commonly held to go for condemnation to the galleys or the mines, although this was not universally the case: Gabriel Vázquez took a line more like Soto's in arguing that someone condemned to perpetual imprisonment or servitude could not licitly escape.[93]

Whereas for Soto, then, the point at which the human law cannot oblige is bodily hurt—wounds or death—the Jesuits generally took a broader view of what makes human life unbearable, morally impossible.[94] They were thus enabled to connect the position on criminals with their position on the limited character of human law generally, and the broader discussion whether it can oblige with the danger of death. This connection is clear in Salas, as we have seen, and also in Lessius's discussion of the rights of criminals: "for the guilty man could, even on the scaffold or under the blow of the sword, take flight: for so great is each man's right of preserving his life, that no power can oblige him not to do so ... unless some public good demanded it: for example if the city was in danger; for the part can be sacrificed for the sake of the whole. But where there is no such cause, it would be too hard and inhuman."[95] Moreover—and Lessius followed the common opinion here—this right of criminals to preserve their own lives does not extend simply to running away if they

[92] Salas, *Tractatus de legibus*, disp. 1, sect. 9, n. 56, fo. 22.
[93] Vázquez, *Commentarii in primam secundae*, disp. 174, cap. 1, n. 7, fo. 136, col. 1.
[94] See Höpfl, *Jesuit political thought*, p. 210, for this point.
[95] Lessius, *De iustitia et iure*, lib. II, cap. 31, dub. 5, fo. 399, col. 1.

can, but to breaking their chains and their prisons in so doing. "Because if the end is licit," Lessius continued, "then so is the means.... Nor is this a case of acting forcibly against the public power: because this power is not in stones, or chains, but in the judge and his ministers, against whom force is not licit when the condemnation is just. But it is otherwise with chains and prison: just as someone who is thrown to a lion, can defend himself against it"—"as long as he can," added the mid-seventeenth century Jesuit author Cardinal Juan de Lugo, somewhat grimly.[96]

Now it is not only we who may be feeling a slight sense of the oddness of an argument that allows the sovereign to put people to death and yet insists that, so strong is the right to the preservation of life, the condemned cannot be obliged not to preserve it, or at least try to. Rodrigo de Arriaga took the contrary view that the condemned man *can* be obliged to cooperate in his own death, if he has been justly condemned, because it is no more morally difficult voluntarily to ascend the steps of the scaffold than to be dragged up there.[97] Arriaga somewhat reluctantly followed the general opinion on the moral licence of escape from prison, but confessed that he could not see any good reason for the thesis. Despite a certain asymmetry, however, I am not sure that we are dealing with any bigger problem of a conflict in Jesuit thought between the rights of subjects and of the state, nor, in consequence, with the idea that natural rights are not a structuring element of their political thought.[98] The natural right to life, or the natural law demand to preserve life, *is* a limit on what the sovereign is able to command: he can command someone to be put to death, but not command that person in conscience not to try to avoid it. However, the subject cannot, in conscience, actively resist the sovereign and his ministers—*this* is the duty that matches up to the sovereign's right—and the Jesuits clearly feel that thereby they have sufficiently safeguarded the commonwealth and its power, which is, of course, only directed to the *common* good. Attractively, and plausibly, no one seems to feel that an escaped criminal on the loose is such a fundamental threat to the commonwealth—like war or plague—that it could ever take precedence over an individual's right to pursue his *own* fundamental good of

---

[96] Juan de Lugo, *Disputationum de iustitia et iure*, tom. I (Lyon 1642), disp. 40, sect. 4, fo. 674, col. 1.

[97] Arriaga, *Disputationes theologicae in primam secundae*, tom. II, disp. 21, sect. 7, n. 56, fo. 250.

[98] Höpfl, *Jesuit political thought*, p. 296, suggests that that there is something not quite right about the Jesuit arguments here, with the rights of the sovereign "not matched by any duty of compliance on the part of individuals when their self-preservation was involved." He concludes that the "refusal of Jesuits to acknowledge the conflict between the natural right of individuals and the authority of the commonwealth indicates once again how little individual rights, construed as limitations on the authority of governors, featured in their thought."

life. Provided the commonwealth is not threatened, it can live with the anomalous situation of one who does not have a just war against the state but yet has rights to avoid the coercive power of the state if he can.

These arguments offer an interesting comparison with those of Hobbes, whose extensive casuistry of the liberty of subjects in chapter 21 in several of its features resembles that of the Jesuits. Thus, no one can be obliged actively to cooperate in their own death, "though justly condemned," but they can be obliged to fight for the commonwealth if its security is in danger. However, there is a central difference, because here the question is, at least on the surface, handled in terms of the original covenant that is entirely lacking in Jesuit theory—even in Arriaga who, as we have seen, comes the nearest to it. The limit on obligation is the limit involved in what you can actually covenant to, which must—precisely insofar as the covenant is an act of will—be some good to yourself, and in the first place the preservation of your own body. "I have shewn before in the 14.Chapter, that Covenants, not to defend a mans own body, are voyd." This allows him a much neater analysis of those occasions on which there is liberty to disobey the sovereign, extending even to active resistance— the bearing of arms—which would horrify the Jesuits.[99] And yet, equally as for them, it is not in fact a matter strictly of the body, and the casuistry turns out not to be so simple after all. Hobbes argued in chapter 15 that men cannot lay down all their natural rights, but must "retaine some; as right to governe their owne bodies; enjoy aire, water, motion, waies to go from place to place; and all things else, without which a man cannot live, or live well."[100] It is this full and flourishing human life, not mere bodily preservation, which is the ultimate "good to himselfe" that a human being intends. The condition of this life is the peace and security achieved through the establishment of a sovereign; and it is this end, rather than the "Words of our Submission," that governs the casuistry of obligation. "When therefore our refusal to obey, frustrates the End for which the Soveraignty was ordained; then is there no Liberty to refuse: otherwise there is."[101] This explains why a subject may sometimes, "without In-justice,"[102] refuse to obey a command to kill another person, which makes no sense if bare self-preservation is at issue. The "*true* Liberty of a Sub-ject"[103] is the natural liberty that an individual retains to live a life of human integrity *within* the commonwealth, without strain (although not without delicate judgement) of conscience.

---

[99] Hobbes, *Leviathan*, ch. 21, pp. 151–52.
[100] Ibid., ch. 15, p. 107.
[101] Ibid., ch. 21, p. 151.
[102] Ibid., p. 150.
[103] Ibid., emphasis mine.

To sum up, then, neither for Hobbes nor the Jesuits nor indeed for Althusius is the limit of the obligation of civil law the natural body itself. Rather, it is a much broader and more complex matter of a subject's life; and not bare life, either, but what the Jesuits call a "morally possible" life, a life that does not contravene a human being's deepest natural attachments. All agree that such a life must be lived in a commonwealth with others; equally, all agree that it cannot be entirely subject to it. The complex negotiation between law and liberty that this throws up cannot be handled in terms of a simple opposition between nature and the city, the physical and the moral, external and internal. The subject who is an interface between both resists any such easy solution.

CHAPTER SEVEN

LOCALITY

In the last chapter we examined the nature of the state's command over its subjects as physically embodied beings, and the limits of the obligation of its law in that context. In this chapter, I want to consider the limits of obligation in another context, that of subjects travelling from one commonwealth to another. One might think that this is to consider the question of "inside" and "outside" in a completely different, and non-metaphorical, sense. But I hope to show that the essential problematic is the same. Like the body of the subject, the physical movement of the traveller implicates another interface between the civic and the natural, this time the relationship between political space and the space of local motion, the space in which all physical beings, not just humans, move. Thus it raises, in a different context, the same issue of the relationship of the city to the natural lives of its subjects, lives that are irreducibly physical and lived in a physical dimension. Implicitly it also poses a fundamental political question about the city as a juridical entity: whether such a body is spatially limited, and, if so, how it can be that a non-physical body has a spatial location. In this sense, the border between the political and the natural and the border of the commonwealth are mutually under construction.

This fundamental political question had no easy answer in a mediating notion of "territory" that was neither natural place nor civil union but juridical space, the space of jurisdiction. Although our authors certainly possessed, and intermittently deployed, such a concept,[1] they could not use it adequately to solve questions of the obligation of subjects to their sovereign. The new understanding of sovereignty—the metaphysics of the state as the bearer of sovereign, legislative power over subjects—precisely displaced the old medieval concept of jurisdiction and with it the stability of the inherited notion of territory, to which jurisdiction, on the medieval understanding, coheres. The new space of the political did not coincide with the old space of jurisdiction; territory had to be re-conceptualised in relation to sovereignty.[2] Early-modern lawyers, especially in Germany, were increasingly concerned with the nature of boundaries and territoriality more generally. But, as we shall see more fully in the following chapter, most of the authors with whom we are concerned in this study showed very little interest either in the concept of territory, or in place more generally.[3] Situation or locality remained on the fringes of their conception of the state; under precisely what aspect place becomes territory is not clear, and neither do they offer a clear central account of territorial sovereignty. Nevertheless, the world that their treatises addressed and sought to conceptualise contained a profusion of human beings moving outside the borders of the commonwealth: merchants, ambassadors, simple visitors, soldiers, fugitives, migrants and (increasingly importantly, as we shall see further on) religious exiles driven from their homes by confessional divisions.[4] Their handling of the obli-

[1] Insofar as our authors offer a definition of territory at all (and most of them do not), they follow the Roman law definition given in the Digest title *De verborum significatione* (D.50.16.239.8): "'Territory' is the universal body of fields within the boundaries of any city." Territory as the space of jurisdiction was underlined by the etymology, often repeated in the early-modern period, from *terrere*, to terrify: "which [i.e., the word *territorium*] some say is derived from this, that the magistrates of that place have the right, within those boundaries, of terrifying, that is, of driving off" (ibid.).

[2] For the medieval maxim *iurisdictio cohaeret territorio*, and the attempts of early-modern German lawyers to craft a new concept of territorial supremacy, see Dietmar Willoweit, *Rechtsgrundlagen der Territorialgewalt: Landesobrigkeit, Herrschaftsgewalt und Territorium in der Rechtswissenschaft der Neuzeit* (Cologne: Bohlau 1975). See also M. Scattola, "Die Grenze der Neuzeit," in M. Bauer and T. Rahn eds., *Die Grenze. Begriff und Inszenierung* (Berlin: Akademie Verlag 1997), 37–72.

[3] This point is made in relation to Bodin by Lauren Benton, *A search for sovereignty. Law and geography in European empires, 1400–1900* (Cambridge: Cambridge University Press 2010), pp. 287–88. I regret that this book appeared too late for me to be able fully to take account of its arguments.

[4] See the summary of the extensive recent literature on the subject in M. Asche, "Auswanderungsrecht und Migration aus Glaubensgründen," in H. Schilling and H. Smolinsky eds., *Der Augsburger Religionsfrieden* 1555 (Münster: Aschendorff 2007), 75–104.

gations and liberties of these figures shows obliquely how physical place is infiltrated into political space, the "sphere of the city," sometimes at some cost to the main narrative that we have been studying. In this chapter, then, we shall take a look at the state from the sidelines.

The Jesuit literature offers us an illuminating way in through its discussion of the obligations of those who are citizens of one commonwealth but happen, for whatever reason (this is not the focus of this discussion), to be in another. So, the Jesuits ask: Does the law oblige members of the commonwealth when they are "outside" it? And does it oblige members of other commonwealths when they are "inside" it? These queries are part of a more general question about what persons the civil law obliges, which is how our authors translate Aquinas's question concerning human law in the *Prima secundae,* "whether all are subject to the law." Now Aquinas had not raised the issue of travellers; he had said simply that "those, who are of one city, or realm, are not subject to the laws of the prince of another city, or realm."[5] However, the late-medieval casuistic literature had extensively discussed the question whether those who travel between parishes or dioceses are obliged to follow church customs and laws that differ from their own. This discussion was incorporated and developed by the Dominicans and Jesuits of the later sixteenth century in their commentaries on the fourth book of the *Sentences* and on the *Pars tertia* of Aquinas's *Summa*, both of which consider the nature and practice of the sacraments of the church. Thus, the Dominican Martín de Ledesma briefly raised the issue in the context of the difference in the celebration of the mass between the Greek and the Latin churches, in using leavened and unleavened bread respectively;[6] Suárez followed him at much greater length in his commentary on the *Pars tertia*.[7] In his vast and free-standing treatise on marriage, first published in 1602, Suárez's fellow-Jesuit Tomás Sánchez tackled the question in the context of the uneven adoption of the Tridentine marriage laws across Europe,[8] Lessius in the context of differing customs and periods of fasting, the latter a difficulty "which often happens now because of the new calendar, which has not been accepted everywhere."[9] This extensive and detailed casuistry reflects a world of infinite local variability, interestingly exacerbated by new attempts at systematisation, but still a world in which the church—an overtly territorially organised institution—had been at home since ancient times.

[5] Aquinas, *ST*, 1a2ae, q. 96, a. 5.
[6] Martín de Ledesma, *Prima quartae* (Coimbra 1555), q. 15, a. 4, fo. 249, col. 2.
[7] Francisco Suárez, *Commentariorum ac disputationum in tertiam partem D. Thomae* (ed. Mainz 1619; 1st edition Alcalá 1590–95), tom. III, q. 74, a. 4, disp. 44, sect. 3, fo. 494–95.
[8] Tomás Sánchez, *De sancto matrimonii sacramento* (ed. Lyon 1669), lib. III, disp. 18, q. 1., fo. 238–41.
[9] Lessius, *De iustitia et iure*, lib. 4, cap. 2, dub. 7, fo. 657–59; quotation at fo. 659, n. 52.

The sophisticated conversation in which these authors engage had started between Augustine and Ambrose.

On the question whether an incoming visitor is bound by the laws of the place to which he travels, authors distinguished between a traveller and one who, having abandoned his native land (*patria*), comes with the intention of staying and making his home in the new place.[10] The latter *is* obliged by the laws of that new place, because domicile in a place subjects a person to its laws. This was commonly agreed.[11] But in the case of a genuine traveller, opinions differed. One opinion held that he was indeed subject to the laws of the new place. The most important authority for this was a letter from Augustine to Ianuarius, in which he reported Ambrose's reply to his question whether his mother Monica should follow the different customs of Milan on her visit there.[12] Ambrose counselled that one should follow the custom of the church where one happens to be; Ledesma, in the context of the celebration of the mass, elevated this advice into a stricter sense of obligation.[13] "And if you were to say," pursued Sánchez in his exposition of this opinion, "that St. Augustine seems to attribute this obligation on travellers to the necessity of avoiding scandal, and that therefore, if there is no scandal, travellers are not obliged; this solution is no good, because ... he did not attribute it to scandal, but to pact and to the society of citizens."[14]

However, Sánchez in fact rejected this solution. A traveller who is in another place purely for the purpose of a visit is not judged to be "morally" in that place, by analogy with material goods that just happen to be in an estate that has been left to an heir, which are not judged to be legally part of the legacy. Consequently, he is not subject to its laws; Ambrose was indeed just offering counsel, or seeking to avoid scandal. Sánchez allowed certain exceptions to his rule. One was if disobedience would cause harm to the place. Another was the exception of *vagi*, "wanderers," people of no fixed address: "for these are bound to the laws and customs of the place in which they find themselves, even in passing. It is proved,

---

[10] Sánchez, *De matrimonio*, disp. 18, q. 1, n. 3. The importance of intention, or *animus*, is underlined in the common source for all these authors, Mazzolini's *Summa*, s.v. *domicilium*: Silvestro Mazzolini da Prierio, *Summa summarum quae sylvestrina dicitur* (2nd ed., Strasbourg 1518), fo. cxxv r.

[11] It raised the further question, however, of what constitutes domicile; here the common opinion was that residence for half the year or more was sufficient to constitute domicile, as was an extended period of continuous stay, for example the three years of a university student.

[12] This letter is cited as Ep. CXVIII, and it appears as such in the sixteenth-century editions of Augustine's complete works that stem from Erasmus, e.g., Basel 1569, tom. II, col. 556–57. However, in modern editions it appears as letter 54, dating from 400 ce.

[13] Ledesma, *Prima quartae*, q. 15, a. 4, fo. 249, col. 2.

[14] Sánchez, *De matrimonio*, lib. III, disp. 18, q. 1, n. 4, fo. 239.

because since they have no particular home, they acquire it in every respect wherever they are. Again, because otherwise they would seem to be exempt from all laws and customs."[15] (Sánchez took this from Soto, whose attitude to vagabonds we examined in chapter 1.[16]) Suárez also held that it was too strict to oblige a traveller to the laws of a new place, even if he would act meritoriously in observing them. He argued his case partly from the Council of Florence, which had allowed a priest of the Greek church to celebrate mass with leavened bread even while within the bounds of the Latin church; moreover, "everyone admits" that a Latin priest passing through the Greek church would not be obliged to alter his Latin custom, so the converse must also apply. "It would be different, though, if the priest had altogether changed his domicile, because then he would no longer be reputed a Greek priest, even if he had been one before, but a Latin priest, because he would already have become a member of the Latin church."[17]

Lessius took issue with this solution. He agreed that, if one considered purely the nature of laws, one would say that they only bound "subjects and inhabitants." Consequently, to make an exception of *vagi* makes no sense: wanderers and travellers are equally non-subjects and non-inhabitants, and therefore are none of them obliged on this reasoning. "Nor should it appear absurd that someone who does not stay anywhere is not obliged by any laws of particular places." However, in fact the received custom of the faithful is to the contrary: people consider themselves to be obliged by the customs of the new place, and it is morally necessary that they should be so, to avoid the inhabitants themselves being led to break the law, citing hospitality and friendship. Finally, Lessius argued from the common opinion in the reverse case, which was that one who left his home to travel was not bound to obey the laws of his home as long as he was away. Thus, it was fair that he should be obliged by those of the new one, since, citing the *Regulae iuris*, "he who feels the benefit should also feel the burden."[18] Lessius explained the rationale behind the reverse case as follows: "because local laws and customs are as if affixed to the place, and bind by reason of being in that place."[19] His authority was a canon of Boniface VIII in the *Liber sextus*, to the effect that the statutes of a bishop do not bind outside his territory; thus, if he

[15] Ibid., nn. 6, 16, 14, 15.
[16] Domingo de Soto, *Commentarii in quartum sententiarum* (Salamanca 1569), dist. 18, q. 4, a. 2, fo. 801, cols. 1–2. The context is the question whether it is necessary to make confession to one's own parish priest.
[17] Suárez, *Disputationes in tertiam*, tom. III, q. 74, a. 4, disp. 44, sect. 3, fo. 496, agreeing with Ledesma, therefore, to this extent.
[18] Lessius, *De iustitia et iure*, lib. IV, cap. 2, dub. 7, n. 49, fo. 658.
[19] Ibid., dub. 8, n. 54, fo. 659.

passes an excommunication on thieves, this does not bind subjects who commit theft outside his territory, because "one who lays down the law beyond his territory is disobeyed with impunity."[20] In using this authority he followed a whole series of theologians, including Sánchez. The objection would be, as Sánchez put it, that "a person is obliged by the laws of his native land, as long as he has not abandoned it.... these travellers are still citizens of their native land, and are said to be 'in' it" (from the argument concerning legacies, as before).[21] But in fact, "someone who is travelling in a foreign territory by way of transit, even if he has not deserted his native land in the first way [that is, with the intention of changing his residence], has nevertheless deserted it in the second way [that is, in the sense of actual habitation]: which is sufficient for him to be de-obliged from its laws." To the problem that such a traveller would not seem to be obliged by any laws, Sánchez denied this, because he is bound by those laws that oblige both in his place of domicile and in the place in which he finds himself.[22]

This last consideration highlights an important aspect of this entire discourse. The fundamental context is human law in the sense of ecclesiastical law; and because the church is universal (none of these authors considers the case of a Catholic traveller in a heretical land), there is always a body of law to which the traveller will be subject wherever he goes, even if he crosses the borders of commonwealths. This is reflected in the general tenor of the discussion, which does not distinguish between crossing from one regional jurisdiction to another and crossing from one commonwealth to another. It is clear that what is mainly being discussed is what we would call local laws, laws of particular cities or towns within a realm; but Sánchez also offers the example of a Castilian in Portugal, who can eat offal on the Sabbath unlike the Portuguese themselves. The point, however, is precisely the same in this case as in that of the regional traveller; the law of Portugal is equally as "local" as the law of Milan, the "national" or political difference being irrelevant in the context of the common body and common law of the church.[23]

---

[20] Ibid. The relevant passage from the canon law is in the *Liber sextus*, lib. 1, tit. 2, cap. 2: "Subjects who commit theft outside the bishop's diocese are recognised as not being bound ... by his statute, since outside his territory, disobedience to the one who has jurisdiction happens with impunity." A. Friedberg ed., *Corpus iuris canonici, Pars secunda* (Graz: Akademische Druck- u. Verlagsanstalt 1959), col. [938].

[21] Sánchez, *De matrimonio*, lib. III, disp. 18, q. 1, n. 17, fo. 241.

[22] Ibid., n. 24.

[23] We should notice, however, that this feature of their discourse is not peculiar to them. It is part of a much broader medieval and early-modern sensibility in which travellers perceive themselves as moving from place to place (city, town, village) rather than through geographical space. Consequently, it is the local jurisdiction into which they enter that

The challenge, then, for an author who held the same position as Sán-chez on the obligation of travellers, but who was discussing civil rather than ecclesiastical law, was to find an analogue for the common law of the church. The Dominican Bartolomé de Medina is, as far as I know, the first commentator on the *Prima secundae* to have incorporated the discussion of travellers into Question 96, on the obligation of human (i.e., in this context, civil) law. He raises a doubt, "whether travellers, and those who do not have fixed dwelling-places, are bound by the laws of the region to which they tend?"[24] Medina answers with a distinction with which we are already familiar, between those who make their domicile in the new place, and "others who wander, and migrate from province to province, like those who make their way to Santiago"—failing to distinguish between vagabonds and pilgrims in a way that would have aroused Soto's ire. The first are bound by the laws of the new place, because do-micile makes a person an inhabitant and a subject, as we have seen. The second are not bound, "because a particular law does not bind a traveller passing through a town by any right." Nevertheless, such persons "are bound by the common laws of the realm, for otherwise the common-wealth would not be well provided-for." In this case, then, the common laws of the realm provide the community of law that is the backdrop to the local liberty of the traveller.

Medina's discussion is very brief, and he does not justify his conclusion with any further argumentation. It was Francisco Suárez who really made the crucial move in adapting the casuistry of the obligation of church law to the question of civil law. It is in his work (and that of Salas and Arriaga following him) that we encounter, for the first time in these treatises on the laws, the idea of—but also the problem of—territory, which is alien to the categories of the *Prima secundae* that otherwise structure their discussions of law. We saw from the start how Aquinas's han-dling of laws is centred around *agency*. The law is what governs human actions. In the development of commentary on his treatise on laws that we have been tracing, the civil law is theorised as what governs the actions of those individuals who have incorporated themselves into the new body of the commonwealth, and hence subjected themselves to its power. The most decided statement of this is, as we have seen, in Suárez himself. Hence he asserts that "every human law obliges all persons who

---

receives all their attention, while the crossing of a "national" border is scarcely even re-marked. See the analysis of early modern travellers' reports in A. Gotthard, *In der ferne. Die Wahrnehmung des Raums in der Vormoderne* (Frankfurt-New York: Campus 2007), esp. pp. 93–109.

[24] Bartolomé de Medina, *Expositio in primam secundae D. Thomae* (Venice 1580), q. 96, a. 5, fo. 517.

are parts of that community for which the law is passed." If we then ask which persons are to be judged members of the community for these purposes, Suárez responds in the clear language of moral union that characterises his analysis of the commonwealth. "The reply is that … just as in a natural body, its actual members are constituted by their proportionate union with such a body, by means of which they are subjected to the motion of the whole body; just so, in the political body, the members are constituted through a moral conjunction." By the same reasoning, the law does not oblige "those who are wholly outside the community upon which the law is imposed," the reason being, "that no power operates beyond its own sphere. But the power of any community has for its corresponding sphere the community itself."[25]

If this is the case, what happens if a person who is a moral member of one community physically leaves that community to enter into another? Is he still obliged by the laws of the original community? We would expect the answer to be yes, in that such obligation is a matter of moral union, therefore for it to be indifferent whether the subject physically leaves the community or not. However, this is not the case. Suárez argues instead that subjects are no longer obliged by the laws of their city once they leave its territory.[26] The central authority for his position—which is, as we have seen, the *communis opinio*—is again the constitution of Boniface VIII to which Lessius appealed. It is highly significant that such a sophisticated theorist of the civil state as Suárez has to borrow his analysis of the territorial extent of civil obligation from the law and the organisation of the church. It indicates the extent to which territoriality is undertheorised in a conception of the commonwealth that centres on the *moral* incorporation of human beings.

Now this canon of Boniface's was not entirely without ambiguity: for one thing, it directly refers to jurisdiction rather than to legislative competence; for another, the reference to impunity suggests a defect of de facto power, rather than necessarily of right. Suárez appreciated these possible cavils. However, in a clear instance of the new understanding of sovereignty displacing the older legal language of jurisdiction, he had already argued against the lawyers that—whatever may be the case with lesser bodies—the sovereign power to legislate is convertible with sovereign jurisdiction.[27] So, in the current instance, he argued that the intention of the pope was to apply this maxim to legislative power, and not merely to the coercive or physical aspect of that power but also to its directive, that is, its moral aspect. Thus, he concluded that whether we are

---

[25] Suárez, *De legibus*, lib. III, cap. 31, nn. 6, 7, 8.
[26] Ibid., cap. 32, n. 3.
[27] Ibid., cap. 1, nn. 7–10. See above, ch. 5, p. 126.

talking about canon or civil law, the rationale is the same: "the jurisdiction of any city or particular prince does not extend to passing laws outside the city or territory"; "just as in philosophy we say that action does not ensue beyond the sphere of activity ... so the activity of jurisdiction in passing law is limited to territory, and therefore beyond it the law does not oblige."[28] The "sphere" of law here, then, is apparently not the community but the territory. Significantly, his words are "the city or territory"—the city in this context is beginning to slide into territory, something that is confirmed when he comes to consider the opposite case, that of foreigners who enter the city. These, he argued—and this again is the common opinion—are obliged by the laws of the community that they visit. "The real reason is that law is generally passed for such a territory, as we suppose. Therefore it obliges all who are actually staying there for the time that they do."[29] The peace and good moral habits that the law is designed to secure are here described not as those of the community but as those of the *place* (*locus*).

To the question whether the law obliges travellers even in its coercive aspect, Suárez's answer is yes, of course. As we have seen, for him, all laws carry a coercive sanction, so to be obliged to obey a law is necessarily to be obliged to pay the penalty for its breach. But he faced another objection based on an authority of canon law, this time to the effect that a sentence of excommunication passed by a bishop only obliges those who are his "subjects." Suárez's response was not to argue that strangers *are* subjects, strictly speaking—although they are in a sense, as we shall see in a minute—but again to make the distinction between a law and a command.[30] Of itself, "a command only obliges the inhabitants of the *terra* and true and permanent subjects; a law [obliges] all those who are staying there." Hence, he continues, "we may consider another difference" between a law and a command: "that a law is passed upon a territory; for it is 'the right of the city' [*ius civitatis*], as Bartolus considered it to be, or 'the law of the territory' [*lex territorii*], as Panormitanus said. And therefore it obliges persons *as if by the mediation of place*, that is, insofar as they move about in that place."[31] This apparently crucial point—to put the discussion in perspective—occurs thirty-three chapters on from first beginning to talk about the civil legislative power! And Suárez did recognise that these conclusions might seem at odds with his analysis of law, which is passed upon subjects understood as members of a moral community, not a place. This is in fact the first objection he proposed in each case. Thus,

[28] Suárez, *De legibus*, lib. III, cap. 32, n. 3.
[29] Ibid., cap. 33, n. 3.
[30] See above, ch. 6, pp. 142–43.
[31] Suárez, *De legibus*, lib. III, cap. 33, n. 12, emphasis mine.

in the case of a citizen going out: "the reason for doubt is that, although a subject is in actuality absent from or travelling outside the territory, he nevertheless still remains a subject as long as he does not change his home." And of a visiting foreigner: they are not obliged by the laws, because "travellers are not subjects."[32] His response was a scholastic distinction: "the subject who is outside the territory, although he does not lose his habitual, or radical, subjection, so to speak, nevertheless loses his actual subjection."[33] Correspondingly, the traveller who comes in gains actual subjection, which is sufficient for an obligation to obey the laws.

The apparent side issue of travellers, then, turns out to demand fundamental modifications of the initial conception of the moral union and the nature of the obligation of civil law. This is equally so if we turn to look at Rodrigo de Arriaga, who offered a thorough-going critique of much of Suárez's discussion. Let us start with the case of the citizen going out. He began by remarking that the common opinion—that he is no longer obliged to obey the law of his city—is not easy to demonstrate. In the case of canon law—Suárez's principal authority for *civil* law, of course—"there is no great difficulty, because we can reduce it to the will of the pope, who did not give to bishops or to other inferior legislators power beyond their territory."[34] But if we are going to find a rationale that applies universally to all human laws, it had better be a universal rationale. Arriaga offered two thoughts, of which he said the second is better; but the first turns out to be the more fundamental. The first, then, is that "the human community is most of all constituted by living together in one place that belongs to one community: for they must have some sort of common bond, but they have none other than common residence in a common place." "And therefore," Arriaga went on, "when someone is outside it, he now ceases to be a part of the community for that time, and therefore he ceases to be obliged by its laws, because the legislator has no right except in members of the community." The second, "better" reason for this conclusion that Arriaga offered is taken from the end or purpose of civil laws: the common peace and security. In this perspective, what a citizen does when he is away makes absolutely no difference: "for the peace of Spain would not be disturbed, even if in Prague I carried arms at night." Therefore, the legislative power does not extend beyond the territory.[35] As to the rationale offered by Suárez for the case of strangers coming in—that laws are passed on the territory, not on

<hr />

[32] Ibid., lib. III, cap. 33, n. 2.

[33] Ibid., n. 7.

[34] Rodrigo de Arriaga, *Disputationes in primam secundae*, tom. II, disp. 15, sect. 2, subsect. 1, n. 7, fo. 162, col. 2.

[35] Ibid., nn. 7–8, fo. 163, col. 1.

persons—Arriaga denied this, explicitly against Suárez. A law prohibiting the carrying of arms, for example, "cannot be passed directly on a territory, but only upon persons." Rather, "a traveller, by the very fact that he now enters another region, already submits himself to the jurisdiction of its sovereign for the time that he wishes to be there: from which it is proved quasi a priori that there is in the legislator such jurisdiction; for although the sovereign did not receive this jurisdiction from his own community, because the stranger was at that point outside the community, he receives it, however, at the point when he enters the territory."[36]

Arriaga faced the same sort of objections as Suárez. The first is that a subject away from home is surely still a subject. As we have seen, Suárez had solved this by a distinction between "habitual" and "actual" subjection. Arriaga rejected this distinction. A subject away from home loses all subjection.

> If the subject is not a slave or semi-slave—because dominion over such persons is not founded upon being in the place belonging to the master, but on a title that abstracts from place—then, I would say, by being away from the territory his own subjection is totally lost. For example, in a Spaniard who is staying in France there remains no other subjection towards the king of Spain than there is in a Frenchman staying in France with regard to that same king of Spain. For just as the first can go back and become a subject; so can a Frenchman go to Spain, and there become a subject of the Spanish king.... You will reply: the king of Spain can recall his own to Spain, therefore they are still subjects. I respond: they are not bound to return, if they do not want to.[37]

The case is different for ambassadors, because their responsibility to return, and indeed to act for the good of their own commonwealth rather than the one in which they are now staying, rests on the personal commission of the sovereign; they are the exception that proves the rule. In general, he repeated, "citizens, who are not slaves of the prince, are not constituted as belonging to the same commonwealth by any other bond than common habitation."[38] Arriaga did allow that there could be cases, for example if a person still had property in his original country, where the person was still subject in respect of that property to the laws of that land. But, he asked, what if a person has no property? He insists that he is trying to abstract from all such considerations to ask purely about one who was born in one place and then moves to another. The wandering

[36] Ibid., sect. 2 [recte 3], n. 25, fo. 166; n. 30, fo. 167.
[37] Ibid., sect. 2, subsect. 2, nn. 9–10, fo. 163, col. 1.
[38] Ibid., n. 15, fo. 164, col. 1.

beggar, then, turns out to be not the pariah that he is in the generality of the literature, but the purest case of political subjection.

Arriaga's solution is elegant. It does not equivocate on membership of a city and being in a territory. Rather, living in a common place just is membership of a city; title to rule politically, rather than despotically, is founded upon place. But there is still some tension with his original remarks on the nature of civil power, where he argues for the voluntariness of the act of political subjection in Suarezian terms. Human beings, he said, do not have to live in political communities; they can live scattered, as many Indians in fact do, without forming any *respublica* and therefore without being subject to any particular power.[39] Alternatively, they can live together, in which case they must constitute a commonwealth, subject to some form of government as a "head" to the body.[40] But that act is described as an act of free consent, with political power arising from the wills of the individuals who come together to form the commonwealth[41]—as indeed is implicit in his discussion of the stranger coming in, who, by the very fact of entering the territory, is understood to submit himself to the power of its prince. Thus, it is apparently *not* place alone that constitutes a subject. It is, as far as I can see, only Juan de Salas who realises that if we are to take seriously the role of domicile and place in the obligation of the law, we are bound to involve it directly in our understanding of the original constitution of the commonwealth and its legislative capacity. In one of the most original passages in the entire Jesuit political literature, Salas accordingly criticises the very foundation of the Suarezian commonwealth, the idea of moral union. But, because he turns place from a side issue into a central theme, we shall defer this discussion until the next chapter.

By way of coda to this part of the chapter, we may note that Arriaga is very much the exception in these discussions in even considering the will of the (now non-) subject *to* return. They concentrate, as we have seen, on an already-effected change of place in respect of liberty or subjection, and are handled entirely independently of any consideration of any right or liberty to travel or to change domicile. There is one context, however, in which a right to escape from subjection through change of place is defended (if controversially), and that is in the figure of the fugitive slave. It was a given for all our authors that a person who voluntarily sold himself into slavery could not then escape, for this would be equivalent to stealing himself. By contrast, it was also clear to all of them that one taken captive and enslaved in an unjust war had every right to escape,

---

[39] Ibid., disp. 13, sect. 3, n. 13, fo. 140, col. 2.
[40] Ibid., and sect. 1, n. 2, fo. 138, col. 1.
[41] Ibid., sect. 3, n. 14, fo. 140, col. 2.

even with forcible resistance, because he continued to have a just war against the master. However, what about the case of one taken captive in a just war? Here it was agreed that the master justly had *dominium* over his new slave. But, following Soto and his close contemporary, the canon lawyer Diego de Covarruvias,[42] several of the Jesuits allowed that, analogously with the case of the criminal, such a slave could licitly escape if the opportunity presented itself.[43] There was nonetheless a caveat on the slave's escape, which Covarruvias took from the Roman law of captives and *postliminium* in the Digest. This complex and contested law stipulated —with several nuances, which we shall explore later on—that a Roman citizen captured by the enemy lost his citizenship but was restored to it (and *eo ipso* to his liberty) if he later returned, either to his native land or to a friendly city.[44] Thus Covarruvias and the Jesuits who followed him stipulated that flight was only licit with the intention of returning to one's own people, or to a friendly city, and that the fugitive slave achieved his liberty only once there. Whilst still within the commonwealth of his master, he would have no right to resist if he were to be caught by him en route, because he would not have a just war against the master (quite the reverse). However, he would have the right to pursue his liberty nonviolently. Fugitive slaves therefore represent another case of the juridical asymmetry we examined in the case of fugitive criminals, with which that of fugitive slaves is directly paralleled. The point that is clear in this discussion, as not in the former, is that this asymmetry has a *place*.

The loss of citizenship through falling into enemy hands, and its recovery through the operation of *postliminium*, was a part of every treatise on the law of war concerning captives. Alberico Gentili opened his *Hispanica advocatio* (first published posthumously in 1613) with the question "whether there is *postliminium* in the domain of a common friend," the specific issue at hand being "whether certain Portuguese, captured by their Dutch enemies on the Spanish sea, would become free here in England, by way of which they were being taken to Holland."[45] His advocacy in this case is for an affirmative reply to the question, on the general grounds that

---

[42] Soto, *De iustitia et iure*, lib. IV q. 2, a. 2; Diego de Covarruvias, *Variarum resolutionum*, lib. I, cap. 2, n. 10, in *Opera omnia* (Frankfurt 1592), tom. II, fo. 15, and *In regula peccatum, de regulis iuris liber unus*, pars 2, § 11, n. 6, in *Opera omnia*, tom. I, fo. 533.

[43] Lessius, *De iustitia et iure*, lib. II, cap. 5 dub. 5, fo. 45; Arriaga, *Disputationes in primam secundae*, tom. II, disp. 7, sect. 8, subsect. 2, n. 62, fo. 73. Differently, Gabriel Vázquez, *Commentarii in primam secundae*, disp. 174, cap. 1, n. 8, fo. 136; vehemently against, Molina, *De iustitia et iure*, tract. II, disp. 37.

[44] D.49.15, *De captivis et postliminio*, esp. 49.15.19 for the principle of the friendly city.

[45] Alberico Gentili, *Hispanicae advocationis libri duo* (1661) (2 vols., New York: Oxford University Press 1921), lib. I, cap 1 (vol. I, p. 1; vol. II [translation], p. 3).

postliminium is a principle that favours liberty and that therefore the "friend" referred to in the text of the Digest ought to include any common friend of both parties, not simply an exclusive friend of the captive's commonwealth. However, the operation of *postliminium* was not confined to the specific case of captives and therefore to questions of the law of war. In the hands of Protestant Aristotelians and natural lawyers it was part of a much more centrally political issue concerning the right of citizens to migrate or to travel and the security of their persons away from home, in peacetime as well as war. It therefore provides, analogously to the Jesuit question of the territorial limits of obligation, a way of looking at the situated dimension of the commonwealth through the lens of the juridical status of persons who travel outside it.

As we have seen, *postliminium* operated to restore a returning Roman citizen to his citizenship after involuntary capture by an enemy (it was denied to those who voluntarily went over to the enemy). However, a text of Pomponius in the Digest title "On captives and *postliminium*" stated explicitly that *postliminium* operated equally in peacetime, positing a distinction between cities that are formally enemies—*hostes*—and those that are not enemies but do not have a formal friendship or treaty of alliance (*foedus*) with Rome. If a Roman citizen falls into the hands of one of the latter, he will become their slave in the eyes of the Roman law, thus losing his Roman citizenship. In such a case, then, *postliminium* operates just as it does in war.[46] But it is unnecessary in the case of those with whom there is a treaty (*foederati*), "because they retain their liberty and their *dominium* of their property among us equally as they do at home, and the same obtains for us among them."[47] Thus the Roman law appeared to propose a view of what we would call international relations that offered no guarantee of security to any individual outside his home state except if he were in the territory of a city explicitly friendly or allied to his own.[48]

---

[46] D.49.15.5.2.

[47] D.49.15.7. The law speaks not merely of allied (*foederati*) but of "free" (*liberi*) peoples, specifying that by a "free" people is meant one that is not subject to another, but that this is compatible with a treaty of friendship and equally a treaty recognising the superiority of another state (thus Rome's client peoples are nevertheless free). It also states both that such allied and free peoples are "foreigners" (*externi*) to us, and that *postliminium* does not obtain. The sense of this passage was heavily contested in the Renaissance, some defending the "vulgar reading" which inserts a "not" before "foreigners," others insisting that it makes sense as it is. See Favre, *Iurisprudentia papinianea*, tit. XI, princ. 8, illat. 7, pp. 616–17; Jacques Cujas, *Observationum et emendationum libri XXVIII*, in *Opera omnia* tom. 4 (Frankfurt 1595), lib. XI, cap. 23, fo. 263.

[48] See Tuck, *Rights of war and peace*, p. 32, although he does not discuss the extent to which Gentili and Grotius in fact rejected this view; see below, pp. 187–91.

The Roman orator and philosopher Cicero, however, in his speech *Pro Balbo*, had referred to *postliminium* in peacetime in a different context, that of *voluntary* change of citizenship or *mutatio civitatis*. In this speech he defended the Roman citizenship of Cornelius Balbus against the claim of a prosecutor from his native Gades (modern Cádiz) that he had not been at liberty to accept it, accusing the prosecutor of a basic ignorance of the Roman law concerning *mutatio civitatis*, "which depends not merely on public laws but also on the will of private individuals." Cicero accepted the fundamental principle that Roman citizenship excluded any other citizenship equally as it excluded any other subjection. However, he set this in the context of the liberty of any citizen either to reject Roman citizenship and transfer himself to another *civitas*, or conversely to accept Roman citizenship and therefore to leave his former *civitas*. A Roman citizen could change citizenship either by dedicating or "attaching" himself to another city (*dicatio*) while abroad, or by *postliminium* (recovering an original citizenship), or by voluntarily transferring himself to another city (the right of voluntary exile, *exsilium*).[49] Cicero went on to argue that, in parallel, no one could prevent a non-Roman from changing to Roman citizenship if it was offered and it was his will to accept.

These texts form the key points of reference for Henning Arnisaeus in two important chapters of the *De republica* that consider the movement of citizens between commonwealths. The first asks "whether someone can be a citizen of two cities at the same time," the other, "whether it is licit for citizens to change cities at will; otherwise stated, whether a citizen who is absent against the will of the commonwealth can be recalled by right of majesty."[50] Both of these chapters are strongly negative in their answers, deploying the legal importance of individual acts of will *against* the liberty to change citizenship. From the point of view of this study, however, they are remarkable for their simultaneous appeal to the voluntariness of obligation and to the necessity of nature, and for their consistent animus against any kind of "wandering" as a transgression of both.

On the question whether one can be a citizen of two cities simultaneously, Arnisaeus established, with appeal to the *Pro Balbo*, that one who was received as a citizen into Rome lost his original citizenship. For this reason, he went on, there are cases of treaties between Rome and allied cities and also between the cities of present-day Switzerland not to receive others in this way.[51] Arnisaeus specified that this does not apply if the two cities are part of the same *imperium*, for then double citizenship

---

[49] Cicero, *Pro Balbo*, xi. 27, 28.
[50] Henning Arnisaeus, *De republica*, lib. I, cap. V, sect. 7 and sect. 8.
[51] Ibid., sect. 7, nn. 5–7.

is perfectly possible without "change of native land (*patria*)"—an assertion, as we shall see, that significantly links *patria* not with the home city but with the state. The denial of the possibility of dual citizenship, then, relates to his technical sense of the *civitas* as the material of a *respublica*, in which *imperium* inheres; it is a refusal of dual *subjection*.[52] On this basis, Arnisaeus argued from the voluntary nature of subjection that it is impossible for a citizen to undertake the obligations of two cities at once, nor is it licit for him to offer them to another. "He who is wholly obliged to one city cannot be wholly obliged to another, for what has once been given, cannot be given again."[53] As to the second question, whether a citizen can change city at will, "this question is attached to the former, and is handled with the same arguments": just as someone cannot offer himself as a citizen to another commonwealth as well as his own, "by the same reasoning he will not be able to desert it or to renounce it against its will, whether he removes himself to another, or whether he wanders in the manner of wild beasts through any land, without native land, without home."[54] And "if he cannot desert, because he remains, wherever he is, obliged to his fellow-citizens and to majesty—to which he subjected himself in his entirety, and once only—he can be compelled in legitimate ways, by him who has the power to compel, to fulfil his contract."[55] Commonwealths may restrain their subjects from any travel that they consider dangerous in some way to the commonwealth; Arnisaeus mentions especially the practice of the "Muscovites or Russians" and the English, who have learned from their experience of Catholic powers. "I remember when I was living in London five years ago, that, not long after the Gunpowder Plot [*conjuratio pulveraria*], the harbours were closed by King James of Great Britain, in a universal edict, to sworn supporters of the Roman see; and any who had gone to Italy without leave were recalled from there."[56]

---

[52] Ibid., n. 8. Cf. ibid., n. 16: "... much less can someone declare himself for two cities, or, what comes to the same thing, subject himself to two different commonwealths which are not subordinate to each other."

[53] Ibid., n. 10.

[54] Ibid., sect. 8, n. 1.

[55] Ibid. Thus, although it is sometimes claimed that there is no contractual basis to the commonwealth in the *politica* literature, including Arnisaeus, and certainly he does not use it to construct a genetic account of the commonwealth, it is clear that Arnisaeus does see the individual as implicitly having entered into at least a quasi-contractual relation with the state. Cf. R. von Friedeburg, *Self-defence and religious strife in early modern Europe* (Aldershot: Ashgate 2002), p. 106.

[56] Arnisaeus, *De republica*, lib. I, cap. V, sect. 8, n. 6. Arnisaeus gave several more examples from his reading of English history in support of his case, including Elizabeth I who in 1581 "recalled many Englishmen 'remaining beyond the seas, under colour of studie, and yet living contrary to the lawes of god, and of the realme,' as Stowe says in *Elisabeth*. And

However, Arnisaeus supplemented the argument from individual will with an appeal to the necessity of nature: "for the nature of things does not allow for someone who is tied to one place to wander freely about the entire province."[57] There is a certain analogy between the obligation of a citizen to his city and the obligation of a vassal to his lord, but the obligation of the citizen is stronger, and defeats any feudal tie, because "no fortuitous chance, nor human convention subjected him to Majesty, but nature itself."[58] Arnisaeus linked this conception of subjection to sovereign power as a *natural* tie or bond with the notion of *patria*, native land or homeland, a move we have already seen in the context of the possibility of dual citizenship.[59] "And just as Martial says, 'He who lives everywhere, lives nowhere,' thus someone who wants to be a citizen of both commonwealths is a citizen of neither, because he cannot perform the office of a good and useful citizen anywhere." Nature planted (*plantavit*) us in our *patria* or commonwealth, and there can be no obligation antecedent to that.[60] Arnisaeus argued, against the Stoic claim that the whole world is the *patria* of the wise, that "the native soil entices to itself the minds of all with a quiet sweetness"; the Stoics must first overturn nature before they can eradicate this affection. "We live beneath the sky, as a common place, but that does not mean that each thing is not attracted by its own proper place, as Aristotle teaches, *Physics* IV, chapter 1. The circumference of the whole world does not take away the limits of each *patria* imposed by the law of nations."[61] Thus, the geographical

---

she threw Philip Howard, the Count of Arundel, into the tower of London on the 25th of April 1585, 'for attempting to have passed the seas without licence,' *idem ibid.*" See John Stow, *The annales of England* (London N.D. [1605]), pp. 1116, 1182.

[57] Arnisaeus referred here to his dispute with the Scottish metaphysician Thomas Reid, who had listed "Being, Same and Different among Transcendentals," and yet had put them in the category of relation. This, according to Arnisaeus in his *Vindiciae* against Reid, is a contradiction: it is the nature of transcendentals to "wander through" everything, without "the custody of limits," whereas a category is a limit, even "a prison." Thus, the metaphysical principle is defended with civic examples ("you recall a legate to Rome and yet you bid him stay in the province"; or as he puts it in the *De republica*, "what is this other than to condemn home to exile, or to be a wanderer within the walls of a town?"), even as the civic principle is defended from metaphysics. Arnisaeus, *De republica*, lib. I cap. V, sect. 7, n. 10; *Vindiciae secundum veritatem ... contra ... M. Thomae Rhaedi Scoti Pervigilia* (Frankfurt 1611), pp. 137–42.

[58] Arnisaeus, *De republica*, lib. I, cap. 5, sect. 7, n. 17.

[59] There is an increasing literature on the reception, mutation, and significance of the ancient notion of *patria* in early modern political thought: see the editor's chapter of the same title in R. von Friedeburg ed., *"Patria" und "Patrioten" vor dem Patriotismus* (Wiesbaden: Harrassowitz 2005); for early modern Germany in particular, A. Schmidt, *Vaterlandsliebe und Religionskonflikt* (Leiden: Brill 2007).

[60] Arnisaeus, *De republica*, lib. I, cap. 5, sect. 7, nn. 19–20.

[61] Ibid., sect. 8, nn. 18–19.

delineation and separation of states, instituted by the *ius gentium*, paradoxically functions to create or at least to enable the natural tie to native soil.

Arnisaeus considered two possible exceptions to his thesis, both of which were the subject of passionate discussion in contemporary Germany. One was the famous provision of the 1555 Peace of Augsburg that, as part of establishing the principle *cuius regio eius religio*, allowed subjects an apparent right to migrate (*ius emigrandi*) from one region to another—"apparent" because the sense of this "right" was disputed between Lutherans and Catholics at the time, and has been among scholars since. For his part, far from taking the provision to express a general liberty of individuals to change city, let alone an incipient right to freedom of conscience,[62] Arnisaeus related it to the security and stability of the state: "Ferdinand the Roman Emperor granted Germans who do not agree with the religion of their prince the power to change their province and take their substance elsewhere, rather than that the right of the prince should be disturbed by a diversity of religion." The same attitude governed his handling of the celebrated *libertas Germanorum*, "freedom of the Germans." Arnisaeus cited a judgement of the Reichskammergericht of Speier that allowed German nobles to fight for foreign powers, "fremde Potentaten," expressly as a part of a long-held "deutsche Freyheit," so long as it did not harm the "Vaterland."[63] But Arnisaeus took that condition as the main intention of the legislation, and argued in consequence that this liberty is only at the discretion of the prince: it has always been licit for princes, "by right of territory," to forbid subjects to go beyond the borders.[64] Thus, neither common subjects nor the nobility could vindicate a liberty to leave the state at will.

In this perspective the contrary position of Hugo Grotius comes strongly into relief. In Book II, chapter V of the *De iure belli ac pacis*, "On

---

[62] See the discussion in J. Whaley, "Religiöse Toleranz in der Frühen Neuzeit," in G. Schmidt et al. (eds.), *Kollektive Freiheitsvorstellungen im frühneuzeitlichen Europa (1400–1850)* (Frankfurt am Main: Peter Lang 2006), 397–416, at pp. 403–404; R. von Friedeburg, "The juridification of natural law: Christoph Besold's claim for a natural right to believe what one wants," *Historical Journal* 53 (2010), 1–19. The genesis of the provision (which gives some support to Arnisaeus's interpretation) is analysed in A. Gotthard, *Der Augsburger Religionsfrieden* (Münster: Aschendorff 2004), pp. 118–23; B. Schneider, *Ius reformandi* (Tübingen: Mohr Siebeck 2001), pp. 157–61, 301–07; Asche, "Auswanderungsrecht," *passim*.

[63] Arnisaeus, *De republica*, lib. I, cap. 5, sect. 8, n. 10, n. 21. For "deutsche Freyheit," see G. Schmidt, "Die Idee 'deutsche Freiheit,'" in id. ed., *Kollektive Freiheitsvorstellungen*, 159–89. This particular liberty, long controversial in Germany, was finally enshrined in the Peace of Westphalia in 1648. My thanks to Jo Whaley for a helpful discussion of these subjects.

[64] Arnisaeus, *De republica*, lib. I, cap. 5, sect. 8, n. 11.

the original acquisition of a right over persons," he began section 24 with the words: "It is usual to ask here, whether it is licit for citizens to depart from the city without obtaining leave." Like Arnisaeus, Grotius cited the Muscovites as a people that does not allow this; the Romans allowed one to change domicile, but one's duties as a citizen in the original munici- pality remained. Contrary to Arnisaeus, however, Grotius read this as a provision *within* the bounds of the Roman empire. "But we are asking what should naturally be the case, if nothing else has been agreed on; nor about a certain part, but about the whole city or complex under one sovereign power."[65] And in this case, while it is not licit for whole com- panies of citizens to depart—because if so, the city cannot survive, and this is "the end, which is what makes right in moral things"[66]—it is dif- ferent for individuals, to whom Grotius conceded (following the Digest under the title "On captives and *postliminium*") a "free faculty" of choos- ing their city.[67] Like Arnisaeus, Grotius cited Cicero's speech *Pro Balbo*, but (in the spirit of the original) to precisely the converse effect. There might be exceptions even in the case of individuals, for example if the city has contracted a substantial public debt, or if danger looms for the city (in which case, however, the citizen might substitute someone else). But otherwise, "it is credible that peoples have consented in the free de- parture of their citizens, because from that liberty they can feel no less benefit from elsewhere"—that is, from people coming in.[68]

Grotius's sense of the mutual benefit of citizens' liberty to leave their city is connected with his perspective on the benefits of trade and ex- change that govern his broader consideration of the right of free move- ment between peoples. We shall explore this familiar dimension of his thought in the next chapter. Meanwhile, another element in his con- struction of the space between nations is his discussion of the Roman law on *postliminium* in peacetime in Book III of the *De iure belli*. *Postliminium* he defined in general as "the right that arises from a return to the thresh- old, that is, to public boundaries."[69] After a consideration of the operation of the principle in war, he took up the strange practice, "which the Roman

---

[65] Grotius, *De iure belli ac pacis*, lib. II, cap. 5, sect. 24, n. 2.

[66] *In moralibus*, ibid.; this exception was denied by Samuel Pufendorf in what is perhaps the fullest treatment of the subject by an early modern philosophical jurist, his *De obliga- tione erga patriam* of 1663, which falls outside the chronological scope of this study. See the contributions by Michael Siedler and Horst Dreitzel in von Friedeburg ed., *"Patria" und "Patrioten."*

[67] Grotius, *De iure belli ac pacis*, lib. II, cap. 5, sect. 24, n. 2; the relevant text is D.49.15.12.9, which demands intentionality on the part of one who returns by *postliminium*, since each is free to choose his *civitas*.

[68] Ibid., n. 3.

[69] Ibid., lib. III, cap. 9, sect. 1–2.

laws testify, that the right of *postliminium* obtained not only between enemies, but between the Romans and foreign peoples." That is, as he
glossed, it was in Roman times licit and customary for nations that were
not at war to take captive one anothers' citizens should they happen to
be within their borders. Security of stay abroad was not a given, but
something that was provided for by specific treaties of friendship, treaties
that were different from treatises to end hostilities. Peace was not friendship. This law of the Romans, however, was a relic of an age of "the No-
mads," when "customs had drowned out the sense of the natural society
that exists between men" and there was a licence of private war even
where there was no public war between nations.[70] In Book II, Grotius
called this practice *Skuthismos*, "Scythianising,"[71] a licence to rob and prey
upon strangers, with the result that treaties had to be made that simply
restored the law of nature, such as treaties of mutual commerce. It was
as a result of an age dominated by this ethos that "Aristotle thought it
praiseworthy to prey upon barbarians, and the very word 'enemy' in ancient Latium meant nothing except 'foreigner.'"[72] However, he pursued
in Book III, not only among Christians but even among Muslims, "the
right of *postliminium* has, just like the right of capture, disappeared outside
war, the necessity of both having been removed by the renewed force of
the relation that nature wished to be among men."[73] The very possibility
of being a *traveller*, then, is a function of a degree of international civilisation that is in fact a re-naturalisation of individual human relations, one
that abstracts from place and makes a person a subject of rights wherever
he is.

This position is consistent with Grotius's appeal, in the Prolegomena
of the 1631 edition of the work, to the Stoic conception of *oikeiōsis* to
underscore his position on natural, and therefore universal, human sociability.[74] However, his account of *postliminium* in peacetime was not origi-

---

[70] Ibid., sect. 18, n. 1.

[71] His notes explain the source of the term in Epiphanius's massive work against heresies,
recently translated by the Jesuit Dionysius Petavius. See Epiphanius, *Opera omnia* (Paris
1622), tom. I, sig. Iii v; Iiiii v; fo. 5–7. *Scythismus* follows *Barbarismus* in a temporal scheme
of the development of heresy, followed again by *Hellenismus* and *Iudaismus*. *Barbarismus*
was the age from Adam to Noah, when men lived according to their own will with no
consensus among them. *Scythismus* took over when men decided to build the city of
Babylon and construct the tower of Babel. It is clear that it is a time of tyranny and corruption, but Epiphanius does not characterise it as one of robbery and prey. The association of Scythians with such practices was, however, a feature of contemporary literature:
see Montecatini, below, n. 90.

[72] Grotius, *De iure belli*, lib. II, cap. 15, sect. 5, nn. 1–3.

[73] Ibid., lib. III, cap. 9, sect. 19.

[74] Ibid., Prolegomena, n. 6; for a nuanced discussion of this theme, C. Brooke, "Grotius,
Stoicism and 'Oikeiosis,'" *Grotiana* 29 (2008), 25–50.

nal to him. It went back to Alberico Gentili in his *De iure belli* (first published in 1598) and before him to Bodin in the 1586 Latin version of his original *Six livres de la république*. Bodin devoted a chapter of the first book to the subject of allied cities and client states. In it, with reference to the legal texts *De captivis et postliminio* and to the *Pro Balbo*, he offered an analysis of the various different types and degrees of alliance that can obtain between two independent cities. One is the kind that bars travellers who are not enemies from becoming captives, since under the Roman law of *postliminium* this would otherwise (as we have seen) obtain. "But," wrote Bodin, "we do not now use that law, on account of the reason of humanity [*ratio humanitatis*] that falls between between man and man." And, while the Greeks had treaties with other cities to allow their citizens to obtain justice abroad, "it has over time come to be the case, with the highest consensus of all peoples, that justice is given to strangers equally as to citizens."[75]

Bodin's treatment was thoroughly juridical: his primary concern, in that chapter, was with the relationship between alliance and sovereignty, not between human universalism and the geographical boundaries of states. However, his *ratio humanitatis* was deliberately picked up by Alberico Gentili and put into the context of a sophisticated meditation on precisely this issue that he had begun in his treatise on embassies, the *De legationibus*, first published in 1585. Here, the ambassador is a figure of mediation, "both a facilitator of contact between nations and a marker of their difference from each other."[76] He has his origin in the *ius gentium* as characterised by Hermogenianus, that is, "when once the nations were separated, kingdoms founded, domains distinguished, commerce established, then the name of 'legation' came into being," and Gentili proposed an overtly Epicurean story to flesh out the bare bones of Roman law. In the beginning,

> in such rudeness of nature, as Lucretius depicts in his incomparable poem, men were neither able to look to the common good, nor did they know how to use any customs among themselves or laws. But afterwards those who bordered upon each other began to compound friendship among themselves.... And if it was necessary for duties and negotiations to arise between those among whom there is some community of right, as there is between nations, commonwealths, and kings; and if those persons either have no wish to meet,

---

[75] Bodin, *De republica*, lib. I, cap. 7, fo. 70. The phrase concerning the "reason of humanity," *ratio humanitatis*, does not appear in the original French version, in which Bodin accepted the ongoing validity of the Roman law in this respect: *Les six livres*, livre I, ch. 7, p. 161.
[76] T. Hampton, *Fictions of embassy. Literature and diplomacy in early modern Europe* (Ithaca and London: Cornell University Press 2009), p. 8.

or—often—cannot; certainly the cities themselves can never do so; therefore it was absolutely necessary ... for others to be constituted, who, representing [*referendo*] those persons, could enact what was needed.[77]

In this story, geographical situation is a critical element of the public body that is the city. Locality or vicinity itself figures as a driver of legal relations and of political civilisation more generally, while the geographical fixity of commonwealths is compensated by the physical mobility of representative persons. Ambassadors, then, are a function of the very existence of separate commonwealths, and their status abroad marks that distinction. They are not subject to those to whom they are sent, "because otherwise the distinction of *imperia* would not be inviolate. For in the person who represents the prince, the prince himself is subject, if that person is subject."[78] But on the same principle, they can be refused entry if there is due cause: "if it were not licit to forbid legates from being sent to oneself, by this one thing the laws of nations would be sufficiently disturbed, those laws that will and command that the *dominium* of things be distinct and inviolate. For a man (that is, the legate) would be staying on foreign soil against the will of its lord [*dominus*], and a necessity would be imposed by one prince upon another to have a man not subject to him in a land that was subject to him."[79] Nevertheless, the requirement of just cause in the denial of entry to ambassadors on public business was a serious condition on the behaviour of states, protecting the fragile but indispensable channel between separation and communication against arbitrary blockage. And this same principle, in reverse, caused Gentili to deny any right of embassy with *praedones* (brigands or pirates). If states that arbitrarily close their borders violate the principle of communication, brigands or pirates violate that of separation. These people, who behave and live purely according to their own will, and treat as prize anything that fortune puts in their way, drag the world back to "the original savagery of nature, when men conducted their lives in the manner of wild beasts" (with a repeated reference to Lucretius's poem). In failing either

---

[77] Alberico Gentili, *De legationibus libri tres* (London 1585), lib. I, cap. 20, p. 37.

[78] Ibid. However, they are nevertheless under the jurisdiction of the local judge; true to Gentili's conception of liberty that we discussed in the last chapter, the liberty of ambassadors is not a *licentia exlex*: ibid., lib. II, cap. 17, pp. 75–76.

[79] Ibid., lib. II, cap. 5, p. 48. Here a certain conceptual instability is apparent: "foreign soil" apparently belongs to *dominia distincta*—"domains distinguished"—rather than *regna condita*—"kingdoms founded"—and the offence is against the lord or *dominus*. But at the same time the land is said to be "subject to," not owned by, the prince in a manner analogous to the subjection of a man (if the rhetoric of the sentence is to work). We shall consider the distinction between *imperium* and *dominium* in the next chapter: see below, p. 200.

to establish in themselves, or to respect in others, the various separations of the *ius gentium—dominia distincta, regna condita*—they take themselves, precisely, out of its community, breaking "the treaty of the human race" (*foedus humani generis*).[80]

The pan-human unity to which Gentili here appeals is not Stoic but Epicurean. Nature has no normative force, and figures rather as an original barbarism. The civilised conduct of the *ius gentium* is the function of an alliance or treaty—analogous to those between states in the law of *postliminium*—implicitly agreed upon by human agents in the process of establishing a space in which human beings might interact and yet preserve their juridical distinctness intact. However, in his *De iure belli* of 1598, Gentili no less than Grotius took such civilised attitudes as the natural relations of human beings towards one another. In Book I, chapter 12 of his *De iure belli*, which asks whether there are natural causes of war among men, he asserted forcefully that "by nature men are not enemies to each other.... Some say, that they are not friends either. But I do not follow this party." Gentili appealed for support to a text of Pomponius in the title *De captivis et postliminio*: "that nation is not an enemy, with which we have neither friendship, nor hospitality, nor a treaty made for the sake of friendship." However, this was apparently incompatible with the operation of *postliminium* in peacetime which that same jurist had posited: "how can these two stand at the same time, that they are not enemies, and nevertheless there is slavery and *postliminium*?" The answer was to distinguish between two kinds of treaty—one that simply ends war and another that adds friendship on top. But whatever the proper interpretation of the legal authorities, on the subject itself "it is remote from reason that in public peace there should be a place for private injuries. And indeed the laws pronounce a barbaric savagery, and injustice, that outside war anyone should become a slave. And therefore this was not afterwards received law (as Bodin relates) on account of the reason of humanity which falls between man and man."[81]

Famously, however, Gentili insisted that war "is almost by nature between us and the Turks, as it was between the Greeks and the barbarians." Against the theologians, he asserted the autonomy of jurisprudence to decide the question of the demands of humanity, just as in the last chapter we saw him insist that the problem of liberty could be solved within law without reference to philosophy.[82] The reason he gave for continuing war against the Turks is that the Turks themselves always treat "us" as

---

[80] Ibid., lib. II, cap. 8, p. 55.

[81] Gentili, *De iure belli*, lib. I, cap. 12, pp. 88–91.

[82] Ibid., p. 92: *Silete theologi in munere alieno*. See Panizza, *Gentili*, ch. 3, for an analysis of Gentili's stand against the theologians.

enemies, seizing whatever opportunity they can for ambush and rapine without any regard for good faith.[83] Accordingly, they almost entirely lose the status of "public" enemies and verge on that of brigands and pirates, *hostes humani generis*, enemies of the human race, with whom the laws of war do not operate.[84] What the immediate context of the law of *postliminium* adds to this aspect of Gentili's thought is the local dimension of this opposition between natural and public. The concept of a public enemy is part of the same international civilisation that recognises the man in the stranger, and does not simply see him as booty that has happily come their way. To treat such change of place as a reason for attack is to operate, oneself, as a purely local rather than an international actor, and thus to deprive oneself of recognition on the part of other international actors. As in the *De legationibus*, the properly public international sphere is an interplay between the demands of local situation and of the juridical relations that go beyond it, not a collapse either of law into locality or of locality into law.

It is interesting to read Hobbes in the light of these related discussions of *postliminium* and natural enmity. At the end of chapter 21 of *Leviathan*, on the liberty of subjects, Hobbes offered what is effectively a little treatment *De captivis et postliminio* on his own terms. Here he asserted that if a prisoner is captured in war, or in some other way gets into the hands of an enemy, then he is at liberty to submit if this is the condition of his life. But, he stressed, the "case is the same, if he be deteined on the same termes, in a forreign country." Hobbes pursued this thought in a passage that asks the same question as the Jesuits had, and in the same context, that is, whether one who has travelled abroad is still subject to the laws of his original commonwealth. According to Hobbes, he "that is sent on a message, or hath leave to travel, is still subject; but it is, by contract between sovereigns, not by virtue of the covenant of subjection. For whosoever entreth into another's dominion, is subject to all the laws thereof; unless he have a privilege by the amity of sovereigns, or by special licence."[85] Now it is central to Hobbes's political philosophy that the covenant of subjection will not hold when an individual is effectively

---

[83] Gentili, *De iure belli*, lib. I, cap. 12, p. 92.

[84] This point is made in P. Schröder, "Taming the fox and the lion—some aspects of the sixteenth-century's debate on inter-state relations," in O. Asbach and P. Schröder eds., *War, the state and international law in seventeenth-century Europe* (Aldershot: Ashgate 2010), 83–102, at pp. 90–91. For an analysis of the complex relationship between Bodin, Gentili, and Grotius on the question of pirates and the law of war, idem, "Gentili's political theory of war and interstate relations," in B. Kingsbury and B. Straumann eds., *The Roman foundations of the law of nations: Alberico Gentili and the justice of empire* (Oxford: Oxford University Press, forthcoming).

[85] Hobbes, *Leviathan*, ch. 21, p. 154.

protected by another party, here the sovereign of a foreign state. However, we are again presented with the de facto problem that we touched upon in chapter 4: why should Hobbes say that an entrant *is subject* rather than being at liberty to submit? One solution is to suppose an implicit act of self-submission, as in Arriaga, with the crossing of the border a tacit sign of the will. Such a person, supposing he were not in danger at home, would have illegitimately withdrawn himself from his obligation to his own sovereign and be back again in the condition of nature with respect to it, an enemy rather than a traveller. It follows that only persons legitimately leaving the commonwealth ("sent" or with "leave") can possibly retain their original subjection, or, in other words, be "travellers" at all; but Hobbes's argument is that even in these cases, their security (and thus their retention of their original citizenship) depends on a treaty or agreement of some kind. Hobbes nevertheless insisted that the safe-conduct of "all men that mediate peace" was a law of nature.[86]

Does this mean that in the absence of explicit treaties of friendship, or of men sent explicitly to negotiate peace, we are in a world of Grotian *Skuthismos*? In all three of his works, Hobbes, developing the theme of the condition of war as a prelude to the genesis of the commonwealth, referred back to an "old time" in which people practised rapine as "a trade of life." I use the word "people" advisedly: *The elements of law* refers simply to "them that used it,"[87] but in *De cive* it is "nations" (*nationes*)[88] and in *Leviathan* it is men living in "small Families."[89] In *De cive*, Hobbes called the practice by the Greek term *lēstrikē*, characterised as *quasi oeconomia*, "a kind of household management." These references distinctly suggest Aristotle's discussion of the natural ways of making a living in Book I of the *Politics*, of which the *bios lēstrikos* is one, sometimes combined with the *bios nomadikos*: ways that are essentially related to the different physical environments in which both human beings and animals find themselves.[90]

---

[86] Ibid., ch. 15, p. 108.

[87] Hobbes, *The elements of law*, part I, ch. 19, p. 100.

[88] Id., *De cive*, cap.V, sect. II, p. 131.

[89] Id., *Leviathan*, ch. 17, p. 118.

[90] Aristotle, *Politics*, bk. I, ch. 8, 1256b1 (we may note in passing that Aristotle's attribution of a *bios* to animals contravenes Agamben's distinction between *bios* and *zoē*: *Homo sacer*, pp. 3–4, 11). Compare Montecatini's commentary on this passage, *In politica*, fo. 256, 286, 290–91. In the table at fo. 256, Montecatini places "*praedatoria, vel lēstrikē*" under "hunting or war," which together form one category (cf. Aristotle's characterisation of the pursuit of natural slaves as a kind of war or hunting, *Politics*, bk. I, ch. 8, 1256b20–25). *Lēstrikē* then divides into war properly speaking, which is just and natural when it is against natural slaves, and *latrocinia*, robbery, "by which the goods and liberty of men who are by nature free and undeserving of such treatment is snatched from them." This practice is unjust and contrary to human nature, though part of the common nature of animals. It is associated with a nomadic way of life since both of them refuse to engage in the work needed to

However, the contrast with Gentili and Grotius, and with contemporary interpreters of Aristotle, is that while they see piracy and robbery as completely lawless practices, Hobbes insisted that this kind of life is governed by the law of honour that dictates restraint from excessive cruelty just as does the law of nature.[91] Its practitioners leave their enemies with their lives, their oxen for ploughing, and their agricultural tools—in other words, the means to start again to cultivate their own patch of ground. In *Leviathan* he explicitly suggested that it is essentially the same "Trade" that commonwealths, "which are but greater Families," now follow between themselves.[92] Thus, while in both *De cive* and *Leviathan* Hobbes argued that *civitates* or "the Sovereign" are analogous to individuals, the law of nations being consequently simply the law of nature applied to the former, equally in these two works there is the suggestion that the analogy is not complete. *De cive* in particular is clear that the "mode" (*modus*) constituted by the code of honour relates to *nationes* rather than to individuals. War as a "Trade," then, even if now conducted by states, is not entirely "public" in Gentili's terms. It remains essentially a local phenomenon, the practice of a group of people in respect of its neighbours: a group that is united like an individual human being, but is at the same time geographically situated in a way that an individual is not. War is not a way of annihilating or conquering its neighbours, but is, paradoxically perhaps, a way of living alongside them.

---

till the ground; *peregrinatio*, going from place to place without regard for *patria*, is inherently vicious (fo. 286), and is the practice not merely of individuals but of whole nations like the Scythians, and now the Tartars and the Arabs (infamous for their *latrocinium*, fo. 290). It is contrary to Cicero's understanding of the society of the whole human race (fo. 291).

[91] In the passage in *The elements*, Hobbes argued that cruelty is forbidden by the law of nature, but what would in other circumstances be cruel can be justified by fear; it follows that cruelty is a sign of fear, and hence a sense of honour dictates abstaining from it. In *De cive*, Hobbes suggested instead that they were not bound to observe such restraint by the law of nature, but only by the law of honour, lest they be accused of fear.

[92] Hobbes, *Leviathan*, ch. 17, p.118.

CHAPTER EIGHT

RE-PLACING THE STATE

As the multifaceted discussions we examined in the last chapter illustrate, for Hobbes and many of his contemporaries locality or situation is an essential presupposition of the way they think about sovereignty and subjection. However, it is at the same time something that emerges only obliquely as they consider particular figures away from home such as travellers, migrants, fugitives, or ambassadors. In this chapter I want to address the issue of the place of the city directly, and to pursue the broader implications of place in relation to the metaphysics of human agency with which this book has been concerned throughout. As the space of physical movement, or locomotion, place is apparently depoliticised from the outset; for the political depends on the free, which, even if conceived as the voluntary and naturalised, as in Hobbes, is nevertheless contrasted with the external motion that is blocked by force. But the casuistry concerning the local motion of citizens shows how the space of the political has to contend with the space of external movement, the same space in which animals move, which resists even as it supplements the voluntary and juridical construction of the state. In this sense the question of place draws together all the strands that we have been threading throughout this study of the limits of the city in relation to nature, limits that turn out to be frontiers on multiple and inter-connected levels.

I want to begin by looking again at the norms of natural agency that we examined in chapter 3. Natural law, the original juridical norm of mankind, is by definition a norm that is not tied to any particular place or spatial ordering. As the law of reason, it is universal in its scope and application. In Aquinas and in the Thomist tradition after him, it is the natural illumination of each human mind, and accordingly fundamentally a law of individual agency. Men are essentially social and political creatures, and thus the law of their nature dictates that they live in society with others; but natural law is not itself the law of that society. In Protestant and legal humanist discourse, as we saw, natural law is differently conceived, precisely as the law of human society. Its dictates are those of sociability. However, that society is not a placed society, but is the universal community of those who behave according to the dictates of reason. There are, it is true, various groups among whom it is not observed. But they are at the limit of human society or human community, no longer at the limit of Europe or any other known space. They can be in any place: they could be in America, yes; but they could equally be marauding pirates in the Mediterranean, or Turks; they could be the Romans and Greeks of an earlier age. That is not to say they bear no relation to place. Paradoxically, as we saw in the last chapter, they operate *locally*, with a localisation of reason that precisely takes them out of universal society, out of "public" and into natural enmity.

By contrast, in one strand of thinking, the *ius gentium* or law of nations *is* a law of placed societies. The temporal dimension that some of the authors we looked at in chapter 3 gave to the *ius gentium* is paralleled by a spatial dimension, a vision of human beings developing norms of interrelations as part of the same movement by which they spread over and settled the surface of the globe. In the Dominican scholastics, Vitoria and Soto, this story is a function of a complex interplay of authorities, the biblical narrative of the first human beings coupled with the texts of Roman law. The story of Genesis is fundamentally one of displacement: Adam and Eve were expelled from Eden, Cain was forced to wander and went and dwelt in the land of Nod. The Flood elided all previous place, but as the waters receded the ark came to rest in one place, Mount Ararat. Thereafter, according to Augustine's influential account, the progeny of the three sons of Noah founded the *gentes* or the *nationes*, "and by their increase filled even the islands";[1] Abraham and Lot agreed to go their separate ways. Likewise, the text of *Ex hoc iure* spoke of "peoples separated ... *dominia* distinguished, boundaries put on fields, buildings set in place," with the implication of the physical activity of human beings moving over,

---

[1] Augustine, *The city of God*, bk. XVI, chs. 3 and 6.

shaping and marking out geographical space.[2] But the way in which the Dominicans put these together was a function of their specific theological inheritance.

As we saw in chapters 1 and 3, they followed Aquinas in holding that the *ius gentium* is distinguished from natural law in being the law that is dictated by the demands of human life together, not individually. Hence it demands division. But Vitoria and Soto took a stronger position than Aquinas in arguing that it is division of *dominia* that *fundamentally* marks off the *ius gentium* from natural law, "according to which nothing is appropriated."[3] Aquinas had indeed suggested that human life together, the domain of the *ius gentium*, demands the division of things, and his example had been a field (*ager*); but there is no sense in Aquinas that division is the essence of the *ius gentium*. Division had, however, been fundamentally problematised by the Franciscan Johannes Duns Scotus and the later nominalist tradition that followed him, exemplified in particular by the Tübingen theologians Gabriel Biel and Conrad Summenhart.[4] Scotus had argued, in contrast to Aquinas, that the original precept of natural law positively commanded community of property and had been revoked after the Fall. This created a licence to appropriate that had then to be legitimated by the law of the prince. In the direct engagement with the Scotist tradition that constitutes his commentary on Question 62 of the *Secunda secundae*, what Vitoria did, followed by Soto, was to substitute the *ius gentium* for that moment of licence and to find for it a legislator different from either God or the prince: the consensus of all mankind. In this context, the *ius gentium* is a law of division, a division that—differently from Aquinas's conception—clearly happened in historical time, following the Fall and then again the Flood. It is not merely a law of division in the abstract, division of "things," but originally and centrally a law of peoples on the move, seeking, settling, and dividing *lands*.[5] I say "originally," because

---

[2] The text of Isidore given in the *Decretum* spoke not of division, however, but of occupation. "The *ius gentium* is the occupation of ground, building, fortification," D.1.c.9 (Isidore of Seville, *Etymologies*, 5. 6): *Ius gentium est sedium occupatio, edificatio, munitio, bella, captivitates, servitudes, postliminia, federa pacis, induciae, legatorum non violandorum religio, conubia inter alienigenas prohibita.*

[3] Vitoria, *Comentarios a la Secunda secundae*, vol. III, q. 62, a.1, n. 20.

[4] I have discussed this tradition in my *Liberty, right and nature*, ch. 1; see now, on Summenhart, J. Varkemaa, "Summenhart's theory of rights," in V. Mäkinen and P. Korkmann eds., *Transformations in medieval and early-modern rights discourse* (Dordrecht: Springer 2006), 119–47; and on the Tübingen scholastics in relation to early Lutheran legal thought, N. Dauber, "Legal theory, private property, and the state in the Reformation," unpublished paper given Cambridge, 2009.

[5] Vitoria, *Comentarios a la Secunda secundae*, q. 62, a.1, nn. 21–23. Here Vitoria suggested (after canvassing various other options) that the most likely way in which this division occurred was by a process of virtual consent: "not with a clear and formal consent, but a

it is clear from the texts that the division of lands that ensued was a once-and-for-ever act. It *has happened.* The principle derived from the *Institutes* of Roman law, that anyone may now occupy anything that has not been divided up, depends on the framework of "the first division," which limits the activity of subsequent individuals and indeed subsequent cities. Henceforth, no one or no city can acquire land by title of division, or capture a land that has been divided up. As Vitoria wrote, again in the commentary on the *Secunda secundae,* this time considering the possibility of acquiring rights over infidel lands, "once that division was made, those lands belonged to those infidels, and they do not want to give them to us, and neither does any prince of theirs; since, therefore, they are true owners, if they do not want to donate them, it follows that we cannot now retain or capture them. Just as, in the matter of the Indians, certainly no one can capture land from them."[6]

Vitoria and Soto understood division as a function of human movement, but they explicitly did not want to see it as a stop on all movement. As the former wrote in the *De Indis:* "in the beginning of the world, when everything was in common, everyone was allowed to visit and travel through any land he wished. This right was clearly not taken away by the *divisio rerum*: it was never the intention of the nations to prevent men's free mutual intercourse with one another by this division. Certainly it would have been thought inhuman in the time of Noah."[7] However, there is no sense in the Dominicans that division is somehow *for* inter-communication. By contrast, in the commentary on the *Institutes* by the early Lutheran jurist and contemporary of Vitoria, Melchior Kling, this is precisely what we find. The demands of human necessity generate the *ius gentium* as a secondary law of nature, which can essentially be reduced to two fundamental precepts: "divide things up," and "punish the guilty." From the first flow all the things mentioned in *Ex hoc iure* that have to do with division: "peoples separated, kingdoms founded, *dominia* distinguished, boundaries put on fields," and the institutions of commerce. The cause of this precept, wrote Kling, "is the precept of natural law, which holds, use things in common [*rebus communiter uti*]. For this is

---

kind of interpretative consent, so that some began to cultivate certain lands and others, others; and from the use of those things it came about that one man would be content with the lands that he had occupied, and another with others, so that none occupied the lands of another." This is what happened between Lot and Abraham, who thus become the model for the settlement of the globe.

[6] Vitoria, *Comentarios a la Secunda secundae*, vol. III, q. 62, a. 1, n. 28. There is an exception here for capturing an occasional foreign town, should it be necessary for defence, for example by the Spanish against the French.

[7] Id., *De Indis*, q. 3, a.1, ed. Pagden and Lawrance, p. 278.

set down as a first principle, or antecedent, from which the law of nations gathers the consequence, thus: If there ought to be community of things [*rerum communio*], it is necessary for peoples to be separated, and again kingdoms founded. Again, there must be certain means set up, through which that communalising [*communicatio*] can happen, such as are contracts, and the means of acquiring the *dominia* of things."[8]

When Hugo Grotius came to pick up the temporal narrative, he expanded and developed this positive perspective on division as paradoxically fostering community. In Book II of the *De iure belli* he offered a markedly post-Fall narrative of discord destroying the original simplicity of life and with it the original community of things, a narrative in which sacred history and the stories of the poets are said to coincide. The *gentes* began to occupy and appropriate different areas of land, which soon became divided among families as well. But what becomes clear is the *interplay* between distance and vice in the ending of *communio rerum*, with distance being ultimately placed first.[9] In this perspective, the things that were left in common—most prominently the sea, to which we shall return later, and the highways that connect different places—become a necessity of sociability, something that reinstates a lost communication that is nevertheless natural to man. Trade, commerce, and travel—"harmless transit"—thereby acquire theological significance as a *remedium peccati*, restoring fallen humanity nearer to its original condition.[10] The world of the *gentes* is an essentially situated world, a world of peoples dwelling apart from one another in different parts of the globe—*gentes … dissitae*, as Grotius put it[11]—and the *De iure belli ac pacis* as a whole is a deliberately civilising project to restore the cultural norms of that world, which are, in Grotius's handling, none other than the natural norms of sociability. This ancient cultural sensibility is one in which place is central, but also in which for that very reason persons out of their own place, away from home, have to be treated as *hospites*, "guests," with peculiar respect. Hospitality is situated practice, a moral requirement of a world of place and displacement.

[8] Kling, *Enarrationes*, p. 6.

[9] Grotius, *De iure belli*, lib. II, cap. II, sect. 2, nn. 1–5.

[10] For the providential function of commerce, see I. Porras, "Constructing international law in the East Indian seas: Property, sovereignty, commerce and war in Hugo Grotius's *De iure praedae*," *Brooklyn Journal of International Law* 31 (2006), 741–804; J. Thumfart, "Freihandel als Religion," *Archiv des Völkerrechts* 46 (2008), 259–71, although it will be clear from my exposition that I am not sure of the extent to which Vitoria can be drawn into the picture of trade as part of a *Heilsgeschichte*. Porras (p. 756) differentiates between Vitoria and Grotius on the position of commerce.

[11] Grotius, *De iure belli*, lib. II, cap. II, sect. 3, n. 2.

In this later work, Grotius emphasised not merely free trade and travel but also free migration and settlement.[12] As we saw in chapter 1, Vitoria in *De Indis* had argued for the right of strangers to occupy things left unoccupied by native inhabitants—deposits of precious metals, just for example—and also to take up domicile in foreign cities and thereby to acquire citizenship.[13] Clearly distinguishing between *dominium* and *imperium*, Grotius offered them a right to occupy not just "things" but parts of other lands that are currently unoccupied by the native inhabitants, on condition they submit to the jurisdiction of the established people of the region.[14] Importantly, however, this argument does not apply purely to individuals. *Imperium* is, as we saw in chapter 5, a function of human will; accordingly, it primarily has human beings for its subject, and only secondarily "place, which is called territory." There can therefore be *imperium* over human beings without *imperium* over place, "for example in a company [*exercitus*] of men, women and children seeking a new home [*novas sedes*]."[15] Thus, the right of settlement applies both to individuals and to entire political communities that have been displaced for some reason, still protected by the ancient norm of hospitality: "it is barbarous to expel guests [*hospites*]."[16] Moreover, we should note that there is no *imperium* over place if there is no *imperium* over people, the one being a secondary consequence of the other. The original spatial division of the world into peoples differently situated (*gentes dissitae*), then, is secured only by the institution of *imperium*. If there were a people that had not instituted political power, and had not thereby turned their place into territory, Grotius's argument offers nothing against a migrant population coming in and setting up an *imperium* of their own. In what his opponents would see as a typical exercise in double standards, Grotius used the moral norms of the world of the *gentes* to justify contemporary settlement activity and at the same time allowed that activity to overrun it.

This past world with its putative norms is elided in those authors who rejected the temporal story of the *ius gentium*. It is not there in Suárez, for whom commerce is indeed a part of the *ius gentium* but justified on the different basis of international custom; nor is it present in Vázquez, in Arriaga, or in Hobbes. Consistently with his overall position on the *ius gentium* that we examined in chapter 3, Arriaga held that any obligation

---

[12] Tuck, *Rights of war and peace*, p. 104.

[13] Vitoria, *De Indis*, q. 3, a.1, ed. Pagden and Lawrance, p. 281.

[14] Grotius, *De iure belli*, lib. II, cap. II, sect. 16–17. For the importance of this distinction and the following in the colonial context, see E. Keene, *Beyond the anarchical society. Grotius, colonialism and order in world politics* (Cambridge: Cambridge University Press 2002), pp. 56–57.

[15] Ibid., cap. III, sect. 4, nn. 1–2.

[16] Ibid., cap. II, sect. 16.

to permit commerce (and this is severely limited anyway by the sovereignty of the state) is an obligation of natural law; moreover, this is not because of the necessity of communication, but because every individual has a natural right to sell his produce even outside the boundaries of the kingdom, unless there is a just cause for denying it.[17] In *The elements of law*, Hobbes held that it "is also a law of nature, *That men allow commerce and traffic indifferently to one another.*"[18] But this provision is absent from the list of natural laws in both *De cive* and *Leviathan*. Luis de Molina is an interesting case, since he preserved the sense of an original division at the heart of the *ius gentium*.[19] But it is stripped of the moral force it possesses, in their different ways, for Vitoria and for Grotius. For Molina, "the time of Noah" was essentially time to set up a prince. Division of *dominium* in the sense of property was directly accompanied by division of *dominium* in the sense of jurisdiction; "immediately" the human race fell, it was necessary to establish rulers with coercive force to compel the wicked.[20] The world of the *gentes*, then, slips instantly into a world of commonwealths, and it is on this basis that Molina rejected Vitoria's proposition that the denial of inter-communication constituted a just cause of war. His specific case turned on a distinction between the right of hospitality and the right to travel and to trade. The right of hospitality was undeniable, but only existed in a state of extreme necessity. Outside that state, any commonwealth had the power to deny entry to foreigners, especially —but not only—if they feared some harm from them.[21] Molina argued this position by a direct analogy between the power of the commonwealth over things that serve for public revenues, and the power of a private owner over his property.[22] Just as an individual can keep anyone off

---

[17] Arriaga, *Disputationes theologicae in primam secundae*, tom. II, disp. 7, sect. 8, subsect. 2, nn. 58–59, fo. 73.

[18] Hobbes, *The elements of law*, part I, ch. 16, p. 87. The sense is that it is illegitimate to deny commerce to some but allow it to others; cf. Vitoria, *De Indis*, tr. Pagden and Lawrance, 3.1, §4, p. 280.

[19] Molina, *De iustitia et iure*, tract. I, disp. 5, n. 4.

[20] Ibid., tract. II, disp. 20, n. 1. Molina does give the fact of distance a role in the rationale for setting up commonwealths, but it comes in second place.

[21] Ibid., tract. II, disp. 105, n. 2; ed. Fraga Iribarne, p. 337.

[22] Molina had provided for this analogy earlier in the work, in the context of a tripartite distinction within *dominium*, the authority for which he took from the lawyers Covarruvias and Bartolus against the usual scholastic bipartite distinction into *dominium* of jurisdiction and *dominium* of property. Molina distinguished instead between *dominium* of jurisdiction, *dominium locorum* or "*dominium* of places," and "particular *dominium*." The two latter are kinds of property, but the former of these is held only by a *universitas* and specifically in "those places or things that are in such a way proper to the *universitas* that they are deputed to the use of individuals. Of this kind are the meadows of a town or a city, deputed to the pasture of the herds of those who are of that place." By contrast, particular *dominium* can be held both by an individual and by a *universitas*, "no otherwise than if it

from his property, at his own discretion and without any other cause, so can a commonwealth, the exception of extreme necessity applying in exactly the same way to both. Thus, despite the initial temporal element to the *ius gentium*, the division once in place functions to give commonwealths the autonomy of private owners, framed only by the demands of natural law.

Alberico Gentili is a more complicated case. Clearly familiar with the Spanish literature, he accepted that it was contrary to the *ius gentium* to deny harbours and commerce, because this was to take away human society and communication.[23] In common with Grotius, he stressed the barbarism of such practices: "I believe it is common to all barbarians, to drive off guests [*hospites*]." Still, Gentili insisted that not every denial of every aspect of interchange constituted a breach of the *ius gentium* concerning commerce. "For how about if importation was denied of something that seems immoral to the inhabitants?" It is not the place of strangers to contest such decisions, "because they do not have the right to change the customs and institutions of the natives." The same goes if a country allows access only to its edges, not to the interior, "which we hear that the British once did, and that the Chinese now do." This too is not an illicit prohibition of commerce. "For a guest is not said to have been driven away if he is not received into every part of the house; and it is licit to keep hidden the secrets of the realm, and to keep away all those who have either come to investigate them, or who might be able to do so."[24] As for the right of harmless transit, this too is a right under the *ius gentium*. Gentili considered an objection that is similar to Molina's position: "The law gives the owner of an estate the power to prevent the entry of a hunter, which goes against our present definition. For the reasoning that applies to a private person in the case of a private estate also applies to a public person in the case of a public estate, or territory."[25] His response was *not* to differentiate public territory from a private estate, but to distinguish between hunting and transit, in the sense that hunting places a burden on the estate whereas transit does not. Thus, transit through public roads is free, and licit, and its denial is a just cause of war; but this

---

were a particular person." Thus, if a *civitas* has something "not for the use of individuals, but so that the revenues serve for public expenses, then certainly the community will possess that thing, and have *dominium* of it." It is this latter that is in play in Molina's rejection of Vitoria's argument. *De iustitia et iure*, tract. II, disp. 3, nn. 7, 11, 12.

[23] On Gentili's relation to Vitoria and the theme of human society, see D. Panizza, "The 'Freedom of the sea' and the 'modern cosmopolis' in Alberico Gentili's *De iure belli*," *Grotiana* 30 (2009), 88–106.

[24] Gentili, *De iure belli*, lib. I, cap. 19, pp. 144–145.

[25] Ibid., p. 141.

is not from Grotius's "situated world" perspective, a world that *has been* divided and now needs, in some way, to overcome that division.

Nowhere are the political implications of the different frameworks for the *ius gentium* that we examined in chapter 3 more apparent than in the contested question of the freedom of the sea. Through his creative appropriation of the work of Fernando Vázquez in the *De iure praedae*, chapter 12 of which was published anonymously in 1609 as *Mare liberum*, Grotius made the sea key to the temporal-spatial conception of the *ius gentium*, as an unoccupied space in between the lands of the *gentes*. In parallel, he made keeping it free, or in common, central to the communication and thus civility of the human race after the Fall. Elaborating the Ovidian poetry of metamorphosis that Vázquez had so effectively deployed in the *Illustrious controversies*, Grotius used citations from the Roman poets to conjure up a world governed by ancient norms of community, norms that were under threat even then. Thus in a celebrated quotation from Ovid, Latona asks for water and laments its denial: "Why do you forbid the waters? The use of waters is in common."[26] Grotius's use of ancient poetry was a crucial part of his project of creating a new cultural sensibility: these texts were part of the education of all civilised Europeans, and his appeal to his readers to recognise their moral force was an appeal to bring that civilised sentiment to bear on the new world of international relations. He was deliberately reconstructing a lost way of talking as well as a lost time, in a temporal layering that is the key to legal meaning.[27] In the *De iure belli*, Grotius explicitly referred back to these passages of the *Mare liberum*, showing that despite his departure from Vázquez's scheme of law in the later work, the new framework still centrally allowed for the "lost world" perspective that governs his earlier work.[28]

It is only once this voice had been re-established that Grotius tackled the specific legal arguments concerning *dominium* over the sea. His arguments in favour of its freedom were, as is well known, initially culled from

[26] Hugo Grotius, *Mare liberum*, in the contemporary translation by Richard Hakluyt, ed. in D. Armitage, *The free sea* (Indianapolis: Liberty Fund 2004), ch. 5, p. 25; the quotation is from Ovid, *Metamorphoses*, bk. VI, repeated in *De iure belli*, lib. II, cap. 2, sect. 12. A survey of recent approaches to this controversial text can be found in G. van Nifterik and J. Nijmann, "Introduction: *Mare liberum* revisited (1609–2009)," *Grotiana* 30 (2009), 3–19.

[27] Thus, concerning the terminology of "common property," he wrote that what "these words signify shall be most fitly signified if, following all poets from Hesiodus and philosophers and ancient civilians, we distinguish those things into times, which peradventure not a long time, yet notwithstanding by certain reason and their nature, are distinguished." *The free sea*, tr. Hakluyt, ch. 5, p. 20. See J. Tully, *A discourse of property* (Cambridge: Cambridge University Press 1980), pp. 69–70.

[28] Grotius, *De iure belli*, lib. II, cap. 2, sect. 3; "cap. 15" is clearly a misprint for "cap. 5," since the *Mare liberum* has no chapter 15.

Vázquez, supported by his own rather dubious reading of Roman law and a handful of highly selective (and occasionally positively misleading) quotations from other jurists.[29] The fundamental, Vazquezian reason why the sea resists *dominium* is its inexhaustibility, which means that the argument from human necessity, dictating the division of *dominia*, has no purchase on the sea.[30] A second reason is the fluidity of the sea: as a flowing substance, it cannot be grasped in the tactile way that is necessary for the acquisition of *dominium* through occupation.[31] The sea cannot be contained; rather it contains the earth: "the wave that constrains the world," that "more truly possesseth than is possessed."[32] Finally, and again from Vázquez, Grotius argued for the imprescriptibility of navigation as a faculty rather than a right.[33] A faculty that rests (as we saw in chapter 4) purely in the will of its possessor defeats the operation of time upon which legal meaning depends. Although apparently, therefore, a different kind of argument, in that it is not to do with the specific nature of the sea, it is in fact intrinsically connected with the boundlessness, the unmarked nature, of the open ocean. It is a space without legal signs in which human activities have no legal consequences. Grotius kept the freedom of this space in the *De iure belli* even while he conceded there the possibility of *imperium* in territorial waters.[34] His argument here deployed the twin scope of *imperium* that he had elaborated for the land—over persons, and over place—eliding the special status, the placelessness, of the shore that had marked the threshold of the state in the earlier work. But it remains true in both works that the space of *imperium* is limited by the open sea. The poetic world and its distinctive idiom frames the world of cities and the language of civil law as the sea frames the dry land.

Grotius's poetic appeals—his attempt to cast the Dutch republic as a modern-day Latona—cut no ice with his Portuguese and British opponents. Serafim de Freitas explicitly drew attention to the duplicity involved in trying to smuggle the city and its works into the ancient and poetic world of the *gentes*. Latona "was not trying to fish or navigate," as

---

[29] For a thorough analysis of the arguments of the *Mare liberum*, see Peter Borschberg, "Hugo Grotius' theory of trans-oceanic trade regulation: Revisiting *Mare liberum* (1609)," *Itinerario* 29 (2005), 31–53.

[30] Grotius, *De iure belli*, lib. II, cap. 2, sect. 3, n. 1.

[31] Id., *The free sea*, tr. Hakluyt, ch. 5, p. 34.

[32] Id., *De iure belli*, lib. II, cap. 2, sect. 3, n. 1: *unda mundam coercens*; *The free sea*, tr. Hakluyt, ch. 5, p. 32.

[33] Ibid., ch. 6, p. 42.

[34] Grotius, *De iure belli*, lib. II, cap. 3, sect. 13, n. 2. For a concise account of Grotius's developing thought, between *Mare liberum* and *De iure belli*, see the editor's introduction in Armitage ed., *The free sea*, pp. xi–xx.

he remarked acidly.[35] In their different ways, Freitas, the lawyer Bento Gil (Benedictus Aegidius, a source for Freitas's arguments), William Welwod, and John Selden all replaced the "lost world" perspective in which (and in which alone) Grotius's arguments made sense. This involved, as a primary move, getting rid of the inherited Vazquezian framework, the effect of which still governed the argument of *De iure belli*. Both of the Portuguese rejected the division of the *ius gentium* into a primary and a secondary law of nations. For Gil, explicitly against Bartolus, the *ius gentium* as the law of natural reason is simply natural law.[36] Freitas began with an explicit critique of Vázquez, arguing firstly that all the legal authorities argue for a single *ius gentium*, and secondly that on the split scenario all division of *dominia* must belong to the secondary law of nations, whereas in fact the Roman lawyers posit that it began with the beginnings of the human race.[37] The *ius gentium* is, rather, single and constituted by natural reason. There are, however, two stages of human life to take into account: the state of innocence and the state of human necessity after the Fall, in which, with the change of circumstances, the law of reason will also change without a change in principle.[38] These are, then, not different temporal stages of the law; Freitas describes them rather as *capita*, chapters or headings.[39] Freitas allowed a corresponding distinction between positive and negative precepts of natural law. Navigation and commerce belong to the second "chapter," are not a matter of positive precept and therefore a prince can forbid all commerce with strangers.[40] Borrowing from Molina, Freitas argued that this is not the case for hospitality in the case of extreme necessity, because extreme necessity brings back the original community of mankind—but *only* extreme necessity. Outside that state, division stands as a principle of natural reason, and travel can be forbidden.[41]

Nevertheless, neither Freitas nor Gil accepted that the sea could be divided in exactly the same way as the land. Freitas conceded that property in the strict sense cannot be had in the sea, although rights of various kinds—occupation, jurisdiction—certainly can. Territory, the object of

---

[35] Serafim de Freitas, *De iusto imperio Lusitanorum Asiatico* (Valladolid 1625), cap. 11, n. 36, fo. 122r. For details of Freitas's argument, see M. Brito Vieira, "*Mare Liberum* vs. *Mare clausum*: Grotius, Freitas and Selden's debate on the dominion over the seas," *Journal of the History of Ideas* 64 (2003), 361–77.

[36] Benedictus Aegidius, *Commentaria in l. Ex hoc iure* [1620] (Coimbra 1700), Pars I, cap. I, n. 5, fo. 26.

[37] Freitas, *De iusto imperio*, cap. 1, n. 4, fo. 4v–5r.

[38] Ibid., nn. 14–15, fo. 5r.

[39] Ibid., nn. 17–18, fo. 5v. Compare his critique of Gil's solution to the problem of legal institutions, like purchase, which do not seem to have begun with the human race: ibid., cap. 14, n. 4, fo. 153r–v.

[40] Ibid., cap. 1, nn. 22–24, fo. 7v.

[41] Ibid., cap. 2, nn. 3–8 and 9–18, fo. 10v.

jurisdiction, includes the sea, and it extends not merely to the hundred miles that Bartolus had suggested, but even to remote parts of the sea.[42] His fellow Portuguese Gil equally rejected an appeal to division. Whereas the medieval jurist Baldus had asserted that under the law of nations, *regna condita, et distincta*—"kingdoms were founded, and distinguished"— equally in the sea as on the dry land, for Gil the acquisition of rights over water required a much more complicated legal justification.[43] By contrast, Welwod and Selden argued more simply for the inclusion of the sea in the original division. Welwod grounded his case in the original condition of mankind, citing the text of Genesis, and asserted that "the waters became divisible and requiring a partition in like manner with the earth, according to that of Baldus: *videmus, de jure gentium, in mare esse regna distincta, sicut in terra arida*."[44] John Selden offered a much more complicated scheme of law, which included some elements similar to that of temporal-spatial conception: in particular, the division of lands by interpretative consent by the Noachidae following the Flood.[45] However, this division takes place not under the *ius gentium*, but under natural law in its permissive aspect; and that division, he proceeded to argue, can be held to include the seas as well.

All of these opponents combated the specific legal arguments that Grotius offered, sometimes with open derision. One of the main strategies of Freitas, Welwod, and Selden was to challenge the argument from the fluidity and unmarkability of the sea to its recalcitrance to right. "For," as Freitas said, "we need to distinguish between sea, river and air as elements, and their places; for if they are considered as elements, they cannot be held, nor occupied, since they are carried here and there around and about. By contrast, considered as circumscribed by places they can certainly be occupied."[46] Whereas for Grotius, the sea contains the earth, Freitas countered that "the sea is founded in the land, as in its bed."[47] Or as Welwod put it, "howsoever it be liquid, fluid, and unstable in the particles thereof, yet in the whole body it is not so, because it keeps the prescribed bounds strictly enough concerning the precise bounds and limits thereof."[48] But unlike either of the two Portuguese jurists, Welwod

---

[42] Ibid., cap. 10, nn. 30, 33, fo. 105r–106v; cf. cap. 11, n. 15, fo. 114r–115v.

[43] Gil, *Comm. in l. Ex hoc iure*, pars I, cap. 3, n. 13 and 33–34, fo. 49–50 and 58–59.

[44] William Welwod, "Of the community and propriety of the seas," ed. in Armitage, *The free sea*, p. 67. For the arguments of Welwod and Selden in their ideological context, see David Armitage, *The ideological originas of the British empire* (Cambridge: Cambridge University Press 2000), ch. 4, esp. pp. 110–14.

[45] John Selden, *Mare clausum* (London 1635), lib. I, cap. 3–7.

[46] Freitas, *De iusto imperio*, cap. 10, nn. 42–3, fo. 107v.

[47] Ibid., n. 47, fo. 108v.

[48] Welwod, "Community and propriety," p. 70.

and Selden deployed the metaphysics of body that we explored in chapter 5 to characterise the sea. Physically, the sea is in flux, like the ship of Theseus or a human body; but while it is continually restored it remains civilly the same.[49] Equally, the two British writers were far more confident than the Portuguese in rejecting Grotius's argument that property requires tactile possession, as also his "scoff"[50] about the inefficacy of imaginary lines in the sea. The lines of latitude and longitude that divide the land in the new colonies of America can equally well divide the sea; moreover, the sea contains rocky outcrops, islands and so forth that can serve as markers and boundaries.[51] It does not constitute an essentially alien field of signification requiring a different language. Far from being a nature that eternally resists the city, the sea can be assimilated to the language of civil bodies and its space to civil space.

I want now to press on this question of natural place in relation to civil space in the main narrative of the founding of the city that we explored in chapter 5. It is here that the interplay between the two senses of *civitas* outlined in the Introduction plays a critical role. Frequently—although not always—creating the mutual moral or juridical bond that generates the city is described as involving a spatial coming-together, a congregation, a coition, for the needs of life and especially for defence. This story dominates the kind of humanist Aristotelian commentary on Book I of the *Politics* that we looked at in the beginning of chapter 5. So, if we take Pier Vettori's very widely read commentary, we find him saying, "Aristotle affirms that the desire for the goods, which he has just stated, first incited men to build houses and cities, and live there together; divided, and living in remote places, they could not enjoy them: for how, in a dispersed state, could they be of mutual protection in avoiding evils, and obtaining the many advantages of life?" Aristotle's "man without a city," the *apolis*, the savage beast, the Cyclops, is translated as "he who lives far from the city"—a gloss on *apolis* that went back to Aquinas.[52] Likewise, Montecatini wrote that "men came together to live in one place; they surrounded it by walls; and they made certain compacts (*pactiones*) and laws, on the one hand to defend themselves from wild beasts and other, more savage men; on the other to have mutual support in living."[53]

---

[49] Welwod, "Community and propriety," p. 72; Selden, *Mare clausum*, pars I, cap. 25, pp. 85–90.

[50] Welwod, "Community and propriety," p. 70.

[51] Selden, *Mare clausum*, pars I, cap. 22, pp. 93, 92.

[52] Pier Vettori, *Commentarii in octo libros Aristotelis de optimo statu civitatis* (Florence 1576), fos. 13, 11.

[53] Montecatini, *In politica*, fo. 47.

"City" here means, of course, primarily the political community that is surrounded by walls: the community that inhabits the *urbs*, the built city. But the story is repeated at the level of *civitas* that is the commonwealth. So Soto wrote in that famous passage that we quoted in chapter 5: "God through nature gave to individual things the faculty of preserving themselves.... But since in their scattered state they were not able to exercise this faculty conveniently, he added to them the instinct of living together, so that united they might be sufficient each to each other."[54] Compare Grotius in the *De iure praedae*, who spoke of "the increasing number of human beings, swollen to such a multitude that men were scattered about with vast distances separating them and were being deprived of opportunities for mutual benefaction. Therefore, the lesser societies began to gather individuals together into one place ... in order to fortify that universal society by a more dependable means of protection."[55] The city in the sense of commonwealth, then, is also situated, is in a place, just like a city with walls; although that transition does put a pressure on the sense of *apolis* that was recognised by Montecatini, who rejected Vettori's understanding of *apolis* as living "far from" the city.[56] For, he said, those who live physically outside the city can still be members of a political community—Montecatini instanced farmers, but also the northern European landed nobility, whom no one, he hazarded, would call "uncivil" or "non-civil," *apolides*.

However, as both Soto and Grotius went on directly to say, and almost every single one of our authors concurred, the commonwealth is not constituted just by congregating or being together in a certain place, but by some sort of act or will or pact. Hobbes in *The elements of law* put the distinction with his usual force: "the word *people* hath a double signification. In one sense it signifieth only a number of men, distinguished by their place of habitation: as the *people* of England, or the *people* of France, which is no more, but the multitude of those particular persons that inhabit those regions, without consideration of any contracts or covenants among them, by which any of them is obliged to the rest. In another sense, it signifieth a person civil ... in the will whereof, is included and involved the will of everyone in particular."[57] And it is the voluntary act that forms the city into a unity that also in some sense *dis*places it. As a moral, juridical, or artificial union, although it is created by people who are in a place, it cannot itself be defined by place. This is not to say that place does not figure at all. One of Soto's arguments against universal em-

---

[54] Above, ch. 5, pp. 124–25.

[55] Grotius, *De iure praedae*, ch. 2 (Prolegomena), fo. 10'; vol. I, p. 19.

[56] Montecatini, *In politica*, fo. 64.

[57] Hobbes, *The elements of law*, part II, ch. 2, p. 124.

pire was an argument from size: a commonwealth, he said, has certain limits of size, beyond which the prince cannot exercise the ruling function and thus constitute its soul or animating principle.[58] This argument was taken from Aristotle in Book VII of the *Politics*, who had posited that there is a certain limit in size determined by the limit of *taxis* or order, beyond which there cannot be a city, but merely an *ethnos*, a "nation," *gens* in the Latin.[59] But, besides the criticism that Soto's views received at the hands of the apologists of Spanish empire,[60] the very notion that size could limit *respublica* was ridiculed by Jean Bodin in Book I, chapter 2 of his *Les six livres de la république*. It does not matter whether all the subjects of a commonwealth are "enclosed in a small town" or whether the commonwealth is as big as Persia, provided they are united under sovereign power.[61] This argument stops the slide from the coition into an *urbs* and into a *respublica*, the metonymy of *civitas* between city and commonwealth; and it was accepted by the Aristotelian Arnisaeus, who, as we saw in chapter 5, equally argued for the distinction between city and commonwealth, although on different grounds. Arnisaeus nevertheless defended Aristotle against Bodin by ahistorically reading the contemporary distinction between the two senses of *civitas* back into Aristotle's understanding of *polis*. Aristotle, he said, distinguished Athens from Babylon only in the narrow sense of "city" as "a multitude living in one place" or "a people enclosed within a certain circumference of walls."[62]

Arnisaeus had some grounds for his reading, nevertheless, in the book of the *Politics* that is crucial to his overall analysis, that is, Book III. If we look again at the key third chapter of that book, where Aristotle discussed the criteria for the continued identity of the city, we see that he directly addressed the factor of place, walls, and human beings considered as inhabitants of a place (rather than as citizens). These, he suggested, do not make a city: rather, the continued existence of the city is to be measured from the continuity of the constitution, that is, the juridical arrangement of the offices of state. Now in his commentary on Book II—the book in which Aristotle criticised Platonic union—John Case had included place in his defence of the idea of the city as a unity, but a unity of order constituted through obedience. So, he said, "citizens who have one place, one law [*forum*], one voice and one mind, can be called one multitude and a unity of many."[63] But whereas the story about genesis tended to

---

[58] Soto, *De iustitia et iure*, lib. IV, q. 4, a. 1.

[59] Aristotle, *Politics*, bk. VII, ch. 4, 1326a30–1326b5.

[60] See Pagden, *Lords of all the world*, pp. 53–54 and note.

[61] Bodin, *Les six livres*, ed. Fayard, p. 48; *De republica*, fo. 10.

[62] Arnisaeus, *De republica*, lib. I, cap. 5, sect. 6 (*De magnitudine civitatis*), n. 8.

[63] Case, *Sphaera civitatis*, lib. II, cap. 1, p. 101.

run together the *civitas* inside walls with the *civitas* that is the common-wealth, the story about form tended to split them apart. So, in his com-mentary on Book III—the continued identity of the city—Case asserted that "the opinions of the learned and the wise differ on this subject from those of the common people and the crowd: for if the same walls, and the same people remain, the vulgar think that the same city remains; but far otherwise did the Philosopher decide in this place, that the unity of the city depends not on the place but on the form, not on the number of men but on the order of the citizens." He went on to illustrate his point. "If the place changes, it will be a different *urbs*, but not a different *civi-tas*.... If the French were driven to the Indies, but kept the same form of government, there would be France." Case did consider an objection concerning the devastation of place: "if the city did not depend on place, Athens and Babylon, now long devastated, would still be called cities: but that is absurd." He replied that "devastation happens in two ways, either in respect of the matter, which consists in place, or in respect of the form, which consists in order. If Babylon and Athens become dead matter"—literally, corpses, *cadavera*—"they can still be cities if the order and the administration survives. But since in fact a confusion of the people and a dissolution of the order occurred in the devastation of the place, there are now not even the ghosts of those cities."[64]

We find some of the same discussion in Book II of Grotius's *De iure belli ac pacis*. As we have seen, this work is fundamentally more place sen-sitive, so to speak, precisely because it concerns the relations between commonwealths and possible just causes of war. The situatedness of the nations is the context of sovereign power, and it is in this context that Grotius did include territory in his account of it. However, as we have seen, he still argued that *imperium* primarily has for its subject human be-ings, and only secondarily place. Thus sovereign power—the *civitas*—is not essentially situated in the way that the nations are. This is confirmed in the chapter on the ceasing of *dominium* or *imperium*, part of which we looked at in chapter 5. We saw how Grotius distinguished between the body and its *species*, its specific form, consisting in a disposition or spirit that holds the otherwise disparate matter of the body together. So now, he argued, a people can die if either the body or the *species* perishes. "The body dies, either if all the parts, without which the body cannot survive, are taken away simultaneously, or if the *ratio*"—rationale, nature—"of a body is taken away." The first case comprises such things as whole peoples being swal-lowed up by the sea or by an earthquake. The second case is a people so scattered by plague or war that they either spontaneously leave the soci-

---

[64] Ibid., lib. III, cap. 2, pp. 207, 209–210.

ety or are separated by force, "such that they cannot come together."[65] It is of the rationale of the body, then, that individual members are so placed that they *can* come together. However, as for John Case, the situated nature of the body is irrelevant to the continuing identity of the *species*. Physical change of place does not alter a people if its *species* remains: "if a people migrates, either of its own will ... or forced, like the people of Carthage in the third Punic War, if the specific form remains, the people does not cease to be; and still less if only the walls of the city are torn down." By contrast, take away the *species* and there is no *civitas*, only an *urbs*, a physical place of life: "Livy tells us that the Romans decided that Capua should be inhabited as an *urbs*: that there should be no body of the city ... but a multitude without sovereign power; and a prefect sent from Rome would administer justice there."[66]

This account of the city, then, removes it from any necessary connection to a particular place and allows it to move, physically, across the surface of the globe. We have already seen the consequences of this in terms of settlement activity: Grotius used the norms of the situated world to protect the movements of unsituated *civitates*. We may compare a passage from the Jesuit Juan de Lugo, in the context of discussing the right to punish that, for him as for all the scholastics, is necessarily a public power. No private individual has it *as a private individual*. But, he says, if we consider the metaphysical case of individuals who live utterly separately, not even united into families, then each individual would have the power to avenge injuries: not as an individual, but as a public person, a prince, in at least a negative sense, that is, one who is not subject. It is the same, he went on, for an army (*exercitus*) or any society of men,

> who by chance might come, and be guests [*hospites*] in, some province: who, if they were badly and unjustly harassed by the natives, could make war on them, and subject them by the right of war, as the Spanish did in the realm and city of Mexico.... for although they be few, and in another's territory, nevertheless they retain in themselves an independent body politic, as Abraham and Jacob conducted themselves when they were travelling with their own in foreign nations; for they retained the form of a people, and of a different community, which had the sovereign right ... to punish its enemies, whoever they were; for they do not, by reason of the foreign land in which they find themselves, lose their liberty, and the right that

[65] Grotius, *De iure belli*, lib. II, cap. 9, sects. 4, 5. Notice that we are here talking about the body independently of the *species*, so that what makes the *body* is some kind of physical coition.

[66] Ibid., sects. 6–7.

> every commonwealth and free community has to avenge its injuries by its own authority.[67]

Just as for Grotius, then, the unsituated nature of the commonwealth, its possibility to migrate, allows for the operation of the European *civitas* on the soil of foreign *gentes*.

In sum, while the story about the genesis of the city implicitly or explicitly includes place, the story about the form of the city—what makes it a commonwealth—has to abstract from place just as it has to abstract from the physical bodies of its constituents. The drive to define the city as a unity possessed of sovereign power, and to show how that entity and that power can have been created by individual human agents, militates against the definition of the state in terms of place or even of territory. This is starkly illustrated in Hobbes's *Leviathan*, so often taken to be emblematic of the early modern natural law state, in which the silence about territory is almost total. It is clear that the genesis of the commonwealth involves some sense of place: as we have seen, in chapter 17 of *Leviathan* Hobbes gave as one of the reasons why individuals need to create a common power the need to defend themselves from the invasion of their neighbours, as well as their mutual attacks upon one another. But his definition of the commonwealth does not itself make any mention of place or even of territory. The issue only comes up in chapter 24, "Of the nutrition, and procreation of a commonwealth." The matter of nutriment —animals, vegetables, and minerals—"is partly native, and partly foreign: native, that which is to be had within the territory of the commonwealth; foreign, that which is imported from without."[68] Place thus figures only in a consideration of matter; it is not part of the form of the city.[69]

We have seen, then, how the natural law state is parasitic upon conceptions of spatial relations or situation both in its practices and even in its founding narrative, while abstracting from them in its essence. This is a critical dimension of the uneasy frontier between nature and the city that I posed in the Introduction as the central problematic of this way of thinking. But in this final section I want to investigate two alternative

---

[67] Juan de Lugo, *Disputationum de iustitia et iure*, tom. I (Lyon 1646), disp. 10, sect. 2, fo. 269, col. 2.

[68] Hobbes, *Leviathan*, pp. 170–71.

[69] See L. Foisneau, "Security as a norm in Hobbes's theory of war: A critique of Schmitt's interpretation of Hobbes's approach to international relations," in Asbach and Schröder eds., *War, the state and international law in seventeenth-century Europe*, 163–80. Against Schmitt, Foisneau points out that the relation between politics and geographical space that is central to Schmitt's analysis of Hobbes in *Der Nomos der Erde* simply does not correspond to Hobbes's own conception either of the state or the state of nature, which are defined interpersonally rather than spatially.

contemporary understandings of how political space is constructed, both of which share the idea that the primary subject of politics is people who live or have their homes together. In chapter 6 we explored the attractive and complex sense of human life that governs the casuistry of the obligation of the law in some of our authors, a life that cannot be either purely naturalised or purely assimilated to the city; but the context is fundamentally individualistic, that is, when it is that one human being ceases to be obliged by the civil law. In chapter 7 we saw how the fact that human beings live in a certain place turns out to be implicit in the political theory of many of them. By contrast, Johannes Althusius and Juan de Salas, in their different ways, explicitly construct the state around human lives that are shared or juxtaposed with one another, and for this reason they build the place of those lives into the very heart of their political theories in a way that the others do not. Althusius developed this account through a successive refinement of the distinction between "simple" and "mixed" forms of association. In his hands, this became a *relationship* between natural and voluntary forms. Juan de Salas did not appeal to these categories; rather, he offered his account as a critique of Suárez's idea of moral union, created through an act of will. By refusing to accept that political union is voluntary in that sense, Salas equally challenged the essence of the natural law construction of the state.

As we saw in chapter 5, Althusius's key political category was the "consociation." A consociation is that whereby those individuals—or those groups—who must live together for the sake of their needs oblige themselves by implicit or explicit pact to offer each other the mutual services necessary for a social life together. The different types of consociation that are the object of political science are analysed according to a series of Ramist dichotomies, which change interestingly between the first edition of the *Politica* of 1603 and the third (the last that Althusius himself saw through the press) of 1614. The differentiae that he posited are not entirely original to him. The distinction between "simple" and "mixed" forms of human association can be found in John Case's 1588 *Sphaera civitatis*, in which Case, in a Ramist table, divided "every society" into "simple" and "mixed" as the primary differentiae.[70] A "simple" society is one that is "instituted" by nature, and this includes only the natural conjunctions that Aristotle had described as necessary for the basic operation of staying alive: man and woman, parent and child, master and slave. All other societies are "mixed," apparently in the sense of "composite,"[71] and these divide into "private and everyday" (the household) and "common," which further subdivide into blood communities (colonies, the village)

[70] Case, *Sphaera civitatis*, cap. I, p. 17.
[71] Ibid., p. 12: *composita, compacta*.

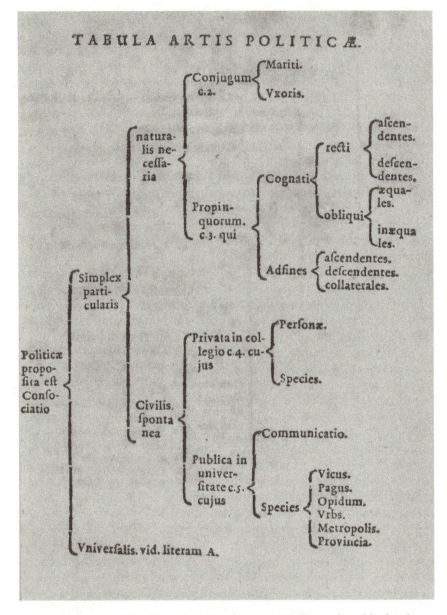

Figure 4 Johannes Althusius, *Politica* (Herborn, 1603). Reproduced by kind permission of the Syndics of Cambridge University Library.

and communities of dignity ("whence the city"). Case did not give any source for the distinction between simple and mixed, but his division of societies follows from and explicitly presupposes a discussion of the distinction in office (*officium*) between master, household manager, statesman (*politicus*), and king, which are the names of respective relationships.[72] These terms suggest a possible source in Simplicius's commentary on the *Enchiridion* of Epictetus, in which different offices are derived from different relationships (*scheseis*), some of which are natural and indissoluble, some voluntary and soluble.[73] This source is explicit in Arnisaeus's justification of the naturalness of the master-slave relationship in his *De republica* of 1615. Here he quoted Simplicius's division of *imperia* into "natural," in which the naturally superior rules the inferior; "voluntary," in which the rich rule and the poor obey "by a certain compact" (*pactione quadam*); and "mixed," "when it has been publicly decreed that the more prudent shall rule."[74] Natural slavery belongs in the first kind, consistent with Arnisaeus's thorough-going defence of it against the lawyers.

In the successive editions of the *Politica*, Althusius worked within these categories to try to stabilise his own specific differentia of the "universal consociation," the *regnum* or *respublica*. In the table to the 1603 edition, consociations are divided into "simple particular" and "universal."[75] "Simple particular" consociations are subdivided into "natural necessary," which further subdivide into those of spouses and those of kinsfolk (no mention of master and slave here), and "civil spontaneous," which further subdivide into "private, in a college" and "public, in a universal body [*universitas*]." "Simple," then, means *either* natural and necessary *or* voluntary and free.[76] A *universitas* is defined as "the collection into one body of several spouses, families and colleges *that live in the same place*."[77] Situatedness, then, distinguishes a public from a private consociation like a college or guild, and also from a natural consociation, none of the definitions of which refer to place. Althusius named as public consociations of this kind

[72] Ibid., p. 11; pp. 16–17.

[73] The work had been translated by Angelus Caninius (Venice 1546) and was translated again by Hieronymus Wolfius (Basel 1563). The translation was reprinted with annotations by Claude Saumaise as *Simplicii commentarius in Enchiridion Epicteti, cum versione H. Wolfii* (Leiden 1640); see ibid., cap. 37, pp. 194–98.

[74] Arnisaeus *De republica*, lib. I, cap. 3, sect. 3, n. 5; *Simplicii commentarius*, cap. 37, pp. 197–98. It should be noted that Arnisaeus was working with a poorer text than the Leiden 1640 version, since it has *publicae* for *publice*.

[75] Johannes Althusius, *Politica* (1st ed., Herborn 1603), *Tabula artis politicae*. See fig. 4. At cap. II, p. 8, "simple" is further contrasted with "mixed," but Althusius does not fill out the sense of this until later on.

[76] The binary distinction between "natural" and "spontaneous" associations is made at p. 11; that "spontaneous" means "voluntary" is clear at p. 29.

[77] Althusius, *Politica* (1603), cap. V, p. 36, emphasis mine.

(which are, it should be remembered, still "simple particular," and not natural but voluntary) a neighbourhood, a village, a town, and a walled city (*urbs*). A *civitas* is a universal body of citizens, a *civium unitas*, living in an *urbs*. Also included in this category of particular public consociations are a metropolis—a city in a dominant relation to other cities—and a province, which contains many cities, towns, and villages. By contrast, the universal consociation, the realm or commonwealth, is "that by which families, colleges, villages, towns, cities and provinces oblige themselves, as members of one political body, to have, constitute, exercise and defend the rights of the realm by their mutual forces and expense within a certain territory."[78] By territory, Althusius specified that he meant "the universal body of fields situated within the boundaries of the covenanting members of commonwealth, in which the laws of the realm are exercised," adapting the Roman legal definition, which refers to the *civitas*, to his own understanding of the *respublica*.[79] Territory as the site of law, then, belongs to the commonwealth, while other public *consociationes* are simply in a certain place as a site of life. However, the difference that Althusius himself highlighted between the universal consociation, the commonwealth or *regnum*, and all other public consociations is that the commonwealth is a "society of life" that is "mixed": "partly necessary, partly spontaneous and dissoluble by its nature, constituted from the species of special, simple and prior society."[80] The *respublica*, then, apparently mixes different species of simple consociation, both natural and voluntary, to create a kind of consociation that is different from all others, even other public consociations like the city. But it seems odd for Althusius to make this the specific differentia of the *respublica* when by his own definition any public consociation, any *universitas*, involves the natural and necessary consociation of the family as well as the voluntary and dissoluble consociations of colleges and guilds.

By the edition of 1614, Althusius had changed his mind. As is clear from the opening table, the distinction between "mixed" and "simple" is now elevated into the primary differentia of all consociations, as it was in Case; but unlike the latter, Althusius made this coincide with the distinction between public and private consociations.[81] A private consociation is always "simple," that is, either natural or voluntary.[82] Apparently, then, any public consociation will be mixed, both natural and voluntary;

---

[78] Ibid., cap. VI, p. 54.
[79] Ibid., cap. VI, p. 57.
[80] Ibid., p. 54.
[81] Id., *Politica* (1614), p. [12]. See fig. 5.
[82] The distinction between natural and "spontaneous, and purely voluntary" societies is developed ibid., cap. 4, p. 33, where Althusius turns from various forms of family and kinship groups to "colleges."

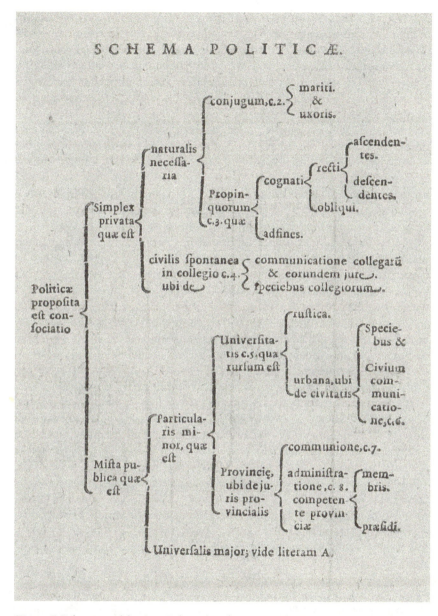

Figure 5 Johannes Althusius, *Politica* (Herborn, 1614). Image courtesy of Herzog August Bibliothek Wolfenbüttel: S: Alv. T 193.

but in fact, when Althusius turned from private to public consociations in chapter V, he made no explicit mention of this mixture at all. He simply said that they will be constituted out of various private consociations, and proceeded to divide them into two: particular and universal. "Particular, which is contained *in certain delimited places*, within which its rights are shared."[83] This contains largely the same list as the 1603 edition, going through various forms of essentially situated community, including the city and the province, with a wealth of detail as to their spatial organisation.[84] By contrast, the definition of the universal consociation does not include any mention of place: "The universal, public and greater consociation is that, by which several cities and provinces oblige themselves to have, constitute, exercise and defend the right of the realm by their mutual sharing of goods, services, forces and expense." Thus, the specific difference of the universal public consociation is that it is not local in the way that the particular public consociations are; it transcends particular situatedness in a trans-local mutuality. As in the 1603 edition, instead of place, the *respublica* or realm has a territory: the law of the realm is "that by which, for establishing the universal sufficiency of life and good order within the territory of the realm, the members of the realm are associated and bound between themselves as one people, into one body under one head." And it is only this universal consociation that is, contrary to the opening table, specifically described as "mixed," which now has a different sense as the mixture of the public and the private: "constituted partly from private, natural, necessary, spontaneous [society]; partly from public."[85]

It is not so clear, then, that Althusius moved from the isolation in 1603 of *maiestas*, the sovereign power that characterises the *regnum* or *respublica* alone, to a conception of *symbiosis* that embraces all forms of public or political consociation in 1614.[86] We can legitimately, I think, infer that the particular public consociations of 1614 are "mixed" in the sense of the 1603 edition, that is, both natural and voluntary. However, this is not the same sense in which the *respublica* is mixed. The *respublica* does not (as the opening table suggests) become one among many political forms of association, but remains isolated in its own specific difference, wherein sovereignty and territoriality lie. However, what is interesting for our pur-

---

[83] Ibid., cap. 5, p. 39, emphasis mine.

[84] Here, as elsewhere in the *Politica* where Althusius considers the situated dimensions of human life and exchange, he draws extensively on the analysis of urban spaces developed in the contemporary "reason of state" literature (see the Introduction, above, p. 8), and likewise in his handling of trade and commerce. However, it is critical to his analysis that political space does not reduce to these dimensions.

[85] Althusius, *Politica* (1614), cap. 9, pp. 88, 90.

[86] See Scattola, "Von *maiestas* zur *symbiosis*," cit. above, ch. 5, p. 131, n. 72.

poses is the role of place or locale that in both editions Althusius gave to the lesser forms of political association. These are "societies of life" that are essentially lived in a particular locality. The mixture of the voluntary and the natural or necessary dimensions of human "life together" (*symbiosis*) that they contain is a mixture that must take place in a certain location, which ties political to physical space. As they are the essential building blocks of the commonwealth, the universalising move of the latter, which also turns place into territory, cannot entirely abstract from the place of the former.

Let me now turn to Althusius's almost exact contemporary, the Jesuit Juan de Salas, who offers us something of the same idea, although without any direct idea of "mixture," in his question on the original location of civil legislative power. It is directed against Suárez's account of moral union that we looked at in chapter 5: political power originally exists in the body of men who have come together for one political end, that is, it exists as a function of their will, and it does not pre-exist the moral union that that will creates. Salas disagreed. "I say ... that of the nature of the thing [*ex natura rei*], political power existed, and still now exists in the whole community of the human race. This is against certain more recent writers"—and there follows the key and as yet unpublished passage of Suárez quoted in chapter 5. He began by asking why this power should not be in the human race. There seems no good reason why, from the beginning, all human beings should not have agreed on various laws that would bind all human beings. "And therefore no union is necessary prior to legislation other than the union of aggregation or congregation, not otherwise impeded."[87] Salas argued that if you deny this, you deny the existence of any positive laws of nations: because these are not simply things that the nations happen all to have agreed on by chance—in that case any nation could decide not to hold them as valid. As genuine laws binding on the whole human race, Salas says, they must originate from a legislative power that is in the whole human race *ex natura rei*. It follows, then, that the thesis that political power is dependent on human will is wrong: "for we have said that independently of human will it is in the whole human race ... and the same is immediately in all human beings who have their domicile together, so that they can pass laws for themselves and for all those who succeed in their domicile, or are staying there for some other reason."[88] Just as for the whole human race, then, there is no necessity of any kind of moral union formed by an act of human will. And it is this same simple cohabita-

---

[87] Salas, *Tractatus de legibus*, disp. 7, sect. 2, n. 19, fo. 114, col. 2; fo. 115, col. 1.
[88] Ibid., n. 23, fo. 117, col. 1.

tion, and not any formation into one body, that generates the principle that the majority can pass laws that bind the whole. For

> those communities that are of people who live in the same place, and having their domicile together, can make laws by the major part, by which all are bound, who wish to stay there, which if any do not wish to keep, they can be expelled, or, if they stay there, punished ... because nature demands that those who live together can be bound by laws pertaining to the common good of the place, and thus just as the unity of the human race is a sufficient foundation for legislative power in the human race: so too the conjunction of domiciles in a community of those who are [so] conjoined.[89]

This is not true for other, non-local—what Althusius would call "spontaneous"—communities, in which the majority principle has to be positively agreed on and does not follow *ex natura rei*.

Thus, differently from Suárez and from practically every other early modern natural law theorist, people do not need to form a moral "one," a mystical body, before they can legislate; all they need is to be living together in the same place. What is interesting, however, is that Salas did not see this as a denial of any idea of unity or community. As we saw at the beginning of chapter 6, he accepted the distinction between law and command based on the perpetuity of the commonwealth as opposed to individuals. Aggregation or congregation is not, therefore, a simple heap or juxtaposition of unconnected domiciles, but itself a kind of unity, a conjunction. Thus, unlike for Arriaga in his virtuoso demolition of Suárez's reasoning concerning travellers, political subjection is not so purely a matter of place that if a person leaves that place, they simply cease to be subject at all. Rather, place and union are interwoven. It was on these grounds that Salas, while reluctantly accepting the *communis opinio* that a traveller leaving the city ceases to be obliged by its laws, nevertheless hedged this around with so many "limitations" that the contrary is effectively the case.[90] It is *domicile*, not simple place, that is the key category, something that is at once a local situation and a moral bond. Salas finished his list of limitations by revisiting Bartolus's analysis of legacies. As we saw, Sánchez and others had concentrated on his statement that things that just happen to be in an estate that has been left to someone are not judged to be legally part of that estate. Salas focused instead on the complementary point, that things that are usually in the estate but happen to be absent *are* part of the legacy. Therefore,

---

[89] Ibid., n. 20, fo. 115, col. 2.
[90] Ibid., disp. 14, sect. 5, fo. 330–38.

since all citizens as long as they do not change their domicile are judged not to be absent, even if they are away by chance, and are reckoned among the citizens and the inhabitants, they will be subject to the prince not just habitually, but actually ... and although Sánchez ... may respond that according to this law, a person who is absent by chance is judged to be present in matters favourable, but not in matters unfavourable, such as is being bound by the laws of his domicile; this does not assist his case, because being subject to the laws is ordained to the common good, and his own; and therefore it is not unfavourable but favourable.[91]

These different ideas of political association offer an alternative conception of "the sphere of the city." Both of them keep, in their different ways, an idea of a union that is both moral and juridical: Salas through his idea of "conjunction," Althusius through keeping the juridical conception of a unity through pact.[92] And yet by focusing their politics on a relation that is not purely juridical or moral, the relationship of living together or alongside, they imply a kind of porosity for the commonwealth that is different from the generous cosmopolitanism of Soto with which we began. Soto's commonwealth was porous in respect of all subjects of rights, but it put up a firm wall against all kinds of natural or seminatural agents, the vagabonds and the roaming bands to which (and only to which) he was prepared to countenance the application of Aristotle's unmodified conception of natural slavery. By contrast, Salas and Althusius allow the physical dimension of human life to penetrate the juridical structure of the commonwealth, and thereby suggest a way to open the gates of the city differently: not merely to the natural dimension of human being, but also, perhaps, to the other kinds of being alongside which human lives must always be lived. Evidently neither Althusius nor Salas had any such idea in mind. But by way of a coda and a metaphor, I want to close this book by looking back out to sea, with *A treatise on islands* published in 1624 by the East Frisian jurist Johannes Gryphiander.

This is a work that can be read as an essentially Grotian contribution to the "free sea" debate. Gryphiander argued that the open ocean, unlike coastal waters, is a free space for navigation, which is a free faculty that can never be prescribed. "For as Seneca says in *De beneficiis*, it was the common good that the commerce of the sea should lie open, and the

<hr />

[91] Ibid., n. 83, fo. 338, col. 2.

[92] Ernst Reibstein, in his *Johannes Althusius als Fortsetzer der Schule von Salamanca* (Karlsruhe: Müller 1955), pp. 88–89, suggested that Althusius's mixing of the "sociological" and the "juridical" is a mistake; on the contrary, I think it is of the essence of his theory.

kingdom of the human race be loosened."[93] But he avoided the dichoto-
mous terms of that debate—free or closed, recalcitrant or assimilated—
by explicitly casting himself as a modern-day Bartolus, whose *Tiberiadis*
constitutes one of the very first tracts on water rights. In this work, Bartolus had argued that the study of law has to admit of geometry in order
to produce the correct legal results concerning alluvial deposits. As Os-
valdo Cavallar points out in his study of the work, however, the openness
is not merely between disciplines, but is a fluidity on many levels. The flow
of the river Tiber is past and through civic space and down to *the* city,
Rome. The river is implicated in the city and the city in the river, and the
justice of the one intertwines inextricably with the justice of the other.[94]
Gryphiander wrote in his preface of Bartolus's motivation, which the
great medieval jurist had himself described in a highly interesting and
unusual proem to the work. "[Bartolus] himself ... writes of the occasion
that moved him to write: that while he was in Perugia lecturing publicly
on the civil law, he took a vacation in a villa near to Perugia on the Tiber,
and, as he contemplated the meanderings of that river, the alluvial deposits, the islands that had sprung up in the river, and the changes of the river
bed, he began to question what was the legal position with regard to
many doubts that arose out of fact.... This cause drove me, as well, to the
same thing, as I once looked out from the islands of Frisia towards the
wide Ocean."[95]

Differently from Bartolus, however, Gryphiander suggested that what
we need in addition to legal science is not geometry but a knowledge of
nature. "This subject cannot be handled purely from the commentaries
of lawyers, since many natural things [*naturalia*] run in between [*intercur-
rant*], the knowledge of which a lawyer must borrow from someone else
if he does not have it himself."[96] He gave a recent example of a lawyer for
the Count of East Friesland, whose denial that there was such a thing as
marine alluvium would have provoked laughter from any Frisian peasant.
The way in which natural processes breach the autonomy of law as a
discipline mirrors the way in which they breach the integrity of the
space of law, the city. Water does not frame the civil space, as in Grotius,
nor is it absorbed into it, as in Freitas and Selden, but runs in between, as

---

[93] Johannes Gryphiander, *De insulis tractatus* (Frankfurt 1624), cap. 25, "On the prescrip-
tion of an island," nn. 53–68.
[94] See O. Cavallar, "River of law: Bartolus's *Tiberiadis* (*De alluvione*)," in J. A. Marino and T.
Kuehn eds., *A renaissance of conflicts. Visions and revisions of law and society in Italy and Spain*
(Toronto: Centre for Reformation and Renaissance Studies 2004), 31–129. My thanks to
Julius Kirschner for directing me to this valuable study.
[95] Gryphiander, *De insulis*, Praefatio, n. 80, p. 12.
[96] Ibid., n. 74, p. 12.

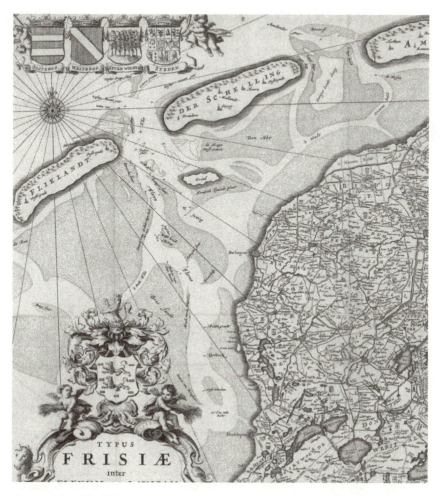

Figure 6 Detail of the East Frisian coast and islands: "Frisia" from the *Atlas Schotanus* (Franeker, 1664). Image courtesy of Tresoar, Leeuwarden.

Gryphiander showed in the opening three chapters, which detail how many cities are in fact islands, and how their very names indicate their genesis from the sea. Thus Zeeland, Selandia, "implies nothing other than the land of the Ocean, or maritime soil," and Leeuwerden in East Fries-land suggests the source of its becoming—German *werden*—from "ma-rine increment."[97] The intercurrent of river and sea allows the physical

[97] Ibid., cap. 1, n. 19, p. 21; nn. 14–15, p. 20.

flux of water the possibility to alter the space of jurisdiction in a way that cannot be assimilated to the human will, even if, and true to his time, it ultimately falls under the divine will.[98] Equally true to his time, and with many references back to Fernando Vázquez's admonitory preface to the *Illustrious controversies* (which, we may note in passing, Grotius never took seriously), the final chapter of the work, "On the loss and death of an island," is awash with the language of mutability: "there is nothing, not the smallest thing in this mortal life, that always remains in the same state." But this does not drown out his central point about the agency of nature. The death of a thing is either natural, "from nature itself," or civil, and "in these two ways not only men perish ... but the very common-wealths, provinces and islands themselves." This death, "albeit common to all created things, nevertheless has dominion in things of the sea, where the returning swell turns everything up and down."[99] The sensibility of constant change combines in Gryphiander's work with a juridical phi-losophy prompted by the watery provinces of the Netherlands and north-east Germany to create an understanding that the sea and the city share the same space. *Mutatis mutandis*, my title is offered in the same spirit.

[98] Ibid., cap. 14 ("On jurisdiction over an island"), n. 96: "if the change of rivers is per-petual, God himself seems to will that the boundaries of an empire or province be changed." Contrast Grotius's treatment of *agri arcifinii* in the *De iure belli*: following Varro's etymology, Grotius suggested that such "fields" are so called because they have boundaries (*fines*) suitable for repelling (*arcendi*) enemies, "that is, natural boundaries: like rivers and mountains." In these cases, if the river changes course, the boundaries of the territory also change, "viz. because each people is credited with having originally occupied their *impe-rium* with the intention that the middle of the river should divide them, as a natural terminus." In this way, the natural change of a river is assimilated to the human juridical world rather than fundamentally challenging it. Grotius, *De iure belli*, lib. II, cap. 3, sect. 16, nn. 1–2.

[99] Gryphiander, *De insulis*, cap. 29, nn. 16, 11, 15, creatively assimilating the constant flow and counterflow (*palirrhoea*) of human life itself, described by the emperor Leo in the proem to his *Novellae*, to the movement of the sea.

BIBLIOGRAPHY OF WORKS CITED

PRIMARY SOURCES

Aegidius, Benedictus. *Commentaria in l. Ex hoc iure* (Coimbra 1700).

Althusius, Johannes. *Iuris romani libri duo* (Basel 1586).

——. *Politica methodice digesta* (Herborn 1603).

——. *Politica methodice digesta*, repr. from the third edition of 1614 with an Introduction by C. J. Friedrich (Cambridge, Mass.: Harvard University Press 1932).

——. *Dicaeologicae libri tres*, repr. of Frankfurt 1649 (Aalen: Scientia Verlag 1967).

Aquinas, Thomas, *Summa theologiae* (Rome: Forzani 1894).

——. *Sententia libri ethicorum*, in *Opera omnia iussu Leonis XIII P.M.edita*, tom. XLVII, vol. 1 (Rome: Ad Sanctae Sabinae 1969).

Aquinas. Political writings, ed. R. W. Dyson (Cambridge: Cambridge University Press 2002).

The Arminian Confession of 1621, ed. Mark A. Ellis (Eugene, Oregon: Pickwick Publications 2005).

Arnisaeus, Henning. *Vindiciae secundum veritatem … contra … M. Thomae Rhaedi Scoti pervigilia* (Frankfurt 1611).

——. *De republica seu relectionis politicae libri duo* (Frankfurt 1615).

Arriaga, Rodrigo de. *Cursus philosophicus* (Antwerp 1632).

——. *Disputationes theologicae in primam partem S. Thomae* (Antwerp 1643).

——. *Disputationes theologicae in primam secundae Divi Thomae* (Antwerp 1644).

Bartolus of Sassoferrato. *In universum ius civile commentaria* (Basel 1562).

Caietanus, Tommaso de Vio. *Secunda secundae cum commentariis Cardinalis Caietani* (Lyon 1552).

Case, John. *Sphaera civitatis* (Oxford 1588).

Bellarmine, Robert. *Disputationum de controversiis Christianae fidei, adversus huius temporis haereticos*, tom. II (Ingolstadt 1611).

Bodecherus, Nicolaus. *Sociniano-Remonstratismus* (Leiden 1624).

Bodin, Jean. *Les six livres de la république* (Paris: Fayard 1986).

——. *De republica libri sex* (Paris 1586).

Bolognetti, Alberto. *Tractatus de lege, iure et aequitate*, in *Tractatus illustrium iurisconsultorum* (Venice 1584), vol. I.

Bozio, Tommaso. *De iure status* (Cologne 1625).

Bramhall, John. *A discourse of liberty and necessity*, in V. Chappell ed., *Hobbes and Bramhall on liberty and necessity* (Cambridge: Cambridge University Press 1999).

Calvinus, Johannes. *Lexicon iuridicum iuris romani* (Frankfurt 1600).

Cellarius, Christianus. *Oratio pro pauperibus, ut eis liceat mendicare* (Antwerp 1530).

——. *Oratio contra mendicitatem pro nova pauperum subventione* (Antwerp 1531).

Chemnitz, Martin. *Examen concilii Tridentini* (Frankfurt 1574).

————. *Loci theologici*, ed. Polycarp Leyser (Frankfurt/Wittemberg 1653).

Connan, François. *Commentariorum iuris civilis libri decem* (Lyon 1566).

Covarruvias, Diego de. *Opera omnia* (Frankfurt 1592).

Cujas, Jacques. *Opera omnia* (Frankfurt 1595).

Doneau, Hugues (Hugo Donellus). *Commentarii de iure civili* (Frankfurt 1589).

Epiphanius. *Opera omnia*, tr. D. Petavius (Paris 1622).

Episcopius, Simon. *Collegium disputationum theologicarum* (Dordrecht 1615).

————. *Collegium disputationum theologicarum in Academia Lugdunensi privatim institutarum* (Dordrecht 1618).

[Episcopius, Simon] *Apologia pro confessione* (NP 1630).

Faber, Antonius. *Iurisprudentiae papinianeae scientia* (Geneva 1631).

Filmer, Robert. *Patriarcha and other writings*, ed. J. P. Sommerville (Cambridge: Cambridge University Press 1991).

Forma subventionis pauperum, quae apud hyperas flandrorum urbem viget (Ypres 1531).

Freitas, Serafim de. *De iusto imperio Lusitanorum Asiatico* (Valladolid 1625).

Gentili, Alberico. *Lectionum et epistolarum quae ad ius civile pertinent libri IV* (London 1583).

————. *De legationibus libri tres* (London 1585).

————. *De iure belli libri tres* (Hanover 1598).

————. *Hispanicae advocationis libri duo* (1661) (2 vols., New York: Oxford University Press 1921).

Giffen, Hubert van (Obertus Giphanius). *Commentarii in decem libros ethicorum Aristotelis ad Nicomachum* (Frankfurt 1608).

————. *Commentarii in politicorum opus Aristotelis* (Frankfurt 1608).

Grégoire, Pierre. *Syntagma iuris* (Lyon 1582).

————. *De republica libri sex et viginti* (Pont-à-Mousson 1596).

Grotius, Hugo. *De iure belli ac pacis*, ed. J. Barbeyrac (Amsterdam 1720).

————. *De iure praedae commentarius* (Oxford: Clarendon 1950).

————. *The free sea*, ed. D. Armitage (Indianapolis: Liberty Fund 2004).

————. *The rights of war and peace*, ed. R. Tuck (Indianapolis: Liberty Fund 2006).

Gryphiander, Johannes. *De insulis tractatus* (Frankfurt 1624).

Hemmingius, Nicolaus. *De lege naturae apodictica methodus* (Wittemberg 1577).

Hilliger, Oswald. *Donellus enucleatus* (Lyon 1619).

Hobbes, Thomas. *The elements of law*, ed. F. Tönnies (London: Frank Cass 1969).

————. *De cive*, ed. H. Warrender (Oxford: Clarendon 1987).

————. *Leviathan*, ed. R. Tuck (Cambridge: Cambridge University Press 1996).

————. *Of liberty and necessity*, in Chappell ed., *Hobbes and Bramhall on liberty and necessity*.

————. *The questions concerning liberty, necessity and chance* (London 1656).

Isocrates. *Isocrates Graeco-Latinus*, tr. H. Wolfius (Basel 1567).

Kling, Melchior. *In quattuor Institutionum libros enarrationes* (Lyon 1566).

Lambinus, Dionysius. *In Q. Horatium Flaccum commentarii* (Frankfurt 1577).

Ledesma, Martín de. *Prima quartae* (Coimbra 1555).

———. *Secunda quartae* (Coimbra 1560).

Lessius, Leonardus. *De iustitia et iure caeterisque virtutibus cardinalibus* (Antwerp 1612).

Lipsius, Justus. *Sixe bookes of politickes or civil doctrine* (London 1594).

———. *Politicorum libri sex*, ed. J. Waszink (Assen: Van Gorcum 2004).

Lugo, Juan de. *Disputationum de iustitia et iure*, tom. I–II (Lyon 1642–1646).

Mazzolini, Silvestro da Prierio. *Summa summarum quae sylvestrina dicitur* (Strasbourg 1518).

Medina, Bartolomé de. *Expositio in primam secundae D. Thomae* (Venice 1580).

Melanchthon, Philip. *Philosophiae moralis epitome* (N.P. 1538).

Mendoza, Fernando de. *Disputationum iuris civilis in difficiliores leges ff. de pactis libri tres* (Alcalá 1586).

Molina, Luis de. *Liberi arbitrii concordia cum gratiae donis, divina praescientia, providentia, praedestinatione et reprobatione* (Antwerp 1609).

———. *De iustitia et iure* (Mainz 1614).

———. *On divine foreknowledge (Part IV of the Concordia)*, tr. with introduction and notes by Alfred J. Freddoso (Ithaca, N.Y.: Cornell University Press 1988).

Montecatini, Antonio. *In politica, hoc est, in civiles libros Aristotelis progymnasmata* (Ferrara 1587).

Moulin, Pierre du. *The anatomy of Arminianisme* (London 1620).

Oldendorp, Johannes. *Eisagōgē juris naturalis sive elementaria introductio juris naturae gentium et civilis* in *Tractatus universi iuris* (Lyon 1549), vol. I.

Rivière, A. [Théophile Raynaud]. *Calvinismus bestiarum religio* (Lyon 1630).

Robles, Juan de. *De la orden que en algunos pueblos de España se ha puesto en la limosna* (1545), ed. in F. Santolaria Sierra, *El gran debate sobre los pobres en el siglo XVI. Domingo de Soto y Juan de Robles 1545* (Barcelona: Ariel 2003).

Rutherford, Samuel. *Exercitationes apologeticae pro divina gratia* (Franeker 1651).

Salas, Juan de. *In primam secundae divi Thomae* (Barcelona 1609).

———. *Tractatus de legibus, in primam secundae S. Thomae* (Lyon 1611).

Sánchez, Tomás. *De sancto matrimonii sacramento* (Lyon 1669).

Selden, John. *Mare clausum* (London 1635).

Simplicius. *Simplicii commentarius in Enchiridion Epicteti, cum versione H. Wolfii* (Leiden 1640).

Soto, Domingo de. *Deliberación en la causa de los pobres*, ed. in Santolaria Sierra, *El gran debate sobre los pobres*.

———. *In causa pauperum deliberatio* (Salamanca 1566).

———. *De iustitia et iure* (Salamanca 1556).

———. *Commentarii in quartum sententiarum* (Salamanca 1569).

Stow, John. *The annales of England* (London [1605]).

Suárez, Francisco. *Varia opuscula theologica* (Lyon 1600).

———. *Commentariorum ac disputationum in tertiam partem D. Thomae* (Mainz 1619).

———. *Tractatus quinque theologici* (Lyon 1628).

————. *Defensio fidei*, ed. E. Elorduy and L. Peña (Madrid: CSIC 1965).

————. *De legibus ac Deo legislatore*, ed. L. Pereña (6 vols., Madrid: CSIC 1971–1981).

Valentia, Gregory de. *Commentariorum theologicorum tomi quattuor* (Ingolstadt 1591–97).

Vázquez, Gabriel. *Commentariorum ac disputationum in primam secundae S. Thomae* (Lyon 1631).

Vázquez de Menchaca, Fernando. *Controversiarum illustrium libri tres* (Frankfurt 1572).

Vettori, Pier. *Commentarii in octo libros Aristotelis de optimo statu civitatis* (Florence 1576).

Vitoria, Francisco de. *Comentario al tratado de la ley*, ed. V. Beltrán de Heredia (Madrid: CSIC 1952).

————. *Comentarios a la Secunda secundae de Santo Tomás*, ed. V. Beltrán de Heredia (Salamanca: Apartado 17 1934).

————. *Political writings*, ed. and tr. A. Pagden and J. Lawrance (Cambridge: Cambridge University Press 1992).

————. *Vorlesungen*, eds. Ulrich Horst, Heinz-Gerhard Justenhoven and Joachim Stüben (2 vols., Stuttgart-Berlin-Köln: Kohlhammer 1997).

Walaeus, Antonius. *Responsio Antoni Walaei ad censuram Ioannis Arnoldi Corvini, in cl. Viri, Petri Molinaei Anatomen Arminianismi* (Leiden 1625).

————. *Censura in confessionem* (Leiden 1626).

————. *Compendium ethicae Aristotelis ad normam Christianae veritatis revocatum* (Leiden 1644).

Zumel, Francisco. *De Deo eiusque operibus. Commentaria in primam partem S. Thomae* (Salamanca 1590).

————. *Variarum disputationum tomi tres* (Lyon 1609).

SECONDARY SOURCES

Agamben, G. *Homo sacer. Il potere sovrano e la nuda vita*, 2nd edn. (Turin: Einaudi 2005).

Aichele, A. "Moral und Seelenheil. Luis de Molinas Lehre von den zwei Freiheiten zwischen Augustin und Aristoteles," in Kaufmann and Schnepf eds., *Politische Metaphysik*, 59–83.

Anghie, A. *Imperialism, sovereignty and the making of international law* (Cambridge: Cambridge University Press 2002).

Armitage, D. *The ideological origins of the British empire* (Cambridge: Cambridge University Press 2000).

————. "Hobbes and the foundations of modern international thought," in A.S. Brett and J. Tully eds., *Rethinking the foundations of modern political thought* (Cambridge: Cambridge University Press 2006), 219–35.

Arrizabalaga, J. "Poor relief in Counter-reformation Castile: An overview," in Ole Peter Grell, Andrew Cunningham, and Jon Arrizabalaga eds., *Health care and poor relief in Counter-reformation Europe* (London and New York: Routledge 1999), 151–76.

Asbach, O., and Schröder, P., eds. *War, the state and international law in seventeenth-century Europe* (Aldershot: Ashgate 2010).

Asche, M. "Auswanderungsrecht und Migration aus Glaubensgründen," in H. Schilling and H. Smolinsky eds., *Der Augsburger Religionsfrieden 1555* (Münster: Aschendorff 2007).

Belda Plans, J. *La escuela de Salamanca* (Madrid: Biblioteca de Autores Cristianos 2000).

Benton, L. *A search for sovereignty. Law and geography in European empires, 1400–1900* (Cambridge: Cambridge University Press 2010).

Bergfeld, C. *Franciscus Connanus (1508–1551). Ein Systematiker des römischen Rechts* (Köln-Graz: Böhlau 1968).

Borschberg, P. "Hugo Grotius' theory of trans-oceanic trade regulation: Revisiting *Mare liberum* (1609)," *Itinerario* 29 (2005), 31–53.

Breiskorn, N. "Lex aeterna," in Grunert and Seelmann eds., *Die Ordnung der Praxis*, 49–73.

Brett, A. *Liberty, right and nature. Individual rights in later scholastic thought* (Cambridge: Cambridge University Press 1997).

———. "Natural right and civil community: The civil philosophy of Hugo Grotius," *Historical Journal* 45 (2002), 31–51.

Brito Vieira, M. "*Mare Liberum* vs. *Mare clausum*: Grotius, Freitas and Selden's debate on the dominion over the seas," *Journal of the History of Ideas* 64 (2003), 361–77.

Brooke, C. "Grotius, Stoicism and 'Oikeiosis,'" *Grotiana* 29 (2008), 25–50.

Burns, J., ed. *The Cambridge history of political thought 1450–1700* (Cambridge: Cambridge University Press 1991).

Burns, J., and Izbicki, T., eds. *Conciliarism and papalism* (Cambridge: Cambridge University Press 1997).

Caney, S. *Justice beyond borders* (Oxford: Oxford University Press 2005).

Cavallar, G. *The rights of strangers. Theories of international hospitality, the global community, and political justice since Vitoria* (Aldershot: Ashgate 2002).

Chantraine, G. "Le surnaturel: Discernement de la pensée catholique selon Henri de Lubac," *Revue Thomiste* 101 (2002), 31–51.

Coing, H. "Zur Geschichte des Begriffs 'subjektives Rechts,'" in id. ed., *Das subjektives Recht und der Rechtsschutz der Persönlichkeit* (Frankfurt: Metzner 1959).

Courtine, J. F. *Nature et empire de la loi. Études suaréziennes* (Paris: Vrin 1999).

Craig, W. *The problem of divine foreknowledge and future contingents from Aristotle to Suárez* (Leiden: Brill 1988).

Crowe, M. "St. Thomas and Ulpian's natural law," in A. Maurer ed., *St. Thomas Aquinas 1274–1974. Commemorative studies* (Toronto: Pontifical Institute of Medieval Studies 1974), 261–82.

Damrosch, L. "Hobbes as reformation theologian," *Journal of the History of Ideas* 40 (1979), 339–52.

Dauber, N. "Legal theory, private property, and the state in the Reformation," unpublished paper given Cambridge, 2009.

Deckers, D., *Gerechtigkeit und Recht. Eine historisch-kritisch Untersuchung der Gerechtigkeitslehre des Francisco de Vitoria (1483–1546)* (Freiburg: Herder 1992).

Dekker, E. "Was Arminius a Molinist?" *Sixteenth Century Journal* 27 (1996), 337–52.

Des Chene, D. *Physiologia: Natural philosophy in late Aristotelian and Cartesian thought* (Ithaca and London: Cornell University Press 1996).

Deuringer, K. *Probleme der Caritas in der Schule von Salamanca* (Freiburg: Herder 1959).

Dibon, P. "Die Republik der Vereinigten Niederlande," in *Grundrisse der Geschichte der Philosophie. Die Philosophie des 17. Jahrhunderts*, Bd. II: *Frankreich und Niederlande*, ed. J.-P. Schobinger (Basel: Schwabe 1993).

Doyle, J. "Francisco Suárez on the law of nations," in M. W. Janis and C. Evans eds., *Religion and international law* (The Hague–London: Nijhoff 1999), 103–20.

Dreitzel, H. *Protestantischer Aristotelismus und absoluter Staat* (Wiesbaden: Franz Steiner 1970).

————. *Absolutismus und ständische Verfassung in Deutschland* (Mainz: Philipp von Zabern 1992).

Eisenberg, J. "Cultural encounters, theoretical adventures: The Jesuit missions to the New World and the justification of voluntary slavery," in Kaufmann and Schnepf eds., *Politische Metaphysik*, 357–83.

Flynn, M. *Sacred charity. Confraternities and social welfare in Spain, 1400–1700* (London: Macmillan 1989).

Foisneau, L. "Omnipotence, necessity and sovereignty," in P. Springborg ed., *The Cambridge companion to Hobbes's* Leviathan (Cambridge: Cambridge University Press 2007).

————. "Security as a norm in Hobbes's theory of war: A critique of Schmitt's interpretation of Hobbes's approach to international relations," in Asbach and Schröder eds., *War, the state and international law in seventeenth-century Europe*, pp. 163–80.

Foucault, M. *Sécurité, territoire, population. Cours au Collège de France, 1977–1978* (Paris: Seuil/Gallimard 2004).

Fraga Iribarne, M. *Luis de Molina y el derecho de la guerra* (Madrid: CSIC 1947).

Friedeburg, R. von. *Self-defence and religious strife in early modern Europe* (Aldershot: Ashgate 2002).

———— ed. *"Patria" und "Patrioten" vor dem Patriotismus* (Wiesbaden: Harrassowitz 2005).

————. "The juridification of natural law: Christoph Besold's 1625 claim for a natural right to believe what one wants," *Historical Journal* 53 (2010), 1–19.

Friedeburg, R. von, and Seidler, M. J. "The Holy Roman Empire of the German Nation," in H. A. Lloyd, G. Burgess, and S. Hodgson eds., *European political thought 1450–1700* (New Haven: Yale University Press 2007), 103–72.

Garrán Martínez, J. *La prohibición de la mendacidad. La controversia entre Domingo de Soto y Juan de Robles en Salamanca (1545)* (Salamanca: Ediciones Universidad Salamanca 2004).

Gelderen, M. van. "Aristotelians, monarchomachs and republicans," in M. van Gelderen and Q. Skinner eds., *Republicanism*, vol. I (Cambridge: Cambridge University Press 2002), 195–217.

Gemmeke, E. *Die Metaphysik des sittlich guten bei Franz Suárez* (Freiburg: Herder 1965).

Giers, J. *Die Gerechtigkeitslehre des jungen Suárez. Edition und Untersuchung seiner römischen Vorlesungen De iustitia et iure* (Freiburg: Herder 1958).

Gotthard, A. *Der Augsburger Religionsfrieden* (Münster: Aschendorff 2004).

———. *In der ferne. Die Wahrnehmung des Raums in der Vormoderne* (Frankfurt-New York: Campus 2007).

Grunert, F., and Seelmann, K., eds. *Die Ordnung der Praxis. Neue Studien zur Spanischen Spätscholastik* (Tübingen: Niemeyer 2001).

Haggenmacher, P. *Grotius et la guerre juste* (Paris: Presses Universitaires de France 1983).

Hampton, T. *Fictions of embassy. Literature and diplomacy in early modern Europe* (Ithaca and London: Cornell University Press 2009).

Hoekstra, K. "The *de facto* turn in Hobbes's political philosophy," in T. Sorell and L. Foisneau eds., *Leviathan after 350 years* (Oxford: Clarendon 2005), 33–73.

Höpfl, H. *Jesuit political thought. The Society of Jesus and the state, c. 1540–1630* (Cambridge: Cambridge University Press 2004).

Hübener, W. "Praedeterminatio physica," in J. Ritter and K. Gründer eds., *Historisches Wörterbuch der Philosophie* (Basel: Schwabe 1989), Bd. 7, cols. 1216–25.

Ittersum, M. van. *Profit and principle: Hugo Grotius, natural rights theories and the rise of Dutch power in the East Indies (1595–1615)* (Leiden: Brill 2006).

Jackson, N. *Hobbes, Bramhall and the politics of liberty and necessity* (Cambridge: Cambridge University Press 2007).

Justenhoven, H.-G. *Francisco de Vitoria zu Krieg und Frieden* (Köln: Bachem 1991).

Karr, Susan Longfeld, "Nature, self and history in the works of Guillaume Budé, Andrea Alciati and Ulrich Zasius," unpublished Ph.D. thesis (Chicago 2009).

Kaufmann, M. "Luis de Molina über subjective Rechte, Herrschaft und Sklaverei," in Kaufmann and Schnepf eds., *Politische Metaphysik*, 205–26.

Kaufmann, M., and Schnepf, R., eds. *Politische Metaphysik. Die Entstehung moderner Rechtskonzeptionen in der Spanischen Scholastik* (Frankfurt: Peter Lang 2007).

Keene, E. *Beyond the anarchial society. Grotius, colonialism and order in world politics* (Cambridge: Cambridge University Press 2002).

Knebel, S. *Wille, Würfel und Wahrscheinlichkeit. Das System der moralischen Notwendigkeit in der Jesuiten-scholastik 1550–1700* (Hamburg: Felix Meiner Verlag 2000).

Kraye, J. *Classical traditions in Renaissance philosophy* (Aldershot: Ashgate 2002).

Kremer, M. *Den Frieden verantworten. Politische Ethik bei Francisco Suárez (1548–1617)* (Stuttgart: Kohlhammer 2008).

Kusukawa, S. *The transformation of natural philosophy* (Cambridge: Cambridge University Press 1995).

Lloyd, H. "Constitutionalism," in Burns ed., *The Cambridge history of political thought 1450–1700*, 254–97.

Lloyd, S. *Morality in the philosophy of Thomas Hobbes. Cases in the law of nature* (Cambridge: Cambridge University Press 2009).

Long, A., and Sedley, D. *The Hellenistic philosophers*, vol. 1 (Cambridge: Cambridge University Press 1987).

Lubac, H. de. *Surnaturel: études historiques* (Paris: Aubier 1946).

———. *Augustinisme et théologie moderne* (Paris: Aubier 1965).

Ludwig, B. *Die Wiederentdeckung des epikureischen Naturrechts. Zu Thomas Hobbes' philosophischer Entwicklung von "De cive" zum "Leviathan" im Pariser Exil 1640–1651* (Frankfurt: Klostermann 1998).

Malcolm, N. "Hobbes's theory of international relations," in id., *Aspects of Hobbes* (Oxford: Clarendon 2002).

Martínez Casado, A., ed. *La causa de los pobres* (Salamanca: Editorial San Esteban 2006).

Martz, L. *Poverty and welfare in Habsburg Spain* (Cambridge: Cambridge University Press 1983).

Mortimer, S. *Reason and religion in the English Revolution: The challenge of Socinianism* (Cambridge: Cambridge University Press 2009).

Nifterik, G. van and Nijman, J., "Introduction: *Mare liberum* revisited (1609–2009)," *Grotiana* 30 (2009), 3–19.

Nolf, J. *La réforme de la bienfaisance à Ypres au XVIe siècle* (Ghent: E. van Goethen & Co. 1915).

Nussbaum, M. *Frontiers of justice: Disability, nationality, species membership* (Cambridge, Mass.: Belknap Press 2006).

Ordóñez, V. "Juan de Salas junto a Suárez," *Revista española de teología* 13 (1953), 159–213.

Overhoff, J. *Hobbes's theory of the will* (Lanham: Rowman and Littlefield 2000).

Pagden, A. *The fall of natural man. The American Indian and the origins of comparative ethnology* (Cambridge: Cambridge University Press 1982).

———. "Dispossessing the barbarian," in A. Pagden ed., *The languages of political theory in early-modern Europe* (Cambridge: Cambridge University Press 1987), 79–98.

———. *Lords of all the world. Ideologies of empire in Spain, Britain and France, c. 1500–c. 1800* (New Haven: Yale University Press 1995).

Panizza, D. *Alberico Gentili, giurista ideologico nell'Inghilterra elisabettiana* (Padua: La Garangola 1981).

———. "The 'freedom of the sea' and 'modern cosmopolis' in Alberico Gentili's *De iure belli*," *Grotiana* 30 (2009), 88–106.

Pasnau, R. *Thomas Aquinas on human nature* (Cambridge: Cambridge University Press 2002).

Pettit, P. "Liberty and Leviathan," *Politics, philosophy and economics* 4 (2005), 131–51.

———. *Made with words* (Princeton and Oxford: Princeton University Press 2008).

Pink, T. "Suarez, Hobbes and the scholastic tradition in action theory," in T. Pink and M.W.F. Stone eds., *The will and human action. From antiquity to the present day* (London: Routledge 2004), 127–53.

Porras, I. "Constructing international law in the East Indian seas: Property, sovereignty, commerce and war in Hugo Grotius's *De iure praedae*," *Brooklyn Journal of International Law* 31 (2006), 741–804.

Porter, J. *Nature as reason. A Thomistic theory of natural law* (Grand Rapids– Cambridge: Eerdmans 2005).

Reibstein, E. *Johannes Althusius als Fortsetzer der Schule von Salamanca* (Karlsruhe: Müller 1955).

Rinaldi, T. "L'azione volontaria e la libertà nel pensiero di F. Suárez," in *Francisco Suárez. Der ist der Mann* (Valencia: Edicep 2004), 307–22.

Runciman, D. *Pluralism and the personality of the state* (Cambridge: Cambridge University Press 1997).

Saarinen, R. *Weakness of will in Renaissance and Reformation thought. From Petrarch to Leibniz* (Oxford: Oxford University Press, forthcoming).

Salmon, J. "Catholic resistance theory," in Burns ed., *The Cambridge history of political thought 1450–1700*, 219–53.

Sassen, S. *Territory, authority, rights. From medieval to global assemblages* (Princeton: Princeton University Press 2006).

Scattola, M. "Die Grenze der Neuzeit," in M. Bauer and T. Rahn eds., *Die Grenze. Begriff und Inszenierung* (Berlin: Akademie Verlag 1997).

———. *Das Naturrecht vor dem Naturrecht. Zur Geschichte des «ius naturae» im 16. Jahrhundert* (Tübingen: Niemeyer 1999).

———. "Naturrecht als Rechtstheorie: Die Systematisierung der «res scolastica» in der Naturrechtslehre des Domingo de Soto," in Grunert and Seelmann eds., *Die Ordnung der Praxis*, 21–46.

———. "Von der *maiestas* zur *symbiosis*," in E. Bonfatti, G. Duso, and M. Scattola eds., *Politische Begriffe und historisches Umfeld in der Politica methodice digesta des Johannes Althusius* (Wiesbaden: Harrassowitz 2002).

———. "Before and after natural law," in T.J. Hochstrasser and P. Schröder eds., *Early modern natural law theories* (Dordrecht: Kluwer 2003), 1–30.

Schmidt, A. *Vaterlandsliebe und Religionskonflikt* (Leiden: Brill 2007).

Schmidt, G. "Die Idee 'deutsche Freiheit,'" in id. ed., *Kollektive Freiheitsvorstellungen*, 159–189.

Schmidt, G., et al., eds. *Kollektive Freiheitsvorstellungen im frühneuzeitlichen Europa (1400–1850)* (Frankfurt: Peter Lang 2006).

Schmitt, C. *Der Nomos der Erde im Völkerrecht des Ius Publicum Europaeum*, 4th ed. (Berlin: Duncker & Humblot 1997).

Schmutz, J. "La doctrine médiévale des causes et la théologie de la nature pure," *Revue Thomiste* 101 (2001), 217–64.

———. ed., *Scholasticon* (http://www.scholasticon.fr).

Schneider, B. *Ius reformandi* (Tübingen: Mohr Siebeck 2001).

Schnepf, R. "Zwischen Gnadenlehre und Willensfreiheit. Skizze der Problemlage zu Beginn der Schule von Salamanca," in Kaufmann and Schnepf eds., *Politische Metaphysik*, 23–42.

Schröder, J. "Die Entstehung des modernen Völkerrechtsbegriffs im Naturrecht der frühen Neuzeit," *Jahrbuch für Recht und Ethik* 8 (2000), 47–71.

Schröder, P. "Gentili's political theory of war and interstate relations," in B. Kingsbury and B. Straumann eds., *The Roman Foundations of the Law of Nations: Alberico Gentili and the Justice of Empire* (Oxford: Oxford University Press 2010).

———. "Taming the fox and the lion—some aspects of the sixteenth-century's debate on inter-state relations," in Asbach and Schröder eds., *War, the state and international law in seventeenth century Europe*, pp. 83–102.

Seelmann, K. "Selbstherrschaft, Herrschaft über die Dinge und individuelle Rechte in der spanischen Spätscholastik," in Kaufmann and Schnepf eds., *Politische Metaphysik*, 43–57.

Senellart, M. *Les arts de gouverner. Du regimen médiéval au concept de gouvernement* (Paris: Seuil 1995).

Skinner, Q. *Liberty before liberalism* (Cambridge: Cambridge University Press 1998).

———. "Hobbes on the proper signification of liberty" in id., *Visions of politics*, vol. III (Cambridge: Cambridge University Press 2002), 209–37.

———. "Hobbes on representation," *European Journal of Philosophy* 13 (2005), 155–84.

———. *Hobbes and republican liberty* (Cambridge: Cambridge University Press 2008).

Sparn, W. "Die Schulphilosophie in den lutherischen Territorien," in *Grundrisse der Geschichte der Philosophie. Die Philosophie des 17. Jahrhunderts*, Bd. IV: *Das heilige Römische Reich*, eds. H. Holzhey and W. Schmidt-Biggemann (Basel: Schwabe 2001), 475–97.

Stintzing, R. *Geschichte der deutschen Rechtswissenschaft. Erste Abteilung* (Munich-Leipzig: Oldenbourg 1880).

Straumann, B. *Hugo Grotius und die Antike* (Baden-Baden: Nomos 2007).

Strohm, C. "Melanchthon-Rezeption in der Ethik des frühen Calvinismus," in G. Frank and H. J. Selderhuis eds., *Melanchthon und der Calvinismus* (Stuttgart-Bad Canstatt: Frommann Holzboog 2005), 135–57.

———. *Calvinismus und Recht* (Tübingen: Mohr Siebeck 2008).

Thumfart, J. "Freihandel als Religion," *Archiv des Völkerrechts* 46 (2008), 259–71.

Tierney, B. "Aristotle and the American Indians—again. Two critical discussions," *Cristianesimo nella storia* 12 (1991), 295–322.

———. *The idea of natural rights* (Atlanta, Ga.: Emory 1997).

Tricaud, F. "'Homo homini Deus,' 'Homo homini Lupus': Recherche des sources des deux formules de Hobbes," in R. Koselleck and R. Schnur eds., *Hobbes-Forschungen* (Berlin: Duncker and Humblot 1969), 61–70.

Tuck, R. *Natural rights theories. Their origin and development* (Cambridge: Cambridge University Press 1979).

———. *The rights of war and peace* (Oxford: Oxford University Press 1999).

Tully, J. *A discourse of property* (Cambridge: Cambridge University Press 1980).

———, ed., *Meaning and context* (Cambridge: Cambridge University Press 1988).

————. *Public philosophy in a new key* (2 vols., Cambridge: Cambridge University Press 2008).

Varkemaa, J. "Summenhart's theory of rights," in V. Mäkinen and P. Korkmann eds., *Transformations in medieval and early-modern rights discourse* (Dordrecht: Springer 2006), 119–47.

Vereecke, L. *Conscience morale et loi humaine selon Gabriel Vazquez S.J.* (Tournai: Desclée 1957).

Walker, R. *Inside/outside: International relations as political theory* (Cambridge: Cambridge University Press 1993).

Walther, M. "*Potestas multitudinis* und *potentia multitudinis*. Zur Transformation der Demokratietheorie zu Beginn der Neuzeit," in Grunert and Seelmann eds., *Die Ordnung der Praxis*, 281–97.

Westerman, P. *The disintegration of natural law theory. Aquinas to Finnis* (Leiden: Brill 1988).

Whaley, J. "Religiöse Toleranz in der Frühen Neuzeit," in Schmidt et al., eds., *Kollektive Freiheitsvorstellungen*, 397–416.

Willoweit, D. *Rechtsgrundlagen der Territorialgewalt: Landesobrigkeit, Herrschaftsgewalt und Territorium in der Rechtswissenschaft der Neuzeit* (Cologne: Bohlau 1975).

Witte, J. *Law and Protestantism. The legal teachings of the Lutheran Reformation* (Cambridge: Cambridge University Press 2002).

————. *The Reformation of rights. Law, religion, and human rights in early modern Calvinism* (Cambridge: Cambridge University Press 2007).

Wyduckel, D. "Recht und Gesetz im Bereich des Reformierten Protestantismus," in C. Strohm ed., *Martin Bucer und das Recht* (Geneva: Droz 2002), 1–28.

Zagorin, P. *Hobbes and the law of nature* (Princeton: Princeton University Press 2009).

INDEX

CPSIA information can be obtained
at www.ICGtesting.com
Printed in the USA
LVHW090308140721
692588LV00012B/2021